Stories, Stats and Stuff About K-State Sports

By Tim Fitzgerald
Research by Bernie Haney

PURPLE PRIDE

Printed in the United States of America by Mennonite Press, Inc.

ISBN 1-880652-62-5

PHOTO CREDITS All photographs were supplied by the Kansas State University Sports Information Department.

ACKNOWLEDGMENTS

I dread microfilm and old musty files. That became a significant problem when my supervisor at Midwest Sports Publications, Bill Handy, asked me to write this book. After all, a book of sports history meant much of the above. That's where Bernie Haney came in.

Bernie is a senior at Kansas State majoring in Journalism and Mass Communications. The Topekan is probably best known as the keeper of Mitch Holthus' statistics during broadcasts on the Wildcat Network. When I started to hunt for a researcher, Bernie came highly recommended.

So off Bernie went, sifting through the numerous folders of the Kansas State Sports Information Department's filing system. The background for virtually all you will read in the *Kansas State Wildcat Handbook* was provided to me by Bernie. For that, he deserves a standing ovation. Bernie did what I dislike, and allowed me to do what I love. Write. Bernie spoon-fed the information to me.

That's not to mean the sole credit for the contents of this book goes to Bernie. He's consistently reminded me to pass on kudos to others deserving attention.

Most notable are the staff of the Sports Information Department. All of the photos in the book came from the K-State Sports Information files. That seems simple enough, but some images date back to the early 1900s. Sports Information staff intern Andy Bartlett made sure the statistics in the back of the book were properly provided. Believe me, no one wanted to retype them.

Also, some of the background for the football section of this book came via Mike Sanders and John Dodderidge, loyal K-State alums who had been doing their own research.

Once the writing was completed, the copy passed through three crucial filters, one volunteer and two official. All the text was read by my wife, Becky, an efficient copy editor and talented journalist herself. After that, Bruce Janssen poured over the copy as the book's editor. Finally, the photos and text went to Jeff Pulaski, who did a marvelous job packaging the product.

Finally, a quick tip of the hat to my parents, Pat and Donna, for letting me become what came naturally, and to an old friend, David Svoboda, who has twice made sure the path of my life led through a newsroom. Thanks to all.

For my father, who once joked I was free to attend any major university in Manhattan, Kansas. A wise man he.

INTRODUCTION

In 1986, Kansas State University veered off course. That's when Jon Wefald became the university's 12th president. Before his arrival, K-State, both athletically and academically, was in a free fall. First, President Wefald stopped the descent, and then he taught K-Staters how to climb the mountain.

When Wefald arrived from the University of Minnesota system, K-State sat on the verge of exiting the Big Eight Conference. Not only had the football program developed an amazing knack for failure, but enrollment in Manhattan had dropped to record lows. Wefald began to preach change, and while many bought into some of what he said, most laughed when he spoke of greatness on the gridiron.

Like all memorable leaders, Jon Wefald provided the vision, found talented people who shared his dreams, offered the tools needed for accomplishment, and then got out of the way.

Maybe only Bill Snyder possessed the needed mix of football brilliance and personal determination to change K-State's football fortunes. Leading the search for the new football coach, Wefald hired the former University of Iowa offensive coordinator in December of 1988. Since then, K-State has steadily climbed up the ladder of Division I-A football. At the time of the writing of this book in 1996, the Wildcats had established themselves as a legitimate Top 20 program.

Probably nothing happening now would have taken place without Jon Wefald. Not only is K-State an athletic power entering the Big 12 Conference, but it's a highly respected academic institution with a soaring enrollment. All K-Staters should be grateful to Jon Wefald and Bill Snyder. They have allowed us to be part of a remarkable resurgence in Manhattan.

Personally, my life would be much different without their contributions to KSU. The school's recent rebirth has led to the existence of *Purple Pride, the Newsmagazine for K-State Sports Fans*, of which I serve as editor. It also made possible the writing of this book.

What you hold in your hands is a testament to the leaders who not only dreamed crazy dreams, but were bold enough to point the way up the mountain.

Fitz.

TABLE OF CONTENTS

Chapter 1: Football

BILL SNYDER *(1989–96)* **6**

Chapter 2: Football

THE PRE-PURPLE PRIDE YEARS *(1896–1966)* **44**

Chapter 3: Football

VINCE GIBSON *(1967–74)* **64**

Chapter 4: Football

THE WAITING PERIOD *(1975-88)* **78**

Chapter 5:

BASKETBALL *(1903-96)* **96**

Chapter 6:

THE BEST OF THE REST **124**

Chapter 7:

BY THE NUMBERS *(Some Wildcat Statistics)* **142**

Wildcat Quiz:

TRIVIA ANSWERS **156**

Bill Snyder: 1989-96

"An architect draws America's toughest job"

Topeka Capital-Journal, Dec. 6, 1988

In the five decades preceding Bill Snyder's hiring as Kansas State's 32nd head football coach on November 30, 1988, the Wildcats had won less than 25 percent of their games. On that day, K-State sat on the verge of becoming the first college football program to lose 500 games.

Anyone associated with K-State football is as familiar with losing as they are with the wind sweeping 'cross the fruited plains. Losing football games had grown into a way of life at K-State.

When Snyder arrived in Manhattan, he met with his players. He saw the history of Wildcat football written across their faces.

"You just don't like to be beaten all the time, within our own professions or our own daily responsibilities, we don't like to be beaten," Snyder said before the start of the 1995 season. "We all know we're going to have some good days and some bad days, but 365 bad days year-in and year-out can beat you down, and that's what I saw in these young guys."

Coach Bill Snyder is introduced as Kansas State's 32nd head football coach on November 30, 1988.

With unprecedented support from the school's administration, Snyder gave the players of Kansas State the tools they needed to succeed. After his first seven years in Manhattan, Snyder had a record of 46-33-1, had

taken his team to three straight bowl games and had transformed Kansas State football from a laughingstock to a respected power.

It hasn't come easily. Snyder took ownership of a house that had burned to the ground, going 2-30-1 the previous three seasons under Coach Stan Parrish. The first Snyder season brought a 1-10 record in 1989, making K-State the first Division I-A program to push past the 500-loss threshold. He never had said it would come quickly.

"It's been gradual, and that's exactly the way we've approached it, and that's what we shared with our players on that first day," Snyder said. "It's going to be one step at a time. There's not going to be any shortcuts. I'm not going to promise you we're going to win one, two, five, seven or 10. All I can promise you is we're going to get a little bit better every day. And that's not just in football, but in all aspects of their life."

The 1-10 beginning was followed by a 5-6 building block in 1990. The breakthrough came in 1991 with a 7-4 mark, which was followed by a slight backward step in 1992 to 5-6.

Since then, the program has been building a head of steam, showing the importance of players being coached within the same system during their entire college careers. The 1993 season brought a 9-2-1 record and a victory in the Copper Bowl. That was followed by two more bowl years: a 9-3 mark in '94 and a 10-2 record in 1995.

"I think the young people who were involved here in 1989 when we won only one ball game were every bit as instrumental with what took place (in the bowl years) as

WILDCAT QUIZ

1. Who is the only Wildcat football coach to be head coach of an NFL team?

Bill Snyder has offered his program a clear vision of expectations.

anybody else," Snyder said. "It was laying the foundation, and all of those young people really had a part in that.

"If the bricks hadn't been put in place in 1989, we wouldn't have won five in 1990 and nine in 1993."

WILDCAT QUIZ

2. In what year did players on K-State's offense actually wear different colored helmets?

THE HIRING

Bill Snyder was a late arrival in the search for Parrish's successor.

Boston College Coach Gene Bicknell was rumored to be a finalist, and then it became known that Memphis State Coach Charlie Bailey topped the search committee's wish list. The names of other Division I assistant coaches popped up in the newspapers: Ron Dickerson (Penn State), Bill Thornton (Texas Christian), John Fox (Pittsburgh) and Milan Vooletich (Navy). Then, came the name of Bill Snyder, the offensive coordinator at the University of Iowa under Coach Hayden Fry.

Kansas State Athletic Director Steve Miller had said throughout the search process that he preferred to hire someone with head coaching experience, but when he traveled to Iowa City to speak with Snyder, he knew there was something special about the man.

"When I walked into (Snyder's) home, I saw all the ingredients that I was looking for in a head football coach," Miller said after hiring Snyder. "What I found that was most important was that he is a person who cares."

Snyder was initially aloof about the K-State job. He had always told friends that if he was going to move on, then the table would have to be perfectly set. However, Miller convinced Snyder to go to Manhattan to speak with the search committee.

"When the committee visited with him, it was a done deal," Miller said just days before Snyder was announced as the school's new coach. "Everyone we talked to had not said anything but great things about him. You will love this guy. He is A-1 cerebral. No one can accuse us of not doing our homework."

WILDCAT QUIZ

3. Who was the last KSU football player to score at Memorial Stadium?

Snyder liked what he saw, and once he took the job, started making immediate changes. He insisted his players, coaches and the school in general begin preparing to win.

"There weren't any goals directed toward lifting the illness of losing, it was just a matter of you get better, all the rest of that stuff will take care of itself," Snyder said.

With the school teetering on elimination from the Big Eight Conference because of the Wildcats' miserable football program, Snyder demanded a financial commitment before he would take the job. It wasn't about how much money he would make, but how much money would be pumped into upgrading the school's abysmal facilities and paying assistant coaches salaries on the same level as the nation's top programs. Miller — and Jon Wefald, the university's president — knew this was the price of winning.

"Bill Snyder asked me, 'How tough is this job?' " Miller said before introducing Snyder for the first time. "I told him it was the toughest Division I-A job in America. Don't let anyone kid you about that. Is it a hard job? It's not a hard job; it's the hardest job in this country.

"But there is a man sitting right here that will surround himself with similar people, he will get the job done. With our help, we'll get this job done."

Snyder has done exactly that using an approach that is simple, yet all inclusive.

■ There's a message as consistent as the sun rising in the morning. "Get a little bit better each day," he repeats.

■ Snyder refuses to let anyone outwork him. The slave to details logs 17-hour days, stopping to eat his one daily meal before going to bed at about 1 a.m.

■ The coach possesses a chess master's knowledge of the game. "If they were giving out Rhodes Scholars to football coaches," said longtime friend, and assistant coach Larry Kramer, "he would get the first one."

■ And, finally, Snyder demands the best. "He expects so much out of his coaches and out of his players," said Tyson Schwieger, a senior receiver on the 1995 Holiday

One of Snyder's first tasks at K-State was teaching his players how to win.

Bowl championship team. "That's probably one reason we've had so much success.

"He expects you to do everything right, whether it's going to class, going to meetings or in practice. That's the kind of person he is."

WILDCAT QUIZ

4. Elmer Hackney was not the only Hackney to produce great achievements in a Wildcat uniform. What was so interesting about his brother Gerald?

1989: THE BEGINNING

CLOSED SHOP The time for Bill Snyder to coach football at Kansas State arrived on March 28, 1989. Spring drills. While many were eager to catch a glimpse of Snyder's team, members of the media and fans quickly learned they would be kept in the dark.

One of Snyder's first acts as K-State head coach was to close spring practice to both the media and public. He had a $2,500 fence erected around the Wildcats' practice facility. He later closed the locker rooms from the media and restricted access to himself, players, assistant coaches, and the team's trainers. Injury reports were put on the permanent disabled list.

With the winless streak at 27, the public didn't seem to mind too much. Anything that would help the program win was all right with most fans. The media, on the other had, didn't like such barricades. Some felt it made doing their job more difficult, and this was a program in need of every bit of publicity possible.

Here are a *Kansas City Star* writer's observations on the policy "The chummy, come-on-over days of previous coaching administrations has been replaced by a no-nonsense guy with a system he thinks will help turn around the mindset at K-State, which has major college's longest winless streak at 27 games. Whether the more structured approach means better football is open to debate."

Snyder insisted the reason for his closed policy was simple. "It is to avoid as many distractions as we possibly can and to put our kids in the best possible learning environment we can. I hope all of you realize that it's not a personal thing."

WILDCAT QUIZ

5. What is the only football number to be retired at Kansas State?

CAN'T STAND THE HEAT Snyder started his first spring practice with only 81 players, but within a few weeks there were 10 fewer players in the camp. Four of the players started spring drills atop the depth chart at their positions.

"I expected attrition to take place," Snyder said. "That's why I felt so fortunate that when we came in and during the off-season conditioning program the attrition rate was still only one."

THE FIRST GAME On September 9, 1989, Snyder's Wildcats took the field for the first time. It was the type of

Bill Snyder walked off the field with his team after suffering through a 31-0 defeat at Arizona State in his first game as K-State's coach.

scheduling the coach would rarely subject his team to in the future. K-State opened the 1989 season at Arizona State, with a crowd of 68,606 on hand at Sun Devil Stadium.

K-State's William Price put the Cats in position to score by intercepting a pass on the first play of the game, but the Wildcats' drive stalled at the 10 and David Kruger missed a 27-yard field goal. That was it for the Cats, as ASU rolled to a 31-0 victory.

PILING ON K-State came home from the loss at Arizona State stinging from defeat, but also still answering questions about a *Sports Illustrated* article headlined: "Futility U." The article, in the magazine's college football preview issue, focused on the past, chronicling the losses of the losingest program in college football history.

"I'm sick of it," said senior safety Erick Harper. "It makes me so sick sometimes I don't sleep at night, just thinking about it." It was thought the streak would come to an end when Northern Iowa visited K-State on September 16, but the Division I-AA opponent beat the Cats 10-8 to prolong the misery.

THE END ARRIVES The winless streak sat at 30 when North Texas rolled into KSU Stadium on September 30. Even in this game, nothing came easily for the Wildcats, but K-State won 20-17 on the final play of the game.

Frank Hernandez caught a 12-yard pass from Carl Straw on the last play of the game against North Texas to end K-State's 30-game winless streak.

Quarterback Carl Straw connected with Frank Hernandez on a 12-yard touchdown pass with no time remaining on the clock. Hernandez's touchdown capped a remarkable nine-play, 85-yard drive that devoured the game's final 95 seconds, turning what could have been just another loss into K-State's 300th all-time victory.

"Gosh, I thought we'd won the damn Super Bowl," defensive end Maurice Henry said after the game. "Little kids were tackling me and biting me on the ankle."

THINNING OUT By mid-season, K-State's small roster had become dangerously thin. At the time, the NCAA allowed teams to carry 95 players on scholarship. By October, injuries had whittled K-State down to 49 players on scholarship, 21 of whom were either freshmen or redshirt freshmen.

IN NORMAN AGAIN K-State's second-to-last game of Snyder's inaugural season wasn't supposed to be played in Norman, Okla., but that's where the Wildcats ended up. The game was originally scheduled to be played in Tokyo as the Coca-Cola Bowl, but the Sooners found themselves on NCAA probation and barred from playing on television. Thus, Coca-Cola Bowl organizers canceled the teams' appearance in Tokyo.

That meant the contest would be moved back to

Manhattan, where it originally had been scheduled to be played. But the athletic department chose to sell the game to Oklahoma so it would be played in Norman. In fact, K-State would play in Norman five straight years (1988-1992).

The Wildcats already had six games scheduled for KSU Stadium, and Athletic Director Steve Miller thought seven games were too many.

"I don't think we can handle that," he told *The Wichita Eagle* before the start of the season. "We charge $15 a game for six games at home last year ... that's $90 for the season. We're not going to say this year's it's $105, even though it is for seven games. Charging $15 more after an 0-11 season ... from a business standpoint, I don't think that's good."

So, the 1989 game went south, and the Wildcats lost, 42-19.

WILDCAT QUIZ

6. What player ran an on-side kick back for a touchdown in 1984, the only time that's happened in Wildcat history?

SEASON ENDER Snyder's first season ended similar to the way in which it had begun — with the Wildcats being manhandled. When the Colorado Buffaloes beat the Cats 59-11 at KSU Stadium, Snyder had compiled a 1-10 record.

1990: THE BUILDING BLOCK

SWITCHAROO The first headline from the 1990 season concerned a game that didn't take place. Kansas State chose to drop Wyoming from its 1990 schedule, and the Laramie-based school sued the Kansas State athletic department. Athletic Director Steve Miller notified Wyoming Coach and Athletic Director Paul Roach that K-State would not play in Wyoming on September 15 nor host the Cowboys on September 14, 1991, in Manhattan. Instead, the Wildcats scheduled a game with New Mexico State.

Eventually, Wyoming filled the open date with Arkansas State, and K-State agreed to pay the school an undisclosed amount of money.

Athletic Director Steve Miller was willing to spend money in the rebuilding process of the K-State football program.

WINNING TRACK When the 1990 campaign opened at KSU Stadium, K-State's football program had won just one game in the previous three seasons, and just 10 games in the past seven seasons. Then, K-State played host to the Western Illinois Leathernecks and routed the visitors 27-6. Next came New Mexico State, which the Cats beat 52-7.

The two wins made K-State 2-0 for the first time since the program had gone to the Independence Bowl in 1982.

BIG EIGHT WIN K-State hadn't won a Big Eight Conference contest in four years when the Oklahoma State Cowboys visited KSU Stadium on October 13. The program that

WILDCAT QUIZ

7. What did Wildcat cornerback Brad Lambert do that was special in the 1984 season?

had become famous through the years for finding a way to lose, found a way to beat the Cowboys. For once, it was the Wildcats making the big play with the game on the line.

Clinging to a precarious 23-17 lead in the fourth quarter, the Wildcats watched the Cowboys march to the KSU 10 in nine plays. Facing a third-and-goal, Oklahoma State quarterback Kenny Ford rolled out and started to sprint for the end zone. Just when it looked as though Ford was headed for a touchdown, K-State linebacker Chris Patterson flew in and stripped Ford of the ball. KSU's Danny Needham pounced on the ball at the 15, and K-State ran out the clock to win 23-17 and move to 4-2 on the season.

"I thought it was an even match-up coming into the game," Oklahoma State Coach Pat Jones said afterward. "We played hard, but I'll be honest with you. I think the better team won."

THE POWERCAT: A SIGN OF THE TIMES

When a new logo for the Kansas State football team was designed in the spring of 1989, it had no name. Most people knew it as the Wildcat football logo that Coach Bill Snyder had the athletic department create for his team.

Today, the stylized, graphic interpretation of a Wildcat is called the Powercat. The name blends Cat with the new attitude that surges through the K-State athletic department since the logo's adoption.

While at first used for only football, the Powercat slowly has been adopted by all of the school's athletic programs. The design's style has drawn many comparisons to the Iowa Hawkeye, but its real intent was to distinguish Kansas State from other schools using Wildcats as their mascot.

"There's a lot of Wildcats across the country," former Assistant Athletic Director Chris Peterson said in April 1989, when the logo was introduced. "We wanted something different and unique, and when you look at it, you don't have to read whether it's K-State or Kentucky or someone else."

The logo, created by Manhattan illustrator Tom Bookwalter, is a prominent feature on the school's new football uniforms — a purple Powercat on the sides of silver helmets replaced solid purple headgear with a white stripe from the Stan Parrish era.

Coach Snyder "wanted something a little bit on the vicious side," Bookwalter said.

The logo appears everywhere, including uniforms, clothing, flags, bottled water, tattoos, and vanity plates for cars.

Previous logos used by the athletic department have been retired. The line drawing of a wildcat head, shared by several Wildcat universities in the past, is no longer seen at K-State, and the cartoonish "Willie the Wildcat" is used only by the Alumni Association.

Pat Jackson rushed for more than 1,000 yards in two years of play.

THE STAMPEDE K-State's season featured just one more win — over Iowa State, 28-14 — leaving the Wildcats with a 5-6 record. Snyder's second season came to an end with a 64-3 loss in Boulder to the Colorado Buffaloes. As bad as it seemed, the game still came complete with a milestone for a K-State player.

Senior running back Pat Jackson became the first player in the program's history to pick up 1,000 yards rushing in a two-year career after transferring from a junior college.

The Columbus, Ohio, native arrived in Manhattan from Waldorf Junior College in 1989 as a quarterback, but the 5-foot-9 athlete played running back, flanker, and split end at K-State.

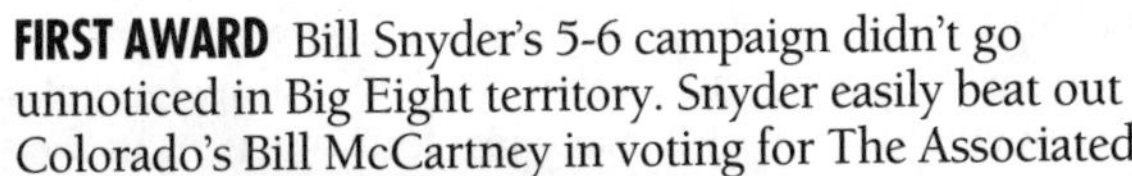

FIRST AWARD Bill Snyder's 5-6 campaign didn't go unnoticed in Big Eight territory. Snyder easily beat out Colorado's Bill McCartney in voting for The Associated

---

A visual boost to school spirit, the Powercat has pumped money into the university. In 1984, the university received less than $2,600 from rights fees to use K-State trademarks. Revenues from school marks in 1995 fell just short of $250,000. All of the money from trademarks at K-State benefits the school's scholarship fund.

K-State's first breakthrough into the national markets came in 1993, when exposure during the Cats' victory at the Copper Bowl sparked interest. Now, major companies may be preparing to nationally market the Powercat just as they would the Kansas Jayhawk.

"We had to change our thinking," said John Fairman, K-State's Assistant Vice-President for Institutional Advancement. "Back in 1987, our major concern was Manhattan. About the time Snyder arrived, we started thinking about being in Wichita, Topeka, and Kansas City. That thought was in place until (the spring of '95, when) I was approached by four big national companies. They said if we could stay in the Top 20 for the next two years, we could be a national team."

Coach Bill Snyder gave the K-State program a new identity with the introduction of the Powercat logo.

Press Big Eight Coach of the Year award. "We had the most talent," McCartney said. "He did the best job. I really feel that way."

"I've seen them before when they were pretty good at Kansas State," Oklahoma State Coach Pat Jones said. "But I've never seen a Kansas State team play with such intensity. They were obviously well organized and well coached."

"We have accomplished some things here," Snyder said. "I appreciate people like Bill and Pat and the kind of things they say. But I'm kind of humbled by this award because there are so many deserving people."

1991: THE BREAKTHROUGH

EARLY SHOT For a year that marked the first winning season for the Cats in nine years, the 1991 campaign got off to an enigmatic start. K-State lost four practices in the fall after an internal investigation discovered three assistants had met with players on four different occasions in April.

"If you're going to put it in a category, maybe careless is somewhat appropriate," Coach Bill Snyder said. "We violated a regulation, and consequently, we feel it's in our best interest to make sure we penalize ourselves to a comparable degree."

William Price was the hero in a win over Indiana State by intercepting a two-point conversion pass and returning it 102 yards for a safety.

PRICE IS RIGHT The most convincing evidence that K-State's football fortunes had changed arrived with the season opener on September 7. K-State led Indiana State 24-19 in the fourth quarter when the Division I-AA Sycamores came up with the kind of rally that would have sent K-State reeling in years gone by. Indiana State scored a touchdown with 3:24 remaining in the game to take a 25-24 lead.

That's when the Indiana State coaching staff made a fateful decision. The Sycamores opted to go for the two-point conversion, and thus put themselves up by three. A possible field goal by the Cats could only tie the game.

What the Indiana State staff forgot to calculate was that the NCAA had implemented a new rule starting with the 1988 season. The rule stated that if a team returned a fumble or interception on a two-point conversion it would be recorded as a safety and be worth two points.

It would be easy for the Indiana State coaches not to think of the rule when making their decision. After all, what were the chances of K-State scoring off of Indiana State's own conversion?

Indiana State quarterback Ray Allen threw a pass in the direction of Charles Swann, a receiver who had sliced up the K-State defense and scored two touchdowns to rally the Sycamores from a 24-13 deficit. Allen's pass didn't find Swann, but instead was picked off by K-State senior cornerback William Price in the end zone. Price cruised 102 yards with the interception and all of a sudden K-State led 26-25.

Game over? Well, not so fast.

Indiana State kicked off to the Cats — don't forget, it had just scored a touchdown — and tried an on-side kick. It worked, with the Sycamores recovering the ball at the KSU 32 with about three minutes remaining in the game.

There was plenty of time for K-State to lose, but the defense rose to the occasion. On first down, Allen bobbled the exchange from center and lost 3 yards. On second down, Allen was sacked by K-State defensive tackle Jody Killian for a 9-yard loss. On a third-and-22 from the KSU 44, Allen threw another pass, and once again Price was in the right spot. Price's interception sealed K-State's victory and put the Cats on the path to a 7-4 season.

"I guess the K-State defense just finds a way to win," junior linebacker Brooks Barta told the Kansas City Star after the game. That statement would hold true for years to come.

WILDCAT QUIZ

8. In what season did the Wildcats attempt the most passes?

IMPRESSIVE K-State had an interesting encounter a few games later. The Wildcats ran headlong into the Washington Huskies. K-State hit the road and was run over, 56-3, by the eventual undefeated national champions.

STRIKING BACK The next game, K-State opened the season's Big Eight schedule with arch-rival Kansas at KSU Stadium. K-State had lost to KU the previous three seasons, with the 1987 season serving up the infamous "Toilet Bowl" game that ended in a 17-17 tie.

Put simply, K-State did everything it could for the first three-and-a-half quarters to hand the Jayhawks a victory. The Wildcats trailed 12-3 in the fourth quarter, had committed six turnovers and Coach Snyder had pulled starting quarterback Paul Watson because of ineffective play.

Lucky for the Cats, Watson wasn't ineffective for the entire afternoon. Snyder reinserted his quarterback with eight minutes remaining and the Wildcats starting at their own 6.

KU might have won the game had Coach Glen Mason made use of his kicker, Dan Eichloff, possibly the best college field goal kicker in the nation that season. Instead, Mason kept going for the end zone on fourth down. The final time he made that decision, he set up K-State at the 6 and in came Watson.

WILDCAT QUIZ

9. What two Kansas State coaches have been inducted into the National Football Hall of Fame?

Quarterback Paul Watson refused to cave-in no matter how tough the pressure.

"When (Snyder) took me out, I was mad at myself. I was hurting the ball club," Watson told the media afterwards. "When he put me back in, I went into the huddle and said, 'Fellas, we're going to get back in the ball game and win.' "

Watson directed a 94-yard scoring march that ended with Eric Gallon dashing in from 10 yards out.

A beleaguered K-State crowd had all but lost hope. Many had left and were driving away from KSU Stadium when the Cats scored. After the Cats cut the Hawks' lead to 12-10, fans now filled with renewed hope starting coming back into the stadium.

K-State forced the Jayhawks to punt after three plays on their next drive. Watson went back to work, and lightning struck when he connected with Andre Coleman for a 34-yard touchdown with 1:58 left in the game. Now up 16-12, the Cats wouldn't put away the victory until they held the Jayhawks out of the end zone as time ran out. KU had the ball at the K-State 19 when the game ended.

The fans stormed the field and tore down the goal posts. The years of frustration against the Hawks were done. K-State was now the team finding ways to win.

OH, SO CLOSE October 19, 1991, will go down as one of those great "what-if" dates in K-State football history. The game went down as a 38-31 Nebraska victory on the Cornhuskers' home field, but ...

What if field goal kicker Tate Wright hadn't missed a 32-yard field goal with 8:35 remaining in the game? The three points would have put the Wildcats up 34-24, and Nebraska's road would have become much steeper. But Wright missed, and all of a sudden NU — still only seven points down — became energized. The Husker faithful at Memorial Stadium got behind their team, and just as quickly as a K-Stater could say "Cornhusker," the Big Red Machine came right back.

Kicker Tate Wright experienced many highs and lows during his four years of play.

"That made a big difference," Coach Snyder said of the missed field goal. "That's a 10-point lead. It's not over until it's over, but that sheds a whole different light on the approach of the rest of the game."

Nebraska responded with two touchdown drives to take a 38-31 lead. K-State didn't roll over. The Wildcats marched down the field, and on a fourth down from the Nebraska 7-yard line, a Paul Watson pass to tight end Russ Campbell was jarred loose at the goal line by NU linebacker Trev Alberts.

"It was in the basket," Campbell said. "I should have had it." The same could be said of the entire game.

CLOSE AGAIN K-State would tease itself once again the next week when the Colorado Buffaloes came to KSU Stadium. Colorado brought its No. 16 national ranking to Manhattan and won a defensive struggle, 10-0.

The Buffaloes scored their touchdown when K-State quarterback Paul Watson fumbled a snap at the KSU 13. Two plays later, Lamont Warren dashed in for CU. Colorado added a 29-yard field goal in the third quarter, but by then the Wildcats had squandered a multitude of chances to score.

Four times in the first half, K-State worked its way inside the CU 25, but came away empty each time. Two interceptions and two missed goals led to zero points. In the second half, K-State fumbled at the CU 22.

"Obviously, turnovers got us again and got us at critical times," Snyder said. "One of them (Watson's fumble) gave up a touchdown and that's seven points."

Yes, K-State's defense was sterling. But this time around, it was the Cats' offense that prevented the upset.

WILDCAT QUIZ

10. Kansas State has won six Defensive Newcomer of the Year Awards in the Big Eight conference, but who is the lone Wildcat to win Offensive Newcomer of the Year award?

FEELING AT HOME When the Wildcats went to Ames,

Iowa, on November 9, K-State hadn't won a road game in six seasons. You got it, six seasons. However, the Wildcats looked perfectly at home in Cyclone Stadium, routing their hosts 37-7, moving their record to 5-4 on the season and 2-3 in the conference.

Quarterback Paul Watson sparkled, connecting on 20 of his 27 pass attempts. Three of those completions came in the form of touchdowns to receiver Michael Smith. The win marked the largest Big Eight road victory for the program since the Cats had won 46-0 at Kansas in 1955.

Running back Eric Gallon gained 1,102 yards during the 1991 season.

POURING IT ON Eric Gallon entered his junior season as an oft-injured fullback who was being asked to switch to tailback in hopes of replacing two-year starter Pat Jackson. Could Gallon get the job done? What he accomplished was simply astounding by K-State standards.

Jackson finished his two-year K-State career with 1,001 yards, but Gallon gained 1,102 in his single season at running back. Only another Jackson, Isaac, ever gained more yards in a single season for the Wildcats, gaining 1,137 in 1973. Gallon would have probably broken that record if he hadn't sat out the final 7:13 of the Cats' season-ending 36-26 victory at Oklahoma State.

"I probably could have broken it, but I'm not too worried about it," said Gallon, who had 176 yards on 33 carries in the game. "We were up (leading 29-12), and I'd already accomplished my goal, so Coach wanted to give somebody else a shot."

BOWL HOPES That win over K-State put the Cats at 7-4 on the season and 4-3 in the Big Eight, good for a fourth-place finish. The record was the school's best since the Wildcats went 7-3 in 1954. That should be good enough for a bowl berth, right? Well, the NCAA had adopted a rule stating that schools must have six victories against Division I-A opponents, so wins over Indiana State and Idaho State didn't count.

K-State appealed to the NCAA, asking for an exemption on the grounds that the game with Indiana State was on the schedule prior to the rule's implementation in 1989. The NCAA's Special Events committee denied the appeal from Athletic Director Milt Richards, and thus the bowls interested in the Cats — Independence and Freedom — were prevented from extending an invitation.

GOOD HANDS GUY Michael Smith exploded on the Big Eight football scene during his sophomore season in 1989. By the close of the '91 season, Smith had rewritten the K-State record books and gone down as one of the best receivers in conference history.

By the time he left K-State, Smith topped the school's

record books in both career pass receptions and receiving yards (179 for 2,457 yards). The New Orleans native also collected 11 touchdowns. Smith finished third on the Big Eight's all-time receiving yardage list, behind All-American Hart Lee Dykes of Oklahoma State and Nebraska's Heisman Trophy winner, Johnny Rodgers.

Michael Smith rewrote K-State receiving records during his playing days.

HONORED AGAIN Not many years had passed since the Kansas State University administration had studied the possibility of dropping out of Division I-A football. Now, however, their new coach was named The Associated Press Big Eight Coach of the Year for a second straight year. Bill Snyder won the award again after leading his program to only its fifth winning season since 1936.

"Seven-and-four is not the ultimate. It's not anything that most coaches are going to jump up and get excited about," Snyder said. "But it was something special to these kids. Just to have regained their self respect. I feel very happy for them."

1992: THE BACKWARD STEP

SCARY ENCOUNTER The 1992 spring practice had just ended when KSU's quarterback during the 1991 season almost lost his life. Paul Watson, who had completed his eligibility, intervened when a group of youths tried to force their way past a doorman at an Aggieville bar. The gang formed a circle around Watson, and eventually piled on top of him. During the scuffle, Watson was stabbed four times. One wound penetrated six inches deep into his chest, just missing his heart. Watson recovered.

Paul Watson survived a knife attack the spring after his final season at K-State.

FUTILITY REVISITED In 1989, just after Bill Snyder's arrival at Kansas State, *Sports Illustrated* writer Douglas Looney had documented the miserable history of the school's football program in an article titled, "Futility U." As the 1992 season drew near, Looney returned to Manhattan, where the Wildcats were coming off a 7-4 season.

In a four-page article, Looney documented how the improvement of the football program helped revitalize the entire university. The article made mention of the enormous number of prestigious academic scholarships K-State students had earned as well as the school's debate program, which had won a national championship.

There wasn't much new in the article to K-Staters, but at least it breathed some fresh air into the tired stereotype of Kansas State football.

TEMPLE OF DOOM K-State opened the 1992 season with a 27-17 victory over Montana, and then Jaime Mendez stole the show the next week in the Wildcats' 35-14

Safety Jaime Mendez intercepted four passes against Temple in 1992.

victory over Temple.

Mendez intercepted four Temple passes and helped set up three K-State touchdowns in the process. The four pickoffs set a new K-State record.

"I'm still in shock," Mendez said after the game. "I can't wait to call my parents. Pro players talk about getting into a zone, but this was amazing."

Even more amazing was the fact that Mendez's performance did not earn him the Big Eight Conference Defensive Player of the Week honor. Instead, a Colorado player won the award.

SHELL-SHOCKED K-State was 3-0 when it traveled to Lawrence to take on the Kansas Jayhawks to open Big

Eight play. It is a game K-Staters won't soon forget because of the dominating performance of the Hawks. KU won 31-7, seemingly spending as much time in the K-State backfield as quarterback Jason Smargiasso.

It only got worse. The next week, K-State traveled to Utah State to play a game the Cats were expected to easily win. They didn't, losing 28-16 in what was the most significant setback in the Snyder era.

STIFLING DEFENSE Following a 54-7 blowout at Colorado, K-State headed to Norman to play the Oklahoma Sooners. Trailing 16-14 at halftime, K-State's defense did everything it could to carry the Wildcats. The Sooners had only five first downs and 86 yards of offense in the second half, but K-State was unable to win.

The difference in the game came with considerable controversy. K-State kicker Warren Claassen missed a 27-yard field goal late in the third quarter during windy conditions. Claassen and many Wildcats thought the field goal was good.

"I sure thought it was good," the kicker said. "I don't think (the official) pointed any direction. He just says that it missed."

Neither team scored in the second half, and the Sooners won the game, 16-14, dropping the Wildcats to 3-4 on the season.

Kicker Warren Claassen was furious when a 27-yard field goal attempt against Oklahoma was ruled no good.

SHOW TIME K-State had not been on national television in 10 years when the Iowa State Cyclones came to Manhattan for a Thursday night game shown nationally on ESPN.

The Wildcats' special teams set up K-State's first two scores in the 22-13 victory by blocking two Cyclone punts. The Wildcats missed both conversions, and then Tate Wright tacked on a 21-yard field goal in the third quarter.

Trailing 15-0, the Cyclones scored a touchdown in the fourth quarter, but running back Eric Gallon broke a 56-yard touchdown run (a career best) in the fourth quarter to put away the win for the Cats and end a four-game losing streak.

"It beats the devil out of what's happened the last four weeks," Coach Snyder said.

WILDCAT QUIZ

11. The Big Eight Conference started having Players of the Week in 1971. Who was the first Wildcat player to receive this award?

FUMBLEROOSKI Carrying a 4-5 record into the 10th game, and still facing a game with Nebraska to close the season, Coach Snyder pulled out all the stops to beat Oklahoma State 10-0 on November 21.

With his team locked in a defensive struggle, Snyder called upon offensive guard Toby Lawrence to score for the Cats.

Using a famed fumblerooski play (during which the

Guard Toby Lawrence scored a touchdown against Oklahoma State on a "fumblerooski."

center leaves the football on the ground by his feet), Lawrence scooped up the ball and rolled 8 yards for a touchdown in the second quarter.

"That's my first touchdown and my last," said Lawrence, a fifth-year senior from Snyder's hometown of St. Joseph, Mo. "It's too scary running. I'd rather block. I tell you what, it's a lot of responsibility holding onto the ball."

The trick play worked, but not as designed. Quentin Neujahr, the center, was actually supposed to squat on the ball until Lawrence tapped him to pick up the ball. Instead, the ball squirted out and Lawrence was forced to scoop up the ball before he took off.

"Quentin kind of got shoved back and the ball popped out," Lawrence said. "I was going to turn around and pick it up, but I was kind of flinching because I thought I was going to get hit.

"I went ahead and turned around, and there was nobody there. It was an excellent call by the coaches."

But it wasn't the first time Snyder's staff had called the play. K-State had used it two years earlier against the Oklahoma Sooners, but the Cats only picked up 3 yards on that attempt.

A LONG JOURNEY If you're going to lose to Nebraska, there are closer places to do it than Tokyo. But that's how K-State closed out a disappointing 1992 campaign, losing 38-24 before 50,000 fans at the Coca-Cola Bowl on December 6.

K-State fell behind 21-0 before senior reserve quarterback Matt Garber breathed life into the Cats. K-State trailed 21-10 at halftime after Garber directed a 76-yard, 8-play drive, and Tate Wright kicked a 40-yard field goal.

Nebraska, however, put the game out of reach with 10 more points in the third quarter before the Cats and Garber closed strong. Garber completed 19 of his 29 passes for 246 yards in his final collegiate game.

The loss was only one thing that went wrong on the trip. Coach Snyder ripped into the event's organizers following the game for a series of small items that added up into an unpleasant experience for the team.

First, K-State gave up a home game to play in Tokyo, and was supposed to have its choice of sidelines as the home team. Snyder selected his side, and then the day before the game, he was told his request was denied because the big-money donors to the contest wanted to be on the Nebraska side. Also, Snyder was told after the game that only he and K-State MVP Andre Coleman needed to stay around for the postgame festivities. K-State had been told the entire team would participate, so Snyder refused to attend the ceremony or the postgame press conference.

WILDCAT QUIZ

12. Who is recognized as Kansas State's first all-league football performer?

"I told them if you don't want my football team, then you don't want me," Snyder said.

A GOOD GUY Brooks Barta arrived at K-State in 1988 as an undersized linebacker from Smith Center High School, a Kansas high-school powerhouse. Barta finished his career in 1992 as a four-year starter and one of the greatest linebackers in school history.

At just 6-foot, 220 pounds, Barta became the program's second all-time leading tackler with 436 stops. Gary Spani, who played from 1974-77, tops the list with 543 tackles. Besides numerous on-field awards, including the Big Eight Newcomer of the Year award during the 1989 season, the math major garnered academic honors.

However, it was Barta's instinctive and knowledgeable

Undersized linebacker Brooks Barta developed into one of the all-time great players in K-State history.

Sean Snyder, son of Coach Bill Snyder, was an All-American punter in 1992.

play that earned him praise and respect.

"Just to look at Brooks, he doesn't have the physical appearance that you look for," fellow linebacker Chris Patterson told the *Manhattan Mercury*. "But as a linebacker, I've never seen anyone with better instincts and the knack for being in the right place at the right time."

ANOTHER SNYDER Sean Snyder was expected to excel at football. After all, his father is none other than K-State Coach Bill Snyder. Sean transferred to K-State from Iowa and punted for the Wildcats for two seasons, ending his senior year in 1992 as an Associated Press All-American. He was the first Wildcat to earn the honor since Gary Spani did so in 1977.

Snyder averaged 40.5 yards as a junior, and then upped his output to 44.7 his senior year. "I worked hard going into the year, and it really couldn't have turned out much better," he said.

1993: THE BOWL BEGINNING

MAY DAY Throughout the struggles of the 1992 season, rumors of a redshirt quarterback with a gun for an arm started to filter out of K-State camp. Chad May had transferred to K-State from California State-Fullerton following the 1991 season when the coaching staff there decided to move toward a more ground-oriented attack. (The school dropped football after the 1992 season.)

May wasn't overwhelming in his first game at K-State, a 34-10 victory over New Mexico State. He threw 30

Chad May debuted as K-State's quarterback in the 1993 season-opener against New Mexico State.

passes, completing 17. He tossed no interceptions, but also had no touchdown passes. In fact, May looked rusty in the game. Coach Bill Snyder described some of May's throws as "helicopter passes," because sometimes it looked as if the ball was twisting end to end.

UNDER THE DOME On September 18, a 2-0 K-State team traveled north to Minneapolis, Minn., to play the program's third game in a domed stadium, against the Minnesota Golden Gophers at the Hubert H. Humphrey Metrodome. The program had lost its other two games in a dome (38-24 in 1992 vs. Nebraska at Tokyo; 20-16 in 1988 vs. Tulane in New Orleans).

On top of that, K-State hadn't won a non-conference road game since beating Air Force in 1979. That losing streak stood at 18. K-State had also lost all four of its games against Big 10 opponents since beating Indiana in 1961.

The streaks ended in Minnesota, with a 30-25 K-State victory that was anything but easy. K-State made the game look like a runaway early by building a 17-0 lead on the Gophers, but Minnesota came roaring back. By

THE FACILITIES: A WISE INVESTMENT

When Bill Snyder was hired as Kansas State's football coach in November 1988, he exacted a promise from University President Jon Wefald that the program's run-down facilities would receive an upgrade.

Wefald has held true to that promise, thanks to millions of dollars donated by loyal K-State fans and, in part, a little luck.

The first order of action was redecorating the football complex. Eventually, money donated by a Saline County couple completed the refurbishment, resulting in the facility being renamed the Vanier Football Complex. Among the improvements are a new 6,500-square-foot weight room, state-of-the-art locker rooms, a new training room, high-tech meeting rooms with the latest video equipment, and a new players' lounge.

Then, a little luck helped the program pay for new turf at KSU Stadium. In 1990, a pair of K-State alumni won $35 million playing the lottery and donated about $800,000 to put in the new artificial turf. The playing surface was dubbed Wagner Field, while the name KSU Stadium remained.

The next step came prior to the 1993 season when a $5.5 million fund-raising campaign financed the construction of a new press box and a full-scale indoor practice facility.

The press box/luxury suites tower on the west side of the stadium replaced a "temporary" press box erected in 1968. In addition to providing comfortable media facilities in a sound-proof environment, the tower was designed with 22 luxury

A multimillion dollar press box/luxury suite complex now dominates the west side of KSU Stadium.

A full-sized indoor practice facility opened prior to the 1993 season.

suites that cost $50,000 each up-front and $10,000 a year in rent, while requiring the purchase of 12 season tickets a year. The suites quickly sold out.

The indoor practice facility measures 230 by 400 feet, one of the largest such facilities in the nation. A regulation football field is housed beneath a roof high enough for the team to practice all facets of the game, including punting.

Two more steps forward came in 1996, the year the Big 12 Conference debuted.

First, a $1 million learning center was attached to the Vanier Football Complex to serve as an academic headquarters for the support services provided to all athletes at Kansas State.

Second, new scoreboards, a Mitsubishi DiamondVision monitor, and a message center sign near the corner of Kimball and College avenues were installed at KSU Stadium. Advertising paid for the $2.5 million project.

The DiamondVision screen, located above the Vanier Complex at the north end of the field, enables the crowd to see replays from the game as well as video highlights. The replay board was only the second in the nation at an all-college facility. New scoreboards were placed at the southeast and southwest corners of the stadium.

Next on the wish list is an expansion of KSU Stadium, which has room for about 39,000 permanent seats, but can host just over 44,000 fans when temporary seating is used. If financing for the expansion is found, the stadium will likely seat more than 50,000 and feature a deck on the east side as well as more luxury seats.

halftime, it was 17-13, and the Cats led 24-19 in the fourth quarter when their hosts went on the march.

Led by quarterback Tim Schade, Minnesota drove 86 yards to take a 25-24 lead with 5:33 remaining, but a two-point conversion attempt failed. With things looking gloomy for the Wildcats, receiver Andre Coleman took the ensuing kickoff 72 yards to set the Cats up at the 24. K-State was in the end zone in just five plays, with junior tailback J.J. Smith dashing in from 7 yards out to put KSU up 30-25 with 3:11 remaining. K-State's two-point conversion also failed.

Game over? Not so quick. Minnesota pushed the ball down field and set up at K-State's 4-yard-line with time running down. K-State's defense held the Gophers out of the end zone on four straight plays to preserve the victory.

BIG EIGHT SCHEDULE K-State opened the 1993 Big Eight slate with a 10-9 win over Kansas at KSU Stadium, and then lost a 45-28 shootout in Lincoln with Nebraska, before tying Colorado 16-16 in Manhattan.

The exclamation mark to the long haul of rugged games came when the Cats stifled Oklahoma 21-7 to move to 6-1-1 on the season. That victory ended a 22-game losing streak against the Sooners. Maybe Mitch Holthus, Voice of the Wildcats, put it best with his sign off that day: "Bill 'Moses' Snyder has parted the Red Sea and says, 'Let my people go' from 23 years of Sooner bondage."

WILDCAT QUIZ

13. In 1954 the Big Eight Conference set up the Phillips 66 All-Big Eight Academic Football Team. Several Wildcats have been recognized for this honor. Who was the first to receive it?

A NAKED LOSS With games against Iowa State, Missouri and Oklahoma State left on the schedule, it was easy for the K-State players to begin dreaming of playing in a New Year's Day bowl. That glance down the road meant the Wildcats didn't see the bump right in front of them.

A little too full of themselves, the Cats went to Ames to take on the lightly regarded Iowa State Cyclones. As the third quarter wound down, K-State led 17-6, and it looked as if the Wildcats' confidence was well-placed.

Then came the streaker. With wind chills dipping near zero, a naked man darted across the field at Cyclone Stadium and headed for the K-State bench. "I think there was somebody from Kansas State he was trying to impress," Iowa State Coach Jim Walden said. "I don't know, but I don't think they were."

The police pinned the man against a brick wall and then carted him from the Wildcat sidelines. But something else left the Cats' sideline at that point: K-State's momentum. A renewed Iowa State team ripped off 21 unanswered points to build a 27-17 lead. KSU quarterback Chad May connected with running back J.J. Smith for a 54-yard touchdown as the game wound down, and after the two-point conversion failed, K-State

Kevin Lockett has become famous for making circus receptions.

trailed 27-23. K-State attempted an on-side kick, but the Cyclones recovered the ball and ran out the clock.

"They hurt a great deal," Coach Snyder said of his shocked team. "They'll take this loss as a team, because it was a team loss. We failed on offense, we failed on defense, and failed on special teams when we had to have it."

THE ACROBAT Kevin Lockett had made more than his share of spectacular catches during his 1993 freshman season, but when the Wildcats beat the Missouri Tigers 31-21 the week after losing at Iowa State, Lockett came up with a show-stopper. With the Cats marching on a crucial drive, Lockett leapt high and snared a bullet pass from Chad May with his right hand. Lockett pulled the ball into his chest with only one hand as a Missouri defender took his legs out and Lockett fell headfirst to the ground. Somehow the freshman from Tulsa, Okla., held on to the ball, and the Cats held on to the victory. It would be one of many amazing catches Lockett would provide during his K-State career.

MAY'S MAGIC Coming off the win over Missouri, K-State had an opportunity to finish the regular season 8-2-1 with a victory at Oklahoma State, but the Wildcats nearly took another tumble. In fact, they would have if not for a little magic delivered by Chad May.

After building a 14-0 lead, K-State watched as OSU tied the game with eight minutes left. Then, with just 58 seconds remaining in the game, Cowboy kicker Lawson Vaughn booted a 43-yard field goal to put Oklahoma State up 17-14.

WILDCAT QUIZ

14. There have been two Kansas State football players to lead the nation in a statistical category: Name them?

K-State took over the ball at its own 20 with 58 seconds and had no time-outs remaining. It seemed like only a miracle would get the job done, but that's what the Cats got and with 17 seconds to spare.

The first play was an incompletion, followed by an illegal procedure penalty that moved the ball back to the 15. Then it was May to Lockett for 18 yards to the 33, but that was followed by another illegal procedure penalty that moved the ball back to the 28.

May and Andre Coleman connected for 24 yards to the OSU 48 with 38 seconds left. May looked to Lockett once more, picking up 26 yards to the 22. That was followed by a 5-yard pass to the 17. May looked back to Coleman on the next play, and his senior receiver was open in the end zone, but the Oklahoma State defender grabbed Coleman's jersey to prevent the catch. The pass-interference call set K-State up at the 2. May found tight end Brad Seib open in the back of the end zone on the next play.

In 41 seconds of action, K-State went 80 yards with no time-outs to win the game 21-17. "The drive Chad put together, in the time frame, was the best I've seen in my career," Coach Snyder said.

QUIET RECORD Place kicker Tate Wright had his ups and downs at K-State, but when the senior kicked three extra points against Oklahoma State in his hometown of Stillwater, Okla., Wright tied Ralph Graham as K-State's all-time leading scorer with 196 points.

Jamie Mendez was named an All-American safety in 1993.

DEFENSIVE ANCHORS By the end of the 1993 regular season, the nation knew Kansas State had one of the finest defensive backfields in college football. Thomas Randolph developed into one of the top cornerbacks in the nation, but it was senior safety Jaime Mendez who earned All-American status for the Wildcats, Every major All-American poll, including The Associated Press, tabbed Mendez as a first-team pick. He ended his K-State career with 15 interceptions in 45 games.

BOWL SELECTION K-State ended the regular season at third in the Big Eight. Following the standings, K-State should have gone to the Aloha Bowl in Hawaii, but the John Hancock Bowl, which was supposed to get the conference's second-place team (Colorado), instead invited Oklahoma, the fourth-place finisher, to El Paso. That angered the K-State players and coaching staff, because the Aloha Bowl then picked Colorado to play in Hawaii. That sent K-State to the Copper Bowl in Tucson, Ariz.

"Our goal was to finish as high as we possibly could in the conference and be rewarded with an opportunity to attend whatever bowl correlates with that," Snyder

Coach Snyder turned K-State's second bowl appearance into the program's first bowl victory at the 1993 Copper Bowl.

said. "That's not the way it played out, and I have some concerns about that."

COPPER CONCLUSION From the start, the Kansas State Wildcats and the Copper Bowl seemed to fit together. The game represented K-State's second bowl game in school history (the first being the 1982 Independence Bowl). The Copper Bowl was a game on the rise looking for a charge. K-State, and the thousands of fans who longed to see their team play in a bowl game, gave the game the energy it needed.

December 29, 1993, will go down as one of the greatest dates in K-State football. The Wildcats may have wanted to go to Hawaii, but the game in Tucson was within driving distance of Kansas, and Wildcat faithful responded to the opportunity to see the Cats play the Wyoming Cowboys of the Western Athletic Conference.

"As the sun begins to set on Tucson tonight," Athletic Director Max Urick said at the luncheon proceeding the night's game, "you're going to see a purple haze on the horizon. Because they're coming, and they're coming by the thousands."

Urick was right, Arizona Stadium was overrun by Wildcat fans, about 20,000. A record crowd of 49,075 saw Wyoming score the first points of the game on a 35-yard field goal. However, by halftime, K-State had grabbed the momentum by taking a 26-10 lead. The big jolt came when receiver Andre Coleman busted loose for a 68-yard punt return for a touchdown.

K-State then tacked on 14 more points in the third quarter to build a 40-10 lead. The big play in that span? Quarterback Chad May rolled to his right, threw across

Andre Coleman broke a 68-yard punt return for a touchdown against Wyoming in the Copper Bowl.

the field and found Andre Coleman wide open. The senior speedster broke away for a 61-yard touchdown.

K-State capped its scoring frenzy with a 37-yard interception return by Kenny McEntyre for a touchdown. The end result was a 52-17 Wildcat romp, and a bowl trip that may have marked the program's breakthrough to football respect.

1994: BACKING IT UP

TICKET COUNT The most convincing evidence that the Copper Bowl represented Kansas State's football breakthrough may have come when the athletic department went to sell season tickets for the 1994 season.

Season ticket sales bottomed out at 7,000 in 1988, Stan Parrish's final year. There was minimal growth in Coach Bill Snyder's first season, followed by gains the next two years. There was a jump to a respectable 15,000 in 1992 from 10,000 the year before, but then in 1993, there was no growth. Coming off the Copper Bowl, officials were able to increase their ticket base by one-third. When K-State opened its season with a 34-6 romp over Southwestern Louisiana, there were about 20,000 season-ticket holders among the crowd of 38,216 at KSU Stadium.

HAWK HUNTING K-State carried a 3-0 record to Lawrence when the Wildcats opened the 1994 Big Eight season against the Kansas Jayhawks. The Thursday night game was nationally televised by ESPN. With the nation watching, K-State raced out to a 21-0 lead behind quarterback Chad May, but then hung on for a 21-13 victory.

Chad May showed a national television audience on ESPN how good he was in helping the Cats beat Kansas in 1994.

Senior quarterback Chad May cut up the Hawks, completing 33 of 44 passes for 379 yards. K-State refused to allow the Jayhawks to complete their rally by playing a little keepaway. K-State had possession of the football for a little more than 40 minutes of the 60-minute game.

SOUND ADVICE The October 6 issue of the *Kansas State Collegian*, the school's student newspaper, offered a little advice for students planning on attending the game in Lawrence. Here's how to escape safely from Lawrence after K-State wins:

"1. Take extra clothing that is not purple. 2. Leave your K-State parking permit at home. 3. Wash off the purple face paint. 4. Disguise yourself in Birkenstocks and flannel. 5. Watch out for grease on the goal posts."

Good advice, but the grease didn't work. K-State fans tore down one set of goal posts at KU's Memorial Stadium following the Wildcat victory.

RAIN ON THE PARADE The table was set for K-State's first victory over Nebraska since 1968 when the Huskers came to town on October 15. The gap between the two programs had closed considerably over the previous three seasons: The average margin of victory had dropped to 12.7 from 41.1 over the 10 seasons prior to 1991. And K-State quarterback Chad May was playing outstanding football.

On top of that, Tommie Frazier, Nebraska's starting quarterback, was injured and wouldn't play. His backup, the star-crossed Brook Berringer, was also injured but entered the game in the second half to help lift the Huskers to victory. The start went to third-string walk-on Matt Turman. A victory parade was surely in store, but then a cold rain began to fall and K-State's downfield passing attack was stifled.

After trailing only 7-6 at halftime, K-State eventually lost 17-6 when Nebraska scored 10 points in the fourth quarter behind Berringer. May was just 22 of 48 for 249 yards in the game, and he threw an interception.

WILDCAT QUIZ

15. What football player became known for his traditional Samoan war dance during the 1982 season?

ADDED FRUSTRATION The frustrations of the Nebraska loss were followed by another near miss with the Colorado Buffaloes. K-State traded punches with the Buffs, going into the fourth quarter tied at 21, but lost 35-21. A goal-line stand by the Buffaloes in the game summed things up. Twice, a camera on the goal-line seemed to indicate running back J.J. Smith had broken the plane of the end zone, but he was ruled down both times, with CU holding the Cats out on the drive.

J.J. Smith ended his career in 1994 as K-State's all-time leading rusher with 2,210 yards.

RUNNING WILD K-State closed the 1994 regular season with a non-conference game in Las Vegas against Nevada-Las Vegas. If you bet on the Wildcats — and senior running back J.J. Smith in particular — then you were a big winner in the game.

K-State won 42-3, with Smith rushing for 227 yards on 34 carries. Those totals made Smith K-State's all-time leading rusher with 2,210 yards. Smith scored 22 touchdowns in his four-year career.

MAY MEMORIES Chad May played only two seasons at K-State, but he will always be remembered as one of the all-time great quarterbacks in school history, joining Lynn Dickey and Steve Grogan in purple hearts.

May's two seasons in Manhattan rank as the school's best two single-season passing seasons. During May's 1993 season, he threw for 2,682 yards. That was followed by 2,571 yards in 1994. May ranks behind only Dickey in career passing yards. But Dickey amassed his 6,208 yards in three seasons (1968-70), while May threw for 5,253 in two seasons. May left atop the school's record books in two categories: Passing efficiency (131.90) and completion percentage (56.04).

CHARACTER STUDY Mike "Crash" Ekeler was one of those personalities too unique to create. Ekeler had to be born a little crazy. This was the guy who first caught the attention of K-State fans by being the "wedge buster" on K-State kickoff coverage teams. The reserve linebacker, often with his face painted for the game, would dive headfirst over the wedge and try to take out the runner. It most often didn't work, but it looked great.

Ekeler had a pet piranha, and when "Carl Lipbalm Spagler" died, he had the fish bronzed and mounted. He named his second piranha, "Kitt Chipowski," deriving the name from a character in the Bill Murray movie *Quick Change*, and teammate Kitt Rawlings.

When told Dan Henning, the coach of the Boston College team the Wildcats were preparing to play in the Aloha Bowl, also was an avid Bill Murray fan, Ekeler said, "Really! I've got to party with that guy. After the game we'll get together. Bill Murray is my idol; *Caddyshack* my bible."

Mike "Crash" Ekeler hung his bronzed pet piranha above his locker.

Joe Gordon blocked a punt that led to K-State's lone touchdown in the 1994 Aloha Bowl.

ALOHA CATS For everything that went right at the 1993 Copper Bowl, things went equally bad at the 1994 Aloha Bowl. Expensive video equipment was stolen from K-State's hotel in Hawaii before the game, and then on the second play of the Christmas Day game against Boston College, Eagles running back David Green broke 51 yards for a touchdown.

The entire day became a study in frustration (BC sacked Chad May eight times in the contest). K-State's lone bright spot was when Joe Gordon blocked a punt that Chris Sublette recovered for a touchdown. Boston College won the bowl, 12-7, ending K-State's season at 9-3.

1995: THE BENCHMARK

TALE OF TWO GAMES In Kansas State's 1995 season opener, the Wildcats manhandled Temple 34-7, and were expected to do the same when they traveled to Cincinnati in Week 2. However, the Bearcats were certainly not a pushover.

With new quarterback Matt Miller at the helm, the

Wildcats' offense began to show some differences from the Chad May years. Miller didn't possess the strong arm of May, but he could scramble and move around much better. When the Cats arrived in Cincinnati, the offense had not fully made the transition between the two quarterbacks. Miller found himself anchored in the pocket and threw four interceptions in the game and also fumbled twice. K-State fell behind 14-0 by halftime.

Yet, Coach Bill Snyder stuck with Miller. By the end of the third quarter, Cincy's lead had diminished to 14-9. K-State took a 17-14 lead in the fourth quarter. With the K-State defense now dominating the Bearcats, it looked as though the game was over. Then Bearcats quarterback Eric Vibberts moved his team down the field and into the end zone with 44 seconds remaining in the game to take a 21-17 lead.

Miller, despite all of his shortcomings in the game, responded with a 38-second drive that rivaled the magic Chad May had delivered during K-State's 1993 trip to Oklahoma State. "He knows he didn't play a good game, and yet he came back for the big drive," senior receiver Mitch Running said of Miller afterward. "When he got in the huddle, his eyes weren't glassy like he was scared. He looked at us and took command."

Quarterback Matt Miller showed his mettle early in the 1995 season with a victory at Cincinnati.

The Cats started their drive at their 41. Miller scrambled for eight and five yards, and K-State was also penalized five yards. He then threw two incompletions before connecting with Tyson Schwieger for 20 yards to the Bearcat 31. K-State's Snyder knew what play he wanted to call but wanted to be closer to the Bearcat end zone. There was one problem: there were only eight seconds left in the game.

So, Snyder patiently asked Miller and his receiving corps to take one more bite out of Bearcat territory with a 9-yard pass to Running. Now with three seconds remaining, Miller and Kevin Lockett hooked up for a little history.

"I thought the play would work, I really did," Miller said.

Schwieger and Running lined up to the left, with Lockett split wide to the right. Miller took the snap and rolled to left with his sights set on his two receivers working against

Kevin Lockett caught a pass on the final play of the game to beat Cincinnati.

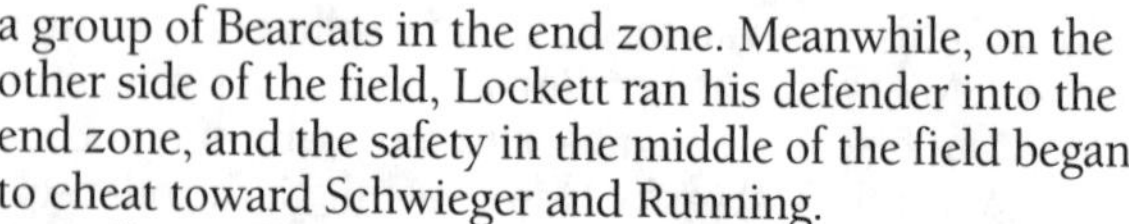

a group of Bearcats in the end zone. Meanwhile, on the other side of the field, Lockett ran his defender into the end zone, and the safety in the middle of the field began to cheat toward Schwieger and Running.

Miller swiftly turned his attention to Lockett and uncorked a pass toward the front corner of the end zone.

"I knew I would have to put something extra on it," Miller said, and he did.

Lockett turned around and waited for the ball to arrive while the Cincinnati defender scrambled to recover. Lockett reached up and grabbed the ball out of the air and ducked into the corner of the end zone. Six points. No time left on the clock. A 23-21 Wildcat victory.

"It was all in slow motion," Running said. "Tyson and I looked back from our routes and saw Matt let it go and Kevin catch it."

LOTS OF ZIPS K-State returned home at 2-0, with the Wildcats knowing they were a better team for having escaped Cincinnati. That's when the K-State defense decided that the Wildcats couldn't lose if the opposition didn't score. Akron, fittingly nicknamed the Zips, came to town and lost 67-0. Northern Illinois followed with a 44-0 loss. Then, Missouri arrived at KSU Stadium to open the Big Eight season. The Wildcats shut out the Tigers 30-0.

"K-State by far has the best defense in the league," Missouri Coach Larry Smith would say by season's end.

Defensive tackle Tim Colston proved himself to be a big-game performer for the Cats.

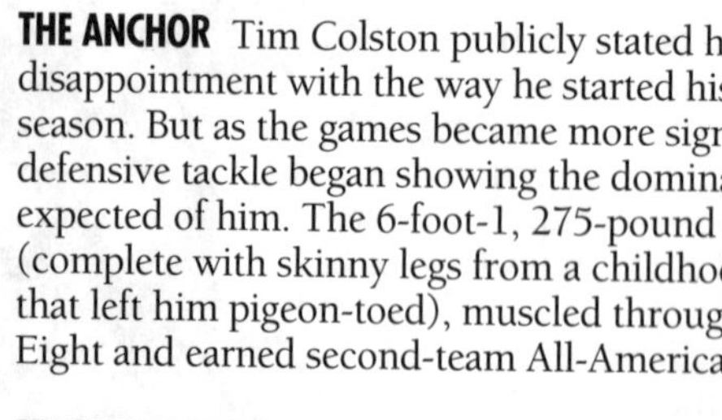

THE ANCHOR Tim Colston publicly stated his disappointment with the way he started his senior season. But as the games became more significant, the defensive tackle began showing the dominance people expected of him. The 6-foot-1, 275-pound Colston, (complete with skinny legs from a childhood ailment that left him pigeon-toed), muscled through the Big Eight and earned second-team All-America honors.

FEATHERED FRIENDS After a close victory at Oklahoma State and a not-so-close loss at Nebraska, K-State returned home with a 6-1 record and a No. 16 ranking. Next up were the sixth-ranked Kansas Jayhawks — a game that would prove to be a turning point for the Wildcats.

KU had already beaten Colorado and stood at 7-0 on the season. This was as good a Kansas team as Lawrence had enjoyed in years. But "nobody had pressured them like we could," safety Chuck Marlowe said. "We knew if we got up in their face it would be a different story."

That's what the Cats did from the start, taking advantage of breakdowns by the KU special teams to build a 27-7 lead at halftime. In the second half, K-State piled on for a 41-7 victory. The win was so convincing that

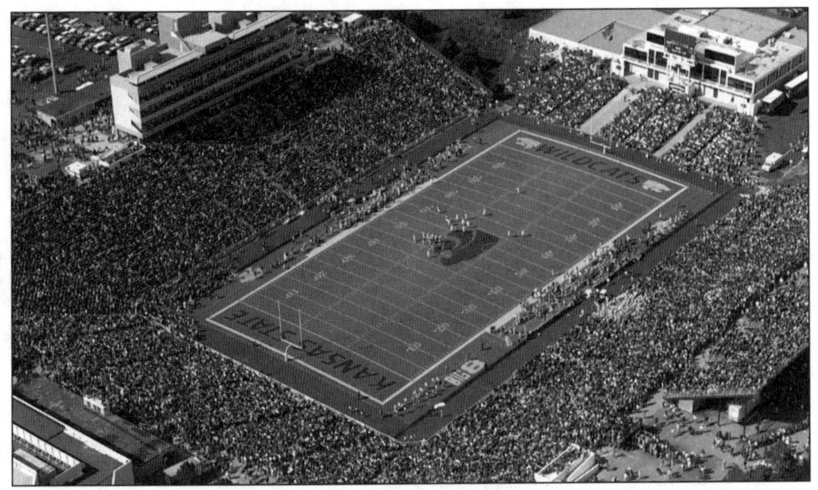

K-State fans packed KSU Stadium to watch the Wildcats dismantle Kansas 41-7 on October 28, 1995.

K-State scored its last points with 13:08 remaining and then shut down the offense to show its opponents mercy.

"I knew they were a good football team," quarterback Matt Miller said. "But I knew we were better. We went out and proved it."

CANTY CAN By the end of the KU game, people around the nation were beginning to take notice of a sophomore cornerback whom defenses were finding unbreakable. Chris Canty, standing only 5-foot-10 and weighing 190 pounds, became a folk hero of sorts to K-Staters.

His knack for making huge plays and his trademark pony step after doing so, earned Canty the nickname "Baby Deion," in honor of NFL standout Deion Sanders. By season's end, the sophomore had earned first-team All-America honors and had been named one of three finalists for the Jim Thorpe Award, given to the nation's best defensive back.

Cornerback Chris Canty was named an All-American as a sophomore following the 1995 season.

BUFFALOED K-State followed the KU showing by dominating Oklahoma and Iowa State. "This is the worst physical beating I've ever been associated with," OU Coach Howard Schnellenberger said after losing 49-10. "I know it could have been worse." With a 9-1 record and ranked No. 7 in the nation, K-State seemed destined to beat the Colorado Buffaloes in the regular-season finale.

When November 18 arrived, the weather was warm and atmosphere at KSU Stadium electric. The Cotton Bowl had announced during the week leading up to the game that the winner would head to Dallas. K-Staters started to make plans for New Year's Day in Dallas.

Colorado ruined the party, playing one of its finest games of the season and taking a 27-17 victory over the

Wildcats. K-State scored with 2:24 remaining to grab a 17-13 lead, but Colorado rose to the occasion with an 80-yard, six-play drive that took only 80 seconds. Now trailing 20-17, Miller looked for some more magic, but all the Wildcats got was a shotgun snap that flew past their quarterback and was recovered for a Buffalo touchdown.

"This is tremendously disappointing, quite obviously," Coach Snyder said, "but collectively we didn't play well enough to win the ball game."

SMOTHERING D "They're a great defense. Probably as good as we've had in the league since some of the Oklahoma teams in the 1970s." Nebraska Coach Tom Osborne knows a few things about great defenses, and his compliment to the 1995 K-State defense was a fitting honor.

The Wildcats ended the season with the nation's top-rated defense, allowing just 250.8 yards per game. The Wildcats finished second in the nation in scoring defense (13.2), and would have also won that category if not for that errant snap that Colorado scored on to end the regular season.

HAPPY HOLIDAY K-State missed its chance to play in the New Year's Day bowl that the players and coaches coveted. But a bid from the Holiday Bowl in San Diego quickly took the sting out of the Colorado defeat. The Holiday Bowl, considered the best bowl not regularly scheduled on New Year's Day, would turn out to be shockingly like the Copper Bowl in 1993.

Many of the estimated 12,000 KSU fans that attended the 1995 Holiday Bowl greeted Coach Snyder and the team the night before the game at a pep rally in downtown San Diego.

No one expected so many K-Staters to make the long and expensive trek to San Diego, but when kickoff time arrived on December 29, there were an estimated 12,000 K-Staters in Jack Murphy Stadium. "We were awestruck by all the purple in the stands," said John Reid, the Holiday Bowl's Executive Director.

By early in the second quarter, Colorado State, K-State's opponent, was awestruck by the Wildcats. The two teams traded punches in the first quarter, ending it tied at 7.

The turning point may have come early in the second quarter, when K-State quarterback Matt Miller was hit so hard he experienced numbness and temporary paralysis. Miller, a native of San Diego playing his final collegiate game, was taken from the field on a stretcher. Seeing their comrade so severely injured (Miller would make a full recovery) lighted a fire under the Wildcats. Back-up Brian Kavanagh entered the game and made use of great field position provided by the Cats' defense and special teams.

Reserve quarterback Brian Kavanagh came in when starter Matt Miller was injured early in the second quarter and became the hero of the Holiday Bowl.

On CSU's next drive, K-State safety Mario Smith, the game's defensive MVP, made the first of his two interceptions and returned it to the CSU 24. On the second play of Kavanagh's first drive, the quarterback handed off to sophomore running back Mike Lawrence who went five yards for the touchdown. CSU's next drive ended after three plays and the Cats blocked the punt, giving the offense the ball at the CSU 32. On the second snap of that drive, Kavanagh handed off to senior fullback Dederick Kelly who went 18 yards up the middle for the touchdown.

Four plays, and Kavanagh had the Wildcats up 20-7. Kavanagh, the game's offensive MVP, helped K-State build a 33-7 lead early in the third quarter. The Cats rolled to a 54-21 victory over their opponent from the Western Athletic Conference. Kavanagh finished 18 of 24 for 242 yards and four touchdowns. The four TD passes tied a Holiday Bowl record set by former Brigham Young great Jim McMahon.

"All season long I haven't been nervous coming in," Kavanagh said. "I just had to go in and do tonight what I've been doing all season."

K-State finished the 1995 season with a 10-2 mark, the program's best record since going 10-1 in 1910. The Wildcats were ranked No. 7 in the final Associated Press Top 25, and No. 6 in the USA Today/CNN Coaches poll.

"We just keep going up every year," junior Nyle Wiren said. "Our goal was the Top 10. Now our goal will be the Top Five."

The Pre-Purple Pride Years: 1896-1966

History has forgotten the actual score of the first football game played at the school now called Kansas State University.

On December 2, 1892, a team from Kansas State Agricultural College played its first game. At "quarter back" was a sophomore from Colfax, Ill., named A.D. Benson. Benson had introduced his schoolmates to football when he arrived at KSAC in 1891.

The sport, however, was quickly banned by the college. Five years later, the school's newspaper, the *K-State Industrialist*, remarked, "It is hoped that our students have the good sense to play even football without violence; but the game as sometimes played is next to barbarism."

Despite that ban, students scheduled a game at nearby Abilene in November 1894. After the game had been scheduled, the faculty gave its permission to play. The team representing KSAC lost, 24-0.

In 1895 a challenge was leveled by a team from St. Mary's, Kans., but the KSAC faculty turned down the challenge on the grounds that the college had no team.

Kansas State Agricultural College played its football games on Ahearn Field on the K-State campus prior to the opening of Memorial Stadium in 1922.

In 1896, KSAC played the first game now recorded in K-State's list of all-time scores. A team coached by Ira Pratt traveled to Fort Riley on Thanksgiving Day and lost to a squad comprised of soldiers, 14-0. Later that fall, KSAC played Fort Riley again, and this time the game ended in a 6-6 tie. It was during the 1896 season that KSAC adopted the mascot "Aggies," and selected royal purple as the school's official color.

A.W. Ehrsam led the school's team to a 1-3-1 record

in 1897, and in 1898 W.P. Williamson directed KSAC to a 1-1-2 mark. Football was beginning to gain acceptance.

Prior to the 1899 season, the faculty raised nearly $100 to cover team expenses. The Board of Regents appropriated $300 to support outdoor sports, building team dressing rooms with showers and lockers. The team, coached by Albert Hanson, a former guard at the University of Nebraska, went 2-3 in 1899.

In each of the first nine "official" seasons of football at Kansas State a different man coached the team. In 1901, Wade Moore took over the program, with the school playing eight games that season. Season tickets were sold for $1, and a rivalry began to develop between KSAC and Bethany College of Lindsborg, Kans.

Moore had been an athlete at the University of Kansas, and he kicked two "goals" in KSAC's season-opener at Bethany, a 12-5 victory. Later in the 3-4-1 season, Bethany came to Manhattan and won 17-0. The school's newspaper, the *Student Herald*, wrote: "Although their team is almost entirely composed of star professional players, they did not outclass our own eleven."

In 1902, the school's rivalry turned to the east, and the Governor's Trophy was established to be given to the winner of K-State's game with Kansas. KU won that initial meeting between the two schools, a 16-0 decision in KSAC's final game of the 1902 season.

After those first nine seasons of constant turnover within the school's football team, the school hired Mike Ahearn to coach. He would hold the position for six seasons — from 1905 to 1910 — also coaching the KSAC basketball team from 1906 to 1911.

By 1905, football was turning into a craze on the Manhattan campus. Six home games were played, and 500 season tickets were sold. More than 600 K-State fans made the trip to Lawrence for the game against Kansas. Ahearn's team finished the season with a 6-2 record.

Ahearn led the Aggies to their first victory over KU, 6-4, in 1906. The Governor's Trophy series has continued with only one interruption — the schools did not schedule each other in 1910, one of the greatest seasons in K-State football history. During Ahearn's six seasons as head coach, KSAC compiled a 29-13 record, culminating with a 10-1 record in 1910.

WILDCAT QUIZ

16. Who scored K-State's last points off a turnover on an opponent's extra-point attempt?

A SEASON TO REMEMBER Captain Croyle. Harvey Roots. Jack Holmes. Merle Sims. "Horse Power" Bates. The names are no longer known, but the 10-1 record compiled by the 1910 Kansas State Agricultural College Aggies remains unmatched in K-State history.

"From the bottom of our left ventrical (sic) we utter the declaration that the football machine of 1910 has

The 1910 team still owns the school's best single-season record with 10-1 mark.

embodied in it more of the elements of perfection than any of its predecessors," the school yearbook, the *Royal Purple*, wrote of the season. "A machine that could participate in eleven melees, and in only one fail to deliver the necessary energy, must have a very low coefficient of friction and a multitude of interchangeable parts."

To put it in more modern terms, the 1910 KSAC Aggies were loaded, and they delivered. In the nine seasons prior to Coach Mike Ahearn's taking over the football program, the Aggies compiled a 15-32-6 record. In Ahearn's first five seasons, the school went 29-11, and his tenure as football coach concluded with the 10-1 mark in 1910.

So complete was the school's dominance early in the season that it took six games before the Aggies were scored upon. The Aggies lined up their under-manned opponents and plowed them under: William Jewell, 57-0; Haskell Institute, 39-0; Kansas State Teachers College-Emporia, 22-0; Arkansas, 5-0; Drury, 75-0; Missouri School of Mines, 23-0.

What followed was a mid-season slump. KSAC escaped with a 6-2 victory over Creighton in Omaha, Nebr. Then the Aggies lost their lone game of the season: a 15-8 setback at Colorado College. "Lamentations would be ineffective at this stage so that we prefer to let this history remain as recorded," the yearbook stated. "It was clearly a case of not living up to possibilities, either because of external or internal circumstances, perhaps a portion of each in combination."

The Aggies roared back in their final three games of the season. KSAC beat Wichita University, 33-6; Baker University, 35-0; and Washburn, 33-0. "Marking the close of so many players' foot ball careers it was only fitting that they should give a final demonstration of their real ability," the *Royal Purple* recorded. "The style of play was perfect and certainly was an appropriate close for such a successful season."

Little did anyone know that the 10-1 season wasn't the beginning of a football dynasty at Kansas State Agricultural College, but the high-water mark. Ahearn stepped down as coach after the season and focused his attention on being the school's athletic director.

During the next 22 seasons, the Aggies would win more games than they lost, but matching the 1910 season remained unattainable.

WILDCAT QUIZ

17. Who is K-State's all-time leader in all-purpose yards?

EVERY MAN A WILDCAT Through its first 19 seasons of athletic competition, Kansas State had used "Aggies" as its mascot. But prior to the 1915 season, new coach John "Chief" Bender gave his squad the nickname "Wildcats." The moniker lasted the one season Bender coached at K-State. Under Coach Z.G. Clevenger in 1917, the school team became known as the "Farmers." In 1920 another new coach, Charles Bachman, took over the program, renaming the team "Wildcats." This time, the nickname stuck.

In 1922, Bachman asked alumni to consider donating an actual Wildcat to the school to serve as a mascot. KSAC alumni Herbert R. Groome and John E. McCoy, both veterinarians in Twin Falls, Idaho, donated "Touchdown I" to the school shortly after the animal was nursed back to health under their care. (The bobcat had had an encounter with a porcupine, and his face and throat were punctured by numerous quills. Unfortunately, Touchdown I never fully recovered from its fight, dying of pneumonia shortly after arriving in Manhattan.)

Although the bobcats have served as K-State's wildcat mascot since 1922, the animals no longer attend K-State games. Touchdown XI, the 11th in the line, currently resides at Manhattan's Sunset Zoo.

NATIONAL ATTENTION Ray Hahn came to KSAC from Clay Center, Kans., in 1918 to serve in the Student Army Training Corps. During his time in Manhattan he joined the football team and quickly became a star. In 1922, Hahn was not only captain of the 5-1-2 Wildcat team but was also named to the Grantland Rice All-America team, making him K-State's first All-American. In 1938, Hahn moved to Lindsborg, Kans., and distinguished himself as a basketball coach before retiring in 1974.

In 1922, Ray Hahn was named K-State's first All-American football player.

At 6-foot-5 and more than 200 pounds, Henry Cronkite was an imposing figure for K-State from 1929 to 1931.

AN ALL-AMERICAN To see Henry Cronkite was to remember him. Standing 6-foot-5 and weighing more than 200 pounds, Cronkite was a massive man in 1929. That was the first season he took the football field for the Kansas State Wildcats. However, he wasn't supposed to be a Wildcat. Cronkite had decided to attend the University of Kansas in 1928, but a visit from new K-State Coach Bo McMillin persuaded Cronkite to attend K-State.

Cronkite didn't play his freshman year, and in 1929, his sophomore season, the Wildcats struggled to a 3-5 record. It was during Cronkite's junior campaign that he began to grab the spotlight. In a 14-0 loss to Kansas, Cronkite and teammate Jim Yeager played the entire game, and Cronkite was widely acclaimed for his staunch defensive efforts.

After the Wildcats opened the 1930 season with a 1-3 mark, they rattled off wins over Missouri, Iowa State, and a team from Centre leading up to their season finale with Nebraska in Lincoln. Starting at tackle against the Cornhuskers, Cronkite intercepted a pass and scored K-State's only touchdown on a pass from Eldon Aucker. Cronkite's efforts led to 10-9 victory, the school's first-ever against Nebraska. K-State ended Cronkite's junior season with a 5-3 record.

Cronkite's senior season was one of the finest in K-State history. The Wildcats raced out to a 5-0 record before heartbreaking defeats to Iowa State (7-6) and Nebraska (6-0) at Memorial Stadium. On November 26, 1931, K-State ended its 8-2 campaign with a 22-0 victory over Washburn. Two days later the accolades for Henry Cronkite began to roll in.

On November 28, Cronkite was named to the Associated Press All-Big Six squad. Two days later, *The New York Sun* and *New York World Telegram* named Cronkite an All-American. By the end of the year, nearly every publication in the nation that selected All-America teams had included Henry Cronkite on theirs, making him K-State's first consensus All-American.

WILDCAT QUIZ

18. In 1993, kicker Tate Wright tied what player atop K-State's career scoring list with 196 points?

LET THERE BE LIGHT On October 8, 1932, the Kansas State Wildcats played the first night football game in school history. The team traveled to Salina, Kans., to play Kansas Wesleyan that evening and won the contest, 52-6, before a crowd of about 4,000.

Fifteen years later, in 1947, K-State played its first night game in Manhattan, a 12-0 loss to Oklahoma at Memorial Stadium.

A LONG WAIT Something happened in 1933 that would take 58 years to repeat. When the Kansas State Wildcats went 6-2-1 and the Kansas Jayhawks put together a 5-4-1 record, the two schools laid claim to winning seasons for the last time until 1991.

A LANDMARK When Coach Bo McMillin accepted the head coaching job at Indiana University prior to the 1934 season, K-State in turn hired away the head coach from Oklahoma A&M to lead the Wildcats. Lynn "Pappy" Waldorf was the chubby son of a Methodist minister, and one heck of a football coach.

In 1934, Coach Lynn "Pappy" Waldorf provided the school with its only Big Six championship.

Waldorf inherited a team that featured some returning lettermen, a talented sophomore class, and a high level of team morale. Waldorf translated that, and his knack for developing talent and using numerous players in each game, into the school's only Big Six championship.

K-State started the season with a sloppy 13-0 victory against Fort Hays State at Memorial Stadium and then embarked on long road swing. K-State played Manhattan (N.Y.) to a 13-13 tie on a muddy Ebbets Field, and then traveled to Milwaukee where the Wildcats lost 27-20 to Marquette. That was followed by a 13-0 victory over Kansas, and then a 21-0 loss at Tulsa.

With their record sitting at 2-2-1, there was little to indicate that this would be a remarkable season for the Cats. Then they won 14-6 over Washburn, 29-0 against Missouri, 8-7 at Oklahoma, and 20-0 at Iowa State. Suddenly, the Wildcats were 6-2-1 and 4-0 in Big Six play.

All that stood between K-State and the league title was a Thanksgiving Day game at Nebraska, the three-time defending Big Six champion.

The game began as had K-State's season. Nebraska marched up and down the field against the Wildcats, with K-State showing little of its ability or determination. But despite muscling around the Wildcats, the Cornhuskers only scored once, leading 7-0 at halftime.

The second half of the game was much like the second half of K-State's season. Waldorf dug into his deep bench, and the war of attrition began to turn the game in K-State's favor. Maurice Elder scored on a 9-yard touchdown dash in the third quarter to tie the game, and the Cats never looked back. Before a crowd of 22,000 at Nebraska's Memorial Stadium, K-State rang up 22 unanswered points to win 22-7.

The victory finished K-State's season at 7-2-1 and provided the Wildcats with a historic league championship. However, Waldorf's romance with Manhattan was short lived. Following his lone season at K-State, Northwestern hired him to coach, and K-State promoted assistant Wes Fry to head coach.

THE LOSING BEGINS Lynn Waldorf's departure from Manhattan marked the end of K-State's football glory.

Coach Wes Fry's winning season in 1936 would be the program's last until 1953. (Under Coach Bill Meek, the Wildcats had 6-3-1 and 7-3 seasons in 1953 and 1954. Those winning season were the program's last until Coach Vince Gibson's 6-5 mark in 1970. That totals three winning seasons from 1935 to 1969, a span of 34 years.)

MR. MUSCLE Elmer Hackney, a multisport star at Kansas State during the late 1930s, was a man of many names — One Man Gang; Mahrajah of Might; Mr. Muscle. It took many nicknames to encompass the legend of Elmer Hackney, because he might have been the greatest all-around athlete ever to wear K-State purple.

Hackney was an All-Big Six football selection in both 1937 and 1938. He also shined in the realm of track and field, winning the NCAA shot put championship in 1938

Elmer Hackney was a powerful fullback who carried multiple nicknames.

and 1939. And, Hackney won three Big Six wrestling championships.

And to think Hackney nearly never made it to college. If not for the efforts of his high-school principal, Dutch Anderson, Hackney may have never earned his high-school degree. As one Hackney legend goes, Anderson made six trips to Hackney's home in Oberlin, Kans., to persuade the student to stay in school.

Hackney got his high-school diploma and then went on to K-State, where he was an outstanding student and adored by his fellow students. Hackney was voted the "Most Glamorous" student on campus, a title he could have used to meet women on campus. But Hackney had married the former Ellen Perrill in 1936, the summer before he came to Manhattan.

WILDCAT QUIZ

19. Who is the only Wildcat to lead the team in tackles all four years of his eligibility?

It was on the football field that Hackney first grabbed the headlines. During his junior season in 1938, K-State played at Northwestern, one of the nation's powerhouse programs at the time. Despite the Wildcats losing 21-0, Northwestern players called the K-State fullback, "the strongest man we've ever seen in a football suit."

Hackney, however, saved his best for the shot put. On his way to winning the NCAA shot put championship in 1939 (for the second consecutive time), Hackney established 18 new shot put records in 12 collegiate meets, including a U.S. record of 55 feet, 11 inches and an NCAA Championship record of 55 feet, 10 3/8 inches. Hackney earned a berth on the 1940 Olympic team, and was one of the favorites to win the gold medal before the games were canceled due to World War II.

Back on the football field, Hackney was being touted as an All-American heading into the 1939 season, but a knee injury ended his final season. That didn't end his football career, though. Hackney went on to play seven seasons in the National Football League, the final five for the Detroit Lions.

Elmer Hackney died at age 52 in 1969. He was survived by Ellen, his wife of 33 years. "I don't believe I've ever seen another athlete like him," Ellen told the *Kansas State Collegian* in 1991. "When it came his turn to do things, he would almost be bored because he did almost everything better than everyone else."

A FIRST FOR EVERYTHING Kansas State and Nebraska had been playing each other since 1911, and in the 30 years leading up to the 1941 season Nebraska had never lost in the state of Kansas. November 1, 1941, marked the end of the Nebraska reign, with the Wildcats taking a shocking 12-6 victory over their Big Six rivals.

It was Homecoming in Manhattan, and with the mighty Cornhuskers coming to town, a smaller-than-

MEMORIAL STADIUM: A LASTING TRIBUTE

As World War I came to a conclusion in 1918, the faculty of Kansas State Agricultural College thought it would be appropriate to build a memorial to the 45 KSAC students who had lost their lives in service to their country.

The next year, that concept was combined with the school's need for a new football facility, and the idea for Memorial Stadium was born. In May 1922, bids were let for construction, and work began on the west side. The east structure was added in 1924.

The original plans for the stadium were impressive, considering the era. The stadium was to seat 22,500, and form a horseshoe on the southwest corner of the campus around a field running north and south.

Each side of the stadium began and ended with a tower that rose 10 feet higher than the 40-foot walls. In between the two, plans called for a third section, complete with two 60-foot towers at the south end of the field and a grand entrance for fans.

Work to enclose the back walls of the east and west structures pressed through the late 1920s, but all work came to a halt when the Depression hit in 1929. After the Depression, the cost of the stadium had risen from $350,000 to $500,000 and the final section to enclose the horseshoe never made it beyond the planning stage.

The stadium was intended to not only serve as a home for the Kansas State Agricultural College's football program, but to also supplement the crowded facilities at Nichols Gymnasium.

Mike Ahearn, the former football coach who served as the school's Director of Athletics in the 1920s, wrote in the February 1, 1923, edition of the Kansas State Agricultural College Bulletin about the need to build the new stadium to replace the field that carried his name.

"The Memorial Stadium will

Crowds packed Memorial Stadium for games from 1922 to 1966.

The original plans for Memorial Stadium called for an enclosed horseshoe.

make it possible to care for the 1,600 young men and the 800 young women who are taking physical education and engaging in varsity and intramural athletics, and will also give seating capacity for the crowds coming to view our games," Ahearn wrote.

With only three sections of the west wing completed in 1922, the first game was played at Memorial Stadium, a 47-0 victory over Washburn University. Forty-six seasons later, K-State played its final game at Memorial Stadium — a 40-6 loss to Colorado.

Beginning with the 1968 season, the team moved to KSU Stadium, and since then, the space and offices beneath the two sides of Memorial Stadium have been used for a variety of academic and administrative purposes.

Memorial Stadium was built long before the K-State Student Union (in the lot to the right) or Ahearn Field House (above the stadium).

usual crowd turned out at Memorial Stadium to watch Coach Hobbs Adams' team. When the Cornhuskers took a 6-0 lead after one quarter, it looked as if defeat was on its way. Then on the first play of the second quarter, Michael "Jug" Zeleznak, K-State's 174-pound quarterback, broke free for a 66-yard touchdown run that tied the score. Later in the second quarter, K-State put together a drive, and Zeleznak dove into the end zone from a yard out to put the Cats up 12-6.

As it turned out, the victory was K-State's only one of the Big Six campaign. The Wildcats ended the 1941 season with a 2-5-2 record.

A GOOD START The 1945 season started with great promise — a 13-6 victory over Wichita University at Memorial Stadium. K-State sealed the victory when freshman back Ted Grimes threw an 11-yard touchdown pass to Bill Weaver. That victory seemed to sum up the age of K-State football.

The promise of the opening victory evaporated over the course of Coach Lud Fiser's 1-7 season. The Cats lost 28 games before winning their next game, a 37-6 victory over Arkansas State in the third game of the 1948 season. That was K-State's lone victory of that season, also.

WILDCAT QUIZ

20. Which Wildcat has gone the highest in the NFL Draft?

THE COLOR BARRIER The year was 1948. World War II was over, and America was experiencing an economic boon. Harry Truman sat in the White House. And all seemed well, if you judge the era by old newsreel footage. Perhaps it was — if you were white. If you weren't, you continued to live the life of a second-class citizen.

One of privileges enjoyed by whites was playing football in the Big Seven Conference, (which had just changed from the Big Six with the addition of the University of Colorado). When Harold Robinson graduated from Manhattan High School that year, he was prepared to become Kansas State's first black athlete. The journey wouldn't be easy.

Robinson was supposed to receive a scholarship from the Blue Key honor society to play football at K-State. However, the battle over the use of blacks in the Big Seven was heated. The universities of Missouri and Oklahoma refused to enroll black athletes. They also pressured other league schools to ban black players. It soon became unclear whether or not Robinson would play at K-State, and Blue Key retracted its scholarship offer.

"They weren't sure if the coaches were going to let us play or if the league was going to let us play," Robinson told the *Manhattan Mercury* in 1991. "I guess they didn't want to blow their money on someone who couldn't help them."

Center Harold Robinson was the first African-American to play football at K-State and the first of his race to be named all-conference in the Big Seven.

That didn't deter Robinson. He enrolled at K-State and found out that Coach Sam Francis would allow him to join the team. But he would have to wait to play, because freshmen were ineligible at the time. Without a scholarship, Robinson worked two jobs to pay his way through school. He washed dishes at Scheu's Cafe and mopped floors at Manhattan's bus terminal. He worked seven days a week, earning around $12 a week that helped him pay rent on his apartment.

Robinson survived that first year, but Coach Francis left K-State after one season, and it was unclear how Ralph Graham, the incoming coach, would handle the situation. Graham went to the owner of Scheu's and asked him to fire Robinson. Graham then put his sophomore on scholarship, making Robinson the first black athlete to receive an athletic scholarship in the Big Seven.

Robinson was named an All-Conference center in 1950, his junior year, despite playing for a 1-9-1 K-State team. Robinson gained the considerable respect of opponents and fans despite the smoldering racism that was so pervasive during his playing days. He wasn't allowed to stay at the same hotel as his teammates on road trips to Oklahoma and Missouri, instead staying in private residences.

Prior to the 1951 season, Harold Robinson made an even bolder move off the gridiron. He fell in love with a white woman. After secretly dating Mary Helm, the daughter of the head of the art department, for more than a year, the two married while in Topeka attending a concert. Robinson had been drafted into military service, and he knew he would soon leave. He didn't want to leave without Mary.

The two kept their marriage a secret from Mary's family for about 45 days before her parents found out. That night, Harold Robinson and his wife loaded his Chevy with all it could hold and left Manhattan prior to his senior season.

Eventually, Robinson served in Korea, earning a Purple Heart. The woman he loved divorced him at the insistence of her family. Not long after returning from Korea, the first African-American to be named an All-Big Seven performer remarried.

Wildcat Bob Mayer died of polio following his sophomore season.

A WILDCAT LOST During his sophomore season in 1950, Bob Mayer rushed for 210 yards on 60 carries. For 1951, the Brewster, Kans., fullback was looking forward to big things. However, his 38-yard touchdown reception in K-State's 28-7 loss to Missouri in 1950 would be Mayer's only touchdown as a Wildcat. As the team prepared for the 1951 season, Bob Mayer died of polio.

The 1951 media guide was dedicated to Mayer, but the Wildcats won only one game that season. The game ball from that contest was signed by the players and Coach Bill Meek, and dedicated in the name of Bob Mayer. That lone win in the 1-7-1 campaign was a 14-12 victory over Missouri.

MR. PERPETUAL MOTION Veryl "Joe" Switzer remains the highest NFL draft pick in the history of Kansas State. In 1954, the Green Bay Packers picked the defensive cornerback and offensive halfback with the fourth pick in the first round of the draft. Switzer earned his spot in the draft after three seasons of outstanding play at K-State.

It was on defense that Switzer earned the nickname "Mr. Perpetual Motion." In 1951, as a sophomore, the Nicodemus, Kans., native earned second-team All-America honors as a defensive back.

After seeing limited time on offense during his first season of action, Switzer emerged as one of the nation's top two-way players in 1952. Switzer not only played both offense and defense, but also returned punts and kickoffs. He rarely missed a single play during the course of a game, earning second-team All-America honors as a junior.

Switzer saved his best for last. He carried the

Veryl Switzer starred on offense, defense and special teams for K-State in the 1950s.

Wildcats, who had finished last in the Big Seven the previous five seasons, to a 6-3-1 record and a second-place finish with a 4-2 conference mark. Switzer not only distinguished himself as one of the nation's best cornerbacks, he also led the Wildcats in rushing, receiving, scoring, and punt returns (averaging 31 yards a return to lead the nation). All of that added up to Switzer being named a first-team All-American by the American Football Coaches Association.

"He's the best defensive back we played against," Oklahoma player Merrill Green said after Switzer had done all he could in a K-State loss to the Sooners. "He was all over the field and made three-fourths of the tackles."

One of Switzer's career highlights was a 167-yard performance against the Kansas Jayhawks during a driving snowstorm in 1953. Switzer scored the lone touchdown in the game, which was being televised on NBC, when he broke a 74-yard run. The TD handed

WILDCAT QUIZ

21. This former Wildcat offensive tackle played on the New York Giants' 1987 Super Bowl team.

K-State a 7-0 victory, its first over KU since 1944.

Switzer played for two years with the Packers and then served from 1956 to 1958 with the Air Force, being named to the Armed Services All-Star team in 1957. When he returned from the service, Switzer played three years in the Canadian Football League before retiring.

Switzer began a career in education in 1960 and returned to K-State in 1969 as the Administrative Assistant to the Athletic Director and Coordinator of Minority and Cultural Programs. Switzer became Dean of Minority Affairs in 1978 and Assistant Vice-President for Student Affairs in 1981. In 1988, Switzer was named an Associate Athletic Director, a position he held until 1996 when he switched duties to oversee K-State's implimentation of a new NCAA academic program.

Now a member of the Kansas State High School Activities Association Hall of Fame, the Kansas State Hall of Fame and the Big Eight Football Hall of Fame, Veryl Switzer stands out as one of K-State's all-time greats.

ORANGE CRUSHED November 20, 1954, marked a giant opportunity missed for the Kansas State football program. The Wildcats traveled to Boulder, Colo., with their eyes set on a victory and a berth in the Orange Bowl. However, the last game of the season proved to be a disappointment for Coach Bill Meek's team. Colorado running back Carroll Hardy ran wild against the Cats — picking up 245 of CU's 493 rushing yards on the afternoon — as the Buffaloes beat the Wildcats 38-14. The loss ended K-State's season with a 7-3 record and snuffed out the Cats' bowl hopes.

FILM STUDY It went into the books as a 46-0 victory over arch-rival Kansas, marking the largest margin by which a K-State team had prevailed over KU in 53 years. The victory on November 5, 1955, seemed like one of those unexplainable blowouts. But there was an explanation. If it looked like the Cats knew exactly where each and every KU play was headed, it's because they did.

While watching films of the Jayhawks, the KSU coaching staff asked the players to study the men they would be working against. Linebacker Andy Stewart kept his eye on KU's right guard. As the film progressed he began to notice a trend. By the end of the film he knew he saw something.

Once the film was over, one of the coaches innocently asked, "Does anybody have something to add?" And Stewart did.

Stewart had noticed the right tackle was tipping the direction of each KU play. If the play was headed right, the right tackle's right foot would be back slightly. If the play was headed straight into the line or to the left, the tackle's feet would be even. That night the K-State coaching staff created a new defense designed to take advantage of the insight, and it led to K-State's total dominance in the contest.

SPARTAN EFFORT K-State closed its 1957 season with a 3-6-1 record, but nearly ended the campaign with a stunning upset of the nation's top-ranked team. K-State traveled to East Lansing, Mich., to play the Michigan State Spartans, who were at the time ranked No. 1. The Wildcats led 9-6 at the end of three quarters, but the Spartans exploded for 21 points in the fourth quarter to post a 27-9 victory.

THE REAL TRUTH Truth be known, Gene Keady wasn't a very good basketball player. Sure, at Purdue University he's distinguished himself as one of college basketball's finest coaches, but Keady was never good enough to crack the starting lineup at Larned (Kans.) High School. Yet, Keady was a great athlete, starring in track, baseball, and as his high school's quarterback.

Gene Keady went on to become a famous basketball coach at Purdue University after playing football at K-State, where he suffered a knee injury.

Yet, he wasn't a good enough athlete to receive an offer from a Big Seven Conference school. So Keady enrolled at Garden City (Kans.) Community College and proved himself as a quarterback. Then the schools came with their offers, and eventually Keady chose to attend K-State over Kansas, New Mexico, Colorado, and Wichita University. But if it had not been for Keady being hit in the head with a 12-pound shot put during high school, he would have never attended K-State. After going to Garden City, Keady received an appointment to the Air Force Academy, but he was rejected because the shot put had years earlier knocked him unconscious and caused a seizure.

So off to K-State Keady went, where he was converted from quarterback to running back and receiver. During the 1956 season under Coach Bus Mertes, Keady led the Wildcats with seven touchdowns. He ran for 310 yards on 43 carries and caught 14 passes for 247 yards.

For his senior season in 1957, Mertes converted Keady to a full-time halfback, and his season started with great promise. He started the first four games of the season, but it was in Game 4 that his life changed. In the 42-14 loss to Colorado, Keady had already picked up 85 yards on a long run for the Wildcats, but fumbled the ball at the 5-yard line. Then he injured his knee, suffering cartilage and ligament damage. His college football career came to an end. Unable to afford an operation to correct the damage, Keady's opportunity to play professional football dried up.

WILDCAT QUIZ

22. Cat Chat, the weekly coach's radio show, started on the Wildcat Network in what year?

That's when he went into coaching. His varied athletic career began to serve him well.

"Track taught me how important running is," he told Purdue's *Gold & Black Illustrated* years later. "Endurance and conditioning are probably why we win a lot of games, because we're in better shape than a lot of teams.

"Football taught me how to get organized. Basketball's the sport I studied the most, especially shooting. Everybody can improve their shooting; I know, because I did it myself.

"Baseball is like golf. It teaches you to be humble and it teaches you there are a lot of things you can't do anything about. ... And all of them taught me about team play, not to be involved in jealousies and to share things and to be for your teammates."

ROUNDING OUT THE FIELD After 10 years as the Big Seven Conference, the league grew into the Big Eight with Oklahoma State's admittance in 1958.

THE BARREN YEARS Doug Weaver came to Kansas State after serving as an assistant football coach for two years

A baby-faced Doug Weaver became the K-State head coach at age 29 in 1959.

each at Michigan State, his alma mater, and Missouri. Weaver was only 29 years old when he became head coach at K-State in December 1959. He looked so young that he later told a story that upon arriving an ambitious paper boy came to sell a subscription to a new customer and asked Weaver, "Are your parents home?"

To say the task Doug Weaver took on was Herculean would be an understatement. The K-State football program had only two winning seasons in the previous 23 years, and had gone a 15-28-1 in five years under Coach Bus Mertes.

When the Wildcats opened the 1960 season, they beat South Dakota State, 20-6, in Weaver's debut. They followed that win with nine-straight losses to end the season 1-9. A 2-8 season in 1961 was followed by a 0-10 campaign. After three years in Manhattan, Coach Doug Weaver's team had won a total of three games.

It can be said that the school gave Weaver plenty of time to grow into the job, which he never did. The Wildcats went 2-7 in 1963, 3-7 in '64, 0-10 in '65, and finally 0-9-1 in 1966. In seven seasons, Weaver compiled an 8-60-1 record.

THE GAME THAT WASN'T Friday, November 22, 1963. Most can remember where they were on the day President John F. Kennedy was assassinated. For members of the Kansas State team, the answer would be

Cornelius Davis was the first Wildcat to rush for more than 1,000 yards in a season with 1,028 in 1966.

on a bus bound for Stillwater, Okla. K-State was scheduled to play Oklahoma State the following day. But that game, like many other games that weekend, was canceled and never rescheduled. The cancellation ended K-State's 1963 season with a 2-7 record.

EMERGING STARS K-State didn't win a game in 1966, but two players emerged as stars on offense. Cornelius Davis became the first K-State running back to gain more than 1,000 yards in a season as the sophomore rushed for 1,028 yards, winning the Big Eight rushing title. His three-season total of 1,873 ranks fourth on K-State's all-time list.

At wide receiver that season was a sure-handed sophomore named Dave Jones. Jones earned the nickname "Mr. Hands" by catching nearly everything thrown his way. He had 721 receiving yards his

Receiver Dave Jones emerged as an offensive star in 1966.

sophomore season, earning him the conference's "Big Eight Sophomore Lineman of the Year" award. By the time Jones was done, he had caught passes for 1,904 yards, placing him third on K-State's all-time list.

ALL TIED UP While the pathetic record Coach Doug Weaver's teams put together over seven seasons seems bad enough, it was actually worse than the numbers would indicate. During Weaver's first six seasons, K-State lost to arch-rival Kansas by a combined score of 188-0. That's right, K-State didn't score for six seasons while giving up an average of over 31 points a game.

In Weaver's final contest against the Jayhawks, his team managed a 3-3 tie. Many remember that game, despite the Wildcats' scoring against the Jayhawks and not losing the game, as the low point of K-State football. K-State led 3-0 for most of the game, and it looked as if the Wildcats would win their homecoming contest and end a 10-season losing streak to the Jayhawks. However, following a K-State fumble in the final minute of the game, KU took possession in K-State territory. When KU's drive stalled with eight seconds remaining in the game, the call went out on the Jayhawk sideline for someone who thought they could kick a 38-yard field goal. Lineman Thermos Butler stepped forward and, despite not kicking since high school, punched a dying effort just over the crossbar to tie the game at 3-3.

Kansas went 2-7-1 that season under Coach Jack Mitchell, and K-State ended the year 0-9-1. Both coaches were fired.

The old saying goes, "If you can't beat 'em, join 'em," and that's exactly what Weaver did with the University of Kansas. After being replaced by Vince Gibson in Manhattan, Weaver earned his law degree from KU, and then joined Coach Pepper Rodgers' KU staff in 1970. That turned out to be Rodgers' final season in Lawrence.

WILDCAT QUIZ

23. From 1977 to 1984, these two men handled K-State's punting duties each as a four-year starter.

Vince Gibson: 1967-74

Vince Gibson took over the K-State program in 1967 and immediately began telling people, "We gonna win."

When a flamboyant football coach from Tennessee arrived at Kansas State in 1967, he took over a football program that had experienced just two winning seasons in the previous 30 years.

It didn't matter to Vince Gibson. He landed in Manhattan saying, "We gonna win." And win the Wildcats did, but not as often as the legend of Vince Gibson would have one believe. For all that Gibson did for the K-State program, his teams posted a winning season only once during his seven-year reign.

While his 33-52 record may not shine, Gibson did bring self-respect to the K-State football program. His teams often lost, but the Cats did it against the likes of Penn State, Arkansas, and Florida. In 1970, with senior Lynn Dickey at quarterback, the Wildcats went 5-2 in the Big Eight (6-5 overall), taking second in the conference.

The following words, spoken in Salina, Kans., soon after he took the K-State job, may sound eerily familiar to K-Staters. Perhaps Vince Gibson was only setting the stage for Bill Snyder.

"I don't think K-State people realize what a great school they have and the potential it offers in the competitive area of collegiate football. Its identification with the state is as strong as any school I've even been associated with. Don't let anyone tell you that this is an impossible job because of the losing tradition here. Quite frankly, the opportunity to excel is at its greatest right now. Now is the time when Kansas State can become a legend in the annals of collegiate football. We have something to sell: a great school, great people, and believe you me, physical facilities that in a short time will hold its own with any in the country. But let me assure you this job is not for the timid, the skeptic or the lazy. I love to compete."

The 1967 media guide also pointed to Gibson's style and commitment to the K-State program. This description, too, could be written of Snyder.

"Vince Gibson is no miracle man. Like any human being, he will make mistakes. He is not the suave type. He does not dispense glamour. He sells sincerity, dedication, and self-discipline. He is a man of boundless enthusiasm. He does not play golf, or fish, or hunt, or worry about the stock market. As Gibson says:

" 'There are three things in my life — my wife, my four children and my football team.' "

Gibson's first K-State team went 1-9, but one of his first accomplishments as K-State coach was attracting the services of a highly recruited quarterback from Osawatomie, Kans. Lynn Dickey was the type of leader around whom Gibson could build his program.

Dickey was one player in an amazing recruiting class that brought to Manhattan some of the school's all-time great players. Mike Montgomery, Mike Kuhn, Manuel Barrera, Clarence Scott, Ron Dickerson, and Charles Collins were all in that 1967 recruiting class.

"I look back over my coaching career, and K-State was my favorite job," Gibson said in 1995. "When I got there, they hadn't won a game in over two years, there were no facilities, and I was 32 years old. It was one of those jobs that no one thought could be done. K-State is a tough job."

Gibson has many fond memories of the people of Manhattan and the Kansas State program.

The "Gibson Girls" gave prospective football recruits tours of K-State while they were in Manhattan.

After that initial season, things started to change. Dickey took control of the offense in 1968, and K-State posted one of its biggest victories in school history during the 4-6 season: a 12-0 victory at Nebraska. Gibson followed that up with 5-5 and 6-5 seasons, both of which featured wins over Oklahoma.

In the end, it was Gibson's bitter rivalry with Kansas Coach Pepper Rodgers that did him in. First, Rodgers accused Gibson's program of NCAA rules violations. That led to similar charges by Gibson concerning KU.

Both programs ended up on probation, but K-State took the brunt of the punishment from the NCAA and the Big Eight Conference.

"My biggest disappointments at K-State both happened in the same week in October of 1970," Dickey recalls of his senior season. "We got socked with probation primarily based upon the allegations of a running back at KU, Vince O'Neil. Then he runs a kickoff back 100 yards and they upset us in Manhattan, 21-15. I played terrible, we all did."

On October 8, 1970, the eve of that game, the Big Eight put K-State on probation for three years. The penalties extended through the 1972 season and prohibited all television exposure and postseason competition. Coach Gibson was formally reprimanded, and violations were cited in four areas: financial aid, unethical conduct, scholastic eligibility, and recruiting practices. KU was put on a less-stringent two-year probation.

"We hated each other," Gibson said in 1995 about Rodgers. "We got put on probation and they were the ones that did it to us. ... I see him once in a while. I don't have any bitterness about it.

"At one time, I tell you what, he killed my program. He hurt my coaching career. He got us on three years probation, and we could never get out from under it."

The glory days of the Vince Gibson era were over. During his final four seasons in Manhattan, his teams went 5-6, 3-8, 5-6, and 4-7. The damage done to the program by the probation couldn't be undone until Snyder arrived in 1989.

Nobody is happier to see the program's present success than Vince Gibson, now living in New Orleans.

"I'm a big, big K-State fan," he said. "I'm so happy for the people. The reason K-State was my favorite coaching job was the people. When I got there, nobody was behind the program.

"But then people got behind the program with all of that purple pride. They wore their purple. They learned how to tailgate. They were great."

It can be said that Vince Gibson laid the foundation upon which Bill Snyder later built a program.

COURAGE Ken Ochs was a 6-foot, 208-pound long shot to make the K-State football team in 1966. The La Crosse, Kans., native made the K-State team but suffered a leg injury during that spring's drills. After his leg didn't respond to treatment, it was discovered that Ochs had a malignant bone tumor. His leg was amputated six inches above the knee.

Cancer claimed the leg and eventually the life of Wildcat player Ken Ochs.

Ochs returned to K-State and earned his degree in the spring of 1969. By then, he was a manager for the football team, and the program had named an honor for personal courage in his name. Ken Ochs died of cancer on October 3, 1969.

THE BATTLER In 1967, the first year the Ken Ochs Courage Award was given, it went to Dan Lankas. The Atwood, Kans., native battled his way through his playing days at K-State. Lankas' first two years at K-State were under Coach Doug Weaver, with the Wildcats compiling a record of 0-19-1. Then, in Gibson's first season, the Cats went 1-9. Despite the team's poor record, the middle linebacker stood out. Lankas' two-year (1966-67) total of 353 tackles is unmatched in K-State history.

Lankas never gave up, playing a significant role in the Cats' win the one time he tasted victory in Manhattan. In

Linebacker Dan Lankas shined during some bleak K-State seasons in the late 1960s.

K-State's 17-7 season-opening victory over Colorado State in '67, Lankas had 16 unassisted tackles, five assisted tackles, and an interception.

"I just knew we were gonna win," the team captain said after the game. "I knew because I could see it in the team's eyes when I met with them Thursday before the game."

An injury prevented Lankas from playing professional football, so he returned to help Gibson coach in 1968 and 1969. Eventually, Lankas wound up back home in Atwood as head football coach, and built his alma mater's program into one of the state's small-class powerhouses.

LITTLE BIG MAN Mack Herron was a sight to behold. Standing just 5-foot-5, Herron electrified Kansas State crowds with his darting moves. "The most amazing

Mack Herron stood just 5-foot-5, but he electrified crowds with his quickness and explosive play.

athlete I ever saw on the football field," is how teammate Lynn Dickey describes Herron. "At only 5-5 and 180 pounds, Mack was the Big Eight 100-yard dash champion and combined his speed with unbelievable strength and balance."

Early in the 1968 season, Herron's first season of action after transferring from Hutchinson (Kans.) Community College, K-State fans found out how exciting Herron could be. He returned a kickoff 99 yards to start the second half against Virginia Tech, and helped spark the Wildcats to a 34-19 victory.

In 1969, Herron scored 126 points — still the highest

total for a season by any Wildcat. His 21 touchdowns during the season also tops K-State's record book. The scoring total was the second-highest in the nation that season behind Oklahoma's Steve Owens.

WILDCAT QUIZ

24. How many Wildcats have rushed for over 1,000 yards in a single season?

By the time Herron completed his two-year career at K-State, his name dotted the record books. In 1969, he led the team in both rushing and receiving. He's eighth all-time in receiving at KSU, second in kickoff returns and third in scoring. His 1,603 all-purpose yards is second-best in school history.

Herron went on to enjoy a brief, but spectacular NFL career. During the 1974 season with the New England Patriots, Herron set a single-season league record for all-purpose yards. During the year, Herron amassed 2,444 total yards from rushing, receiving, and returning kickoffs and punts. Herron's total broke a mark set by Gale Sayers in 1966.

"It goes to show you that anything can happen," Herron said at the time. "It shows you can do anything if you have the desire."

THE RED MENACE The images still linger from K-State's 12-0 victory over Nebraska in 1968. Heading into the 1996 season, the '68 win at Memorial Stadium was K-State's last over Nebraska, and the last time the Huskers were shut out at home.

Many of the details of the game have been lost in time, but some of the players remember certain images like snapshots in their minds. "I remember they had balloons tied down at the end of the field to be released when they scored," said lineman Mike Kuhn. "One of the greatest joys was at the end of the game, I looked back, and they had never got a chance to release those balloons."

"I don't remember a lot of the specifics other than a few pass plays I was involved in," said Mike Montgomery. "The ball coming through the snow with a background of red still sticks out in my mind."

WILDCAT QUIZ

25. Who is the only player to lead the Wildcats in kickoff return yards for four straight years?

The mind can grab the strangest images from the most important days of a person's life. For example, another one of the few details Montgomery remembers from the game was the movie Coach Gibson showed the team the night before the game.

The movie? *Barbarella.* Then again, what college-aged male of the era wouldn't remember when and where he saw the sexy, controversial Jane Fonda movie?

SEASON TWO Gibson's second season at K-State came to an end with a 4-6 record. Dickey set seven school passing records during the course of the year. The four wins were the most for the program since 1955. Five of

K-State's 10 opponents during the season went on to bowls (Kansas and Penn State, Orange; Oklahoma, Bluebonnet; Missouri, Gator; Arizona, Sun).

LAYING OF THE TURF As the Wildcats prepared for the 1969 season, their fans around the state were jumping on the bandwagon. It looked as if great things were in store for the Cats. Gibson capitalized on the enthusiasm by raising $250,000 to put new turf on the KSU Stadium field, replacing the natural grass.

CLOSE SHAVE Penn State arrived in Manhattan the third week of the 1969 season to face a 2-0 K-State team. The Nittany Lions brought with them the nation's No. 2 ranking. A possible win turned into a loss for the Wildcats when a fumble and two pass interceptions choked off three first-half scoring opportunities.

By the end of the third quarter, Penn State led 17-0. The Cats didn't give up. K-State drove 50 yards in 11 plays to make it 17-7. Then, in the game's final minute, Lynn Dickey hooked up with Mike Creed on a 60-yard touchdown pass to push the score to 17-14. But K-State's on-side kick was covered by the Nittany Lions, and they ran out the clock for the 17-14 victory.

CLASSIC CLASH October 11, 1969, marked perhaps the greatest chapter in the rivalry between K-State and Kansas. Coach Gibson's team roared into Lawrence with a 2-1 record, and Coach Pepper Rodgers' Jayhawks were coming off their 9-2 Orange Bowl season.

Quarterback Lynn Dickey pitched the Cats to many wins during his playing days.

KU's Memorial Stadium was packed with 51,000 fans for the game. The environment was among the finest in all of college football. The story of the game was K-State's offense, and one crucial stop by the K-State defense on the game's final play to preserve the Cats' 26-22 victory.

Lynn Dickey directed the Wildcats on scoring drives of 80, 90, and 62 yards. Mack Herron scored three touchdowns. Mike Montgomery broke a 54-yard run that set up K-State's decisive score. But the biggest star of the game may have been K-State receiver Sonny Yarnell, who made a pair of crucial catches for the Wildcats.

"I don't know many names," KU's Rodgers said afterwards, "but the kid who made those two catches deserves a lot of credit for Kansas State's victory."

The offensive heroics aside, K-State's victory came down to a play by defensive backs Clarence Scott and Mike Kolich on the game's final play. KU quarterback Jim Ettinger threw a pass into double coverage, and as the ball settled into the hands of Steve Conley in the end zone, Scott and Kolich unloaded on Conley, jarring the ball loose.

WILDCAT QUIZ

26. Has any K-State quarterback ever led the program in passing for four straight years?

The K-State victory in Lawrence was complete, a feat that wouldn't be duplicated until 1994. The win also lifted a weight off the K-State program. The Cats hadn't beaten the Jayhawks since 1955, and from 1960 to 1965 they had been out-scored 188-0 by their rivals.

K-State fans tore down the Memorial Stadium goal posts, and they were carried into the K-State locker room. "No one can say Pepper and I haven't brought big-time football to Kansas," Gibson said.

ENDING THE MISERY Oklahoma's dominance over the Kansas State football program was amazing. As the Cats prepared to play the Sooners in 1969, K-State hadn't beaten the Sooners since 1934. That streak came to a shocking end, thanks to Lynn Dickey.

Dickey stepped into the national spotlight by smashing virtually all of the conference's single-game passing records in K-State's 59-21 win over the Sooners at KSU Stadium. Dickey threw for 380 yards on 28 completions in 42 attempts before coming out of the game with almost 10 minutes left. He completed passes to 10 different receivers in the game. Jerry Lawson stepped in for injured running back Mike Montgomery, rushing for 77 yards on 11 carries and catching six passes for 37 yards.

The streak was over. Not only had K-State beaten Oklahoma, the Cats had handed the Sooners their worst loss in school history. The win pushed K-State to 5-1 on the season. That would be the high-water mark for the season, though, as the Cats came unraveled. What once looked like a sure bowl season ended with four straight losses and a 5-5 record.

CRAZY LEGS Henry Hawthorne lit up KSU Stadium when the Wildcats played host to nationally ranked Colorado in 1970. The senior wingback rushed nine times for 128 yards, caught four passes for 96 yards and one touchdown, and returned a kickoff 67 yards. For his contributions in the Wildcats' 21-20 victory, Hawthorne was named the Big Eight's Back of the Week.

WILDCAT QUIZ

27. Who is the only quarterback to lead the Wildcats in total offense two straight years?

REVENGE IS THEIRS In 1970, Kansas turned the tables on K-State. The night before the game, K-State was rocked by probation brought on by charges leveled by KU coaches and players. Then, the Jayhawks sneaked into KSU Stadium and swiped a 21-15 victory. K-State out-gained the Hawks 387-232 in the game. The loss dropped K-State to 2-3 on the season.

GREAT SCOTT Clarence Scott came to K-State with the possibility of being a receiver for a fellow recruit named

Lynn Dickey. Scott never played receiver at K-State, but instead recognized the team's need for a defensive back. It was as a defensive halfback that Scott started for three seasons and blossomed into one of the best defensive backs in the Big Eight.

Clarence Scott starred in the Wildcats' defensive backfield before going on to star in the NFL.

Within two games during his senior season, Scott proved his value to K-State. Coming off a loss to Kansas, K-State needed a boost and got it with a 17-0 victory at Iowa State. With a little more than a minute remaining in a scoreless first half, Scott picked off an Iowa State pass and returned it to the ISU 1. That set up K-State's first score of the game.

The next week, in K-State's 19-14 victory at Oklahoma, Scott deflected a pass into the hands of linebacker Oscar Gibson. Three plays later, K-State scored the decisive touchdown.

"Quickness is the main thing a good defensive back must have," Scott said at the time. "It can make up for a lack of great speed. Secondly, a defensive back has to be sharp. There are so many ways an offensive man can beat you that you have to be on your toes."

When Scott finished his eligibility in 1970, he departed with 12 career interceptions. At the time, the total put him atop K-State's record books. (His numbers were surpassed in 1993 by Jaime Mendez's 15.)

Scott left K-State as an honorable mention All-American (without his degree), going into the NFL as the school's first first-round draft selection. He enjoyed a 13-year, injury-free career with the Cleveland Browns. He twice was named the Browns' defensive player of the year, and he started at defensive back in the 1974 Pro Bowl. The next year, Scott returned to K-State in the off-season and completed his degree in social sciences.

RED HOT K-State carried a 6-3 record into its final Big Eight game of the season, a chance to tie for the Big Eight title if it could win at Nebraska. The Wildcats came nowhere close to victory as Lynn Dickey tossed seven interceptions. The 51-13 setback dropped the Wildcats to 5-2 in the Big Eight. The Cats then finished the season the next week with a 31-7 loss at Florida State, closing the year with a 6-5 record.

PAYBACK TIME Obviously, the Oklahoma Sooners weren't happy about losing to K-State for two straight years. In 1971, they rolled into KSU Stadium and won an offensive shoot-out, 75-28. OU's Greg Pruitt rushed for an NCAA record 294 yards in 19 carries. That's an average of more than 15 yards a carry. The Sooners as a team rolled up a devastating 785 yards of total offense and scored on 11 of their 12 possessions.

NO. 11: K-STATE'S RETIRED JERSEY

Only one number has been retired from use in the history of Kansas State football.

Fans will never again see a Wildcat wear No. 11, and for good reason. Lynn Dickey and Steve Grogan, the program's finest quarterbacks prior to the 1990s, both wore the number.

The magic associated with the number started with Dickey. Coach Vince Gibson knew he needed a strong-armed quarterback to help turn his program into a winner. Dickey was a cocky high school standout from Osawatomie, Kans., when Gibson came calling. The recruiting battle between K-State and Kansas was intense. Dickey was won over by Gibson's dynamic personality and a silly statement from the KU coaches that didn't sound appealing to Dickey, a big fan of New York Jets quarterback Joe Namath.

Lynn Dickey looked up to Joe Namath, starting from the tips of the white shoes that Dickey wore in Namath's honor.

"Vince promised me three things," Dickey said. "He said we would have a state-of-the-art athletic dorm, a new stadium, and a pro-style offense where I could throw the ball 40 times a game.

"But the real clincher for me coming to K-State was when the KU coaches told me I would get to run the ball on rollouts just like (KU quarterback) Bobby Douglass."

No thanks, Dickey told KU, and he came to K-State in 1967 with hopes of replicating Namath's flashy passing style. For the most part, he did.

Dickey still holds K-State's record for career passing yards, with 6,208 during his three years (1968-70). Dickey also engineered some of the biggest victories in K-State football history, including 1968's 12-0 victory at Nebraska and back-to-back wins over Oklahoma, in 1969 and 1970.

The 1969 victory over Oklahoma, a 59-21 thrashing of the Sooners, was historic. The victory was the program's first over OU in 35 years. Dickey completed 28 of 42 passes for 380 yards and three touchdowns in the contest.

The quarterback became known for his white shoes — just like Namath used to wear — and his confident demeanor. When informed that he had just engineered K-State to its first win over Oklahoma in 35 years, Dickey responded, "I wasn't playing here for 35 years. I'm playing now."

Yet, some might find it hard to believe that the win over OU doesn't stand out to Dickey.

"Don't get me wrong, that game was fun, but the 1970 19-14 victory over OU when we scored two late, fourth-quarter touchdowns was much sweeter, and so was our 12-0 upset of Nebraska in Lincoln in 1968."

Dickey led the Wildcats to a 6-5 record in his senior season. That record in 1970 was the program's best in 15 seasons. After graduating, Dickey went on to shine in the NFL with both the Green Bay Packers and Houston Oilers.

While Dickey was building his career in the NFL, another quarterback took over his old number.

Steve Grogan came to K-State from Ottawa, Kans., in 1971. He watched Dennis Morrison quarterback the Cats for two years before finally stepping into Dickey's shoes in 1973.

Grogan, however, was a different quarterback from Dickey. He would scramble and pick up yardage with his feet. Grogan's 2,213 passing yards are good for only eighth on K-State's all-time list.

But that doesn't mean he isn't revered by K-State fans. Grogan's scrappy nature stood as a metaphor for the program. The Cats went 5-6 during Grogan's junior year in 1973 and the 4-7 during his senior campaign, Gibson's last season as the Wildcats' coach.

"Anyone who played at K-State during those years, when we weren't winning many, had a lot of character," Grogan said.

"Steve Grogan is a winner," Gibson said of his quarterback at the time. "Don't ever worry about him."

Grogan followed Dickey into the professional ranks, playing quarterback for the New England Patriots from 1969 to 1991. Grogan, who led the Patriots to the Super Bowl in 1986, holds the franchise's records for passing yards (26,886) and touchdowns (182).

Steve Grogan did the No. 11 proud with both his feet and arm.

Both Dickey and Grogan stick out in the memory of Coach Gibson, who now owns the nation's largest sports travel agency, which is based in New Orleans. But Gibson admits that Dickey's decision to attend K-State still stands out as a factor that led to K-State's success during his years at K-State.

"If I had to say one guy that really sticks out in my mind it has to be Lynn Dickey. He had a lot of places he could have gone, and he came to K-State," Gibson said. "That meant something. I still have some great memories of those guys."

So do most K-Staters.

Mo Latimore anchored one of the Cats' offensive guard spots in the early 1970s and is now a K-State coach.

Meanwhile, K-State piled up 542 yards of offense. New quarterback Dennis Morrison completed 29 passes, but threw three interceptions.

MIGHTY MO As the Wildcats slugged their way through a 5-6 season in 1971, a 6-foot, 244-pound senior guard from Byron, Ga., was winding up his playing days at K-State. Mo Latimore had come to K-State from Hutchinson Community College, and before his second year was elected one of the team's offensive captains.

Mo not only protected quarterbacks Lynn Dickey and Dennis Morrison but also handled some of the kicking duties when Max Arreguin was injured. Latimore played four seasons with the Calgary Stampeders of the Canadian Football League and then returned to K-State as an assistant coach. Latimore worked on the K-State staff until 1985, the last three as assistant head coach, leaving when Jim Dickey resigned. In 1994, Latimore returned to K-State to serve under Bill Snyder.

Isaac Jackson set the standard for rushing at K-State with 2,182 yards and now sits in second on the school's all-time list.

A STIFF WIND K-State carried a 2-3 record into its 1972 meeting with Kansas at KSU Stadium. Amazingly, the Wildcats had not beaten the Jayhawks in Manhattan since 1954.

Three factors added up to K-State's 20-19 victory. There was Jim Cunningham stopping KU quarterback David Jaynes just inches short of the goal on a two-point conversion. Also, a stiff 30-mile per hour wind limited the teams throughout the contest and gave a huge advantage to the team with the wind at its back. Finally, there was Roger Stucky's block of a Kansas point-after attempt that proved to be the difference in the contest.

It all added up to a K-State victory that moved the Wildcats to 3-3 on the season. It would be the Cats' last win of the season, as they spiraled downward through the Big Eight slate with five straight losses.

WILDCAT QUIZ

28. In what two states did Coach Bill Snyder coach high school football?

CALL HIM MR. JACKSON Isaac Jackson ran for over 1,000 yards in his first two seasons at K-State despite a series of nagging injuries. Jackson capped his K-State career with 1,137 during 1973, his senior season. Jackson finished his three-year K-State career with 2,182 yards on 492 carries. He sits second on K-State's all-time rushing list.

WHAT A RELIEF Frustrations were mounting by the time K-State carried a 4-6 record into the final game of the 1973 season. Heading to Colorado, prospects didn't look good for a season-ending victory. But that's what the Cats did, winning 17-14 on Keith Brumley's 30-yard field goal with five seconds remaining.

HOW MUCH TIME IS LEFT? Coach Vince Gibson's final tour in Manhattan was 1974. The 4-7 season was epitomized in the Wildcats' 20-13 loss to Kansas at KSU Stadium in first Big Eight game of the year.

KU escaped with the victory when K-State quarterback Steve Grogan was stopped two yards short of the goal line on the game's final play. Compounding the frustration was the fact that the players on the field were unsure how much time was remaining in the game because the scoreboard clock at the stadium had malfunctioned. When Grogan was stopped, the clock ran out and the game was over.

A loss to Kansas in 1974 was one of the most difficult during Steve Grogan's playing days.

END OF AN ERA Vince Gibson went out a winner when his Cats muscled Colorado 33-19 in the final game of the 1974 season. The 4-7 record marked the end of Vince Gibson's eight-season tenure in Manhattan.

The Waiting Period

ELLIS RAINSBERGER: 1975-77

Ellis Rainsberger took over the Kansas State football program in 1975 after Vince Gibson's departure. K-Staters hoped he could return the Wildcats to the winning ways that had slipped away from Gibson after the program was put on probation in 1970.

K-State fans hoped Ellis Rainsberger could propel the Cats back toward the top of the Big Eight when he became head coach in 1975.

Rainsberger came nowhere close to accomplishing that task. His teams won just five games in his three years. A sixth win was later added to the record books when Mississippi State forfeited a victory in 1977.

Worse yet, Rainsberger landed the Wildcats back on probation by inserting some of his varsity players into junior varsity games under false names, a violation he denied. The attempt to get his players more experience only showed how poor the program had become. The misguided Rainsberger finished his tenure with a 6-27 record.

GREAT BEGINNINGS The 1975 campaign started off magically for Rainsberger. K-State opened his coaching tenure with a 17-16 victory at Tulsa, and then backed it up with a 32-0 victory over Wichita State and a 17-16 win at Wake Forest.

The program's 3-0 start matched the same mark by Gibson's team the year before, but Gibson's team had won just one more game in 1974. Rainsberger's Wildcats were a bigger bust, finishing the season with eight straight losses, including a 28-0 defeat at Kansas.

MISSING THE BUS The 1976 season also started with a victory — a 13-3 win over Brigham Young — but it would be the last of the season. The year was summed up by a 51-0 loss at Nebraska on October 16. The Cornhuskers dominated the Wildcats, holding them to a negative 45 yards rushing, but it was how the Huskers got to the game that was the real story.

Coach Tom Osborne's team had converged at a hotel before the game, but the buses scheduled to pick up the Huskers and take them to Memorial Stadium failed to show up. So, the players wandered to the stadium in groups, some hitch-hiking to get rides.

HARD WORK PAYS Paul Coffman wasn't offered a scholarship by Kansas State. The tight end from Chase, Kans., wasn't offered a scholarship by any major college football program. So, he walked on at K-State and became one of the finest tight ends in school history.

Coach Vince Gibson had promised Coffman a scholarship heading into his sophomore year if he survived the 1974 season. Coffman survived, but Gibson didn't. So to win a scholarship, he had to prove himself to Rainsberger; and he did so in the fall of 1975.

Paul Coffman's name doesn't dot the K-State record book. In fact he never led the Wildcats in receptions in any of the three seasons he played. After his college career ended in 1977, Coffman wasn't drafted by any teams in the NFL. So he tried out again, and proved himself once more.

Coffman played for the Green Bay Packers from 1978 to 1985 and remains the team's all-time leading tight end in receptions and yardage. He played two seasons for the Kansas City Chiefs, and finished his career in 1988 with the Minnesota Vikings.

"At K-State," Coffman told the *Kansas City Star* in 1993, "even though we did get beat 50-0 by Oklahoma, the guys played 60 minutes. We played our hardest the whole game. And I think that's something that helped me in professional football.

"I've been through some tough times. Going through some of that helped me to endure some of the things I had to go through to make it in professional sports. And in life."

As a tribute to Coffman's dedication, the K-State football program began giving out the Paul Coffman Award in 1982. The honor is bestowed each spring on a player who has shown outstanding leadership, attitude, and improvement.

WILDCAT QUIZ

29. This former K-State safety now oversees the athletic department's NCAA rules-compliance program.

THE FINAL WIN K-State carried a 12-game losing streak with it as the Cats went to Wichita State on September 24, 1977. The streak came to an end with a 21-14 K-State victory, but the win would be Rainsberger's last on the field. The next week the Wildcats lost 24-21 to Mississippi State, a loss that later became a victory when the Bulldogs forfeited the contest.

JIM DICKEY: 1978-85

The fact he won only one-in-three football games while at Kansas State doesn't really matter in recounting the legacy of Coach Jim Dickey. Dickey went 25-53-2 during his stint in Manhattan, his tenure coming to an end with his resignation following a 10-6 loss to Northern Iowa in the second game of the 1985 season.

However, people don't remember Jim Dickey for the losing as much as for the stunt he pulled in 1981 to give the K-State faithful a taste of success. Dickey redshirted a

WILDCAT QUIZ

30. In what year did K-State adopt it's school alma mater?

GARY SPANI: THE MAN IN THE MIDDLE

The career of Gary Spani, perhaps more than that any other Kansas State football player, reflected what was wrong and right with too many years of K-State football.

Spani was never on television and never played in a bowl game. During his four seasons, from 1974 to 1977, the Wildcats were 10-34, winners of only one Big Eight game.

Yet, despite such adversity, K-State's all-time leading tackler averaged more than 12 tackles a game for his entire four-year career. Spani was an All-Big Eight selection three consecutive years and a UPI All-American his senior year. He was also a leader in the Fellowship of Christian Athletes, and widely respected by teammates, coaches, fans, and opponents.

— Jerry McKee, *Purple Pride*

Gary Spani's exploits remain cherished at Kansas State. The honors that he, Lynn Dickey, Steve Grogan ,and others won replaced the bowls that the program couldn't reach and the national exposure the team wouldn't received.

Spani bridged the gap between how K-State fans wanted to feel about their program and the reality that had become evident by the time the Manhattan native began his freshman season.

The middle linebacker's freshman campaign came in 1974, the last season the Wildcats were coached by Vince Gibson. Gibson had brought some respect to Wildcat Land, but then his program was rocked by probation. In 1974, the Wildcats went 4-7.

Things only got worse for the Wildcats during Spani's career. Ellis Rainsberger took over in 1975 and was gone following 3-8, 1-10, and 2-9 seasons. His teams went 0-21 in Big Eight play.

Despite all of that, coaches around the Big Eight knew they needed to avoid the 6-foot-2,

Even when the Wildcats weren't good in the 1970s, opponents knew they had to worry about linebacker Gary Spani.

222-pound Spani. The linebacker played his position with unparalleled efficiency.

Gary Spani

"Spani ranks with any of the past outstanding linebackers to come out of the Big Eight," Iowa State Coach Earle Bruce said in 1977.

"Gary Spani is an excellent football player," Missouri's Al Onofrio said in 1976. "But then, he proved he was a good one when he was only a freshman."

Spani's biggest fans were his coaches. It boggles the mind to think where the program would have been without its defensive heart during Rainsberger's reign.

"When you consider his range, instinct, and consistency," Rainsberger said, "then you have to think of Spani in the same breath with the all-time great college linebackers."

"Gary has great fluency, movement, and instinct for the football ... the best linebacker's instinct I've ever seen or coached," said defensive coordinator Dick Selcer. "He knows exactly where to go to make the play most effectively."

Spani mixed those instincts with athletic ability.

"He has tremendous speed and acceleration to the football," Selcer continued. "His height and speed make him extremely effective as a pass defender. He makes more than his share of big plays, but at the same time, he's consistently our stopper."

Spani led the Wildcats in tackles his sophomore, junior, and senior seasons, earning All-Big Eight honors each year. Following his senior season, Spani became the school's first consensus All-American, winning the honor from UPI, Kodak, *Football News*, and *Kickoff Magazine*. His total of 543 tackles still sits far above that of anyone else to play football at K-State.

"We were an excellent defensive team most of my career," Spani said. "But we never scored many points."

It would have been easy for Gary Spani to become full of himself, but that wasn't how he operated. He led people on and off the field, and found courage in the bravery of a former teammate.

"Joe Hatcher probably had the biggest influence on me," Spani said. "He showed such courage after being injured in the alumni game of his sophomore year. He lost a kidney and was forced to stop playing.

"He then became a graduate assistant coach, and on game days he worked up in the press box. In a private pact — just between the two of us — I would point to Joe in the press box whenever I was able to make a big play."

Spani continued his sterling play right into the NFL. Picked in the third round of the NFL draft by the Kansas City Chiefs, Spani played 10 years in the NFL before retiring in 1987.

large portion of his senior class in 1981, saving them for the 1982 campaign.

"I guess it was mostly my idea," Dickey said. "I noted that other teams' starting players were always a year or two older than us, and subsequently stronger and more mature. When I suggested redshirting several of our veteran returning players, most of my assistants told me it wouldn't work and the players wouldn't go along."

The players did go along. K-State went 2-9 in 1981 but returned a team full of players with experience, including a group of seniors who had taken a year off and were hungry for success. K-State went 6-4-1 during the 1982 season, earning a berth in the Independence Bowl. The trip to Shreveport, La., was K-State's first-ever bowl trip, but the Wildcats lost 14-3 to Wisconsin.

"Even looking back today," said Dickey, who has since returned to his high school in Texas to coach, "I would probably have done it the same way."

IN THE BEGINNING When 45-year-old Jim Dickey took over the Kansas State football program from Ellis Rainsberger in the 1978 season, he came with strong credentials. "The best you can think of is the best you can say about Jim Dickey," Houston Oilers Coach Bum Phillips said about his fellow Texan. "He's a fine football coach who has what it takes."

It didn't seem much had changed in Dickey's first three games, losses to Arizona, Auburn, and Tulsa. Then, on September 30, 1978, Dickey picked up his first victory as coach of the Kansas State Wildcats, a 34-21 victory over Air Force.

Dickey undertook the tough job of overseeing the Cats in 1978.

ROCKED HAWKS Dickey's Cats beat Oklahoma State to open the Big Eight season, but then lost four conference games as they prepared to end the season with two Big Eight home games.

K-State tossed aside Colorado 20-10 and then wound up the season with a date against the Kansas Jayhawks. Dickey finished his first season with a bang: His Cats dismantled the Hawks 36-20 in front of 45,115 fans at KSU Stadium. K-State raced out to a 16-0 lead, and in the process Jim Ginther kicked K-State's only field goal of the season.

The victory ended a five-game losing streak against the Hawks, and wrapped up Dickey's first season with a 4-7 record.

WILDCAT QUIZ

31. How many NCAA Championships has Kansas State won in athletics?

COMING UNRAVELED The Wildcats opened the 1979 season with a 26-18 loss at Auburn but then returned home to beat Oregon State 22-16. The next week, the Cats won 19-6 at Air Force in what would turn out to be the program's last non-conference road victory for 14 years.

That victory was be followed by losses to Tulsa, Iowa State, and Oklahoma.

A return to the glory days, a la Vince Gibson, would not arrive in 1979. K-State beat Missouri 19-3 in Columbia for its only Big Eight win of the season. The 3-8 campaign included a 36-28 loss at Kansas. (At the time, those 64 points were the most scored in one game during the rivalry's history.)

IN THE DARK The 1980 season opened with a 21-0 loss at LSU and two home victories over South Dakota and Arkansas State. The season seemed to hinge on the outcome of K-State's road game at Tulsa on October 4. K-State's defense did the job, holding the Golden Hurricane to just 160 yards. But the Wildcats played in the dark during the night game, gaining only 188 yards. The final score: Tulsa, 3-0.

RALLY CATS The Kansas Jayhawks came to KSU Stadium on November 1 and manhandled the Wildcats. However, the score didn't show the damage, and the Cats almost pulled off a huge come-from-behind victory.

KU led 20-10 with 2:30 left in the game, and K-State had no time-outs. KU's Bucky Scribner came in to punt from the Jayhawks' 25, but K-State's Monte Bennett blocked the punt and the ball squirted out at the 1. One play later, K-State scored a touchdown. Quarterback Darrell Dickey then passed to John Liebe for the two-point conversion.

Now trailing 20-18 with 2:11 left, K-State tried an on-side kick. Ten players lined up on one side of the field and kicker Jim Jackson angled the ball in front of them.

WILDCAT QUIZ

32. What inter-collegiate sport did Kansas State add for the 1996-97 season?

A mad rush ensued, but KU recovered the kick and held on for the victory. The 20-18 loss later went into the books as a victory after KU forfeited the win.

Punter Don Birdsey booted a 93-yarder during the 1980 game against Nebraska.

GIVING IT THE BOOT Little good came out of K-State's 55-8 loss at Nebraska during 1980. However, K-State punter Don Birdsey booted a ball to remember. Birdsey ripped off a 93-yard punt, which was one yard short of the Big Eight record. Birdsey's kick remains the longest punt in K-State history.

BIG EIGHT WIN K-State won its only Big Eight game of the 1980 season (aside from the KU forfeit) in its final game of the season. And, the Wildcats waited until the last second to get the job done. Jim Jackson kicked a 17-yard field goal with one second left on the clock to give K-State a 17-14 victory over Colorado.

OUT OF CHARACTER By October 31, the 1981 season had turned into a study in frustration for Coach Dickey's Cats. The Wildcats had opened the season with a win over South Dakota, but then lost six straight games through September and October.

The Iowa State Cyclones visited the Cats on Halloween, and the Cats spooked the 'Clones. Using a 109-yard performance by running back Mark Hundley, the Wildcats upset Iowa State 10-7. The Wildcat defense smothered the Cyclones, holding them to 294 yards of offense.

"It was a great performance by our players, both on offense and defense," Coach Jim Dickey said. The win would be K-State's last during the 2-9 campaign.

Mark Hundley rushed for 109 yards against Iowa State in 1981.

SOONER OR LATER On November 7, 1981, K-State put a scare into the mighty Oklahoma Sooners that left OU Coach Barry Switzer saying, "Kansas State took the ball and kicked our butts." However, kicking the Sooners' hindquarters wasn't good enough to earn the victory.

K-State scored first, on a 20-play, 80-yard drive that devoured more than 10 minutes of the first quarter. Mark Hundley plunged in from a yard out to make it 7-0. K-State then kicked off to the Sooners with its first in a series of on-side kicks.

The Wildcats recovered and scored again. By late in the second quarter, K-State led 21-0. Then, the Sooners scored right before half to cut the lead to 21-6 and take the momentum. As it turned out, OU would do the rest of the scoring. But when a two-point conversion failed with 6:47 left in the game, K-State still led 21-20.

Oklahoma scored a final touchdown with 2:36 remaining and escaped Manhattan with a 28-21 victory.

Jim Dickey's highlight was a redshirt program that loaded the team up for the 1982 season and delivered K-State to its first bowl game.

THEY'RE BACK The redshirt experiment left K-State with a 2-9 record in 1981, but the Wildcats headed into the 1982 season with 26 returning starters at 22 positions. Yes, the Wildcats were loaded. The offense was led by senior Darrell Dickey, the son of Coach Jim Dickey, and the defense headed into the season with nine seniors and two juniors in its starting lineup.

WHAT A DIFFERENCE K-State opened the 1982 season with a 23-9 victory over Kentucky and then stuck it to South

Quarterback Darrell Dickey, son of coach Jim Dickey, led the Cats into the 1982 Independence Bowl.

Dakota 42-3. South Dakota had lost to the Wildcats the previous two seasons at KSU Stadium, but this year the Wildcats jumped out to an early lead and turned the game into a blowout.

By the time South Dakota had earned its initial first down of the game — on a K-State penalty at the 6:35 mark of the first half — the Wildcats led 21-0. The Wildcats held the Coyotes to 50 yards rushing in the game.

The 39-point victory was the largest since 1955, when K-State beat Kansas 46-0. The 574 yards of offense set a new school record.

RETIRING THE HARDWARE Wichita State came to Manhattan the next week feeling pretty good about itself. The Shockers had opened the season with a 13-10 victory over Kansas. A win over K-State would give the Shockers the newly-created Wheat State Trophy, a prize given to the winner of the round-robin play between the state's three major football schools.

The trophy was the idea of Governor John Carlin, the first K-State alumnus to serve in the state's highest office. After K-State beat the Shockers 31-7 the Wildcats were on their way to winning the hardware.

WEARING THE GRAY The nation tuned in when superstation WTBS came to Manhattan to televise the Wildcats' game with Kansas. K-State carried a 3-2-1 record into the game, so a victory was crucial to K-State's bowl hopes.

A capacity crowd of 45,595 watched K-State thump Kansas 36-7 under portable lights in 1982.

A crowd of 45,595 packed KSU Stadium to see a game played under portable lights. The Wildcats warmed up in their traditional purple uniforms, but when the team returned to the field before kickoff, they had changed.

The Cats stormed onto the field wearing special gray uniforms that Coach Dickey had ordered for the occasion. KSU Stadium rocked like it had during the Vince Gibson era, and the Wildcats unleashed a whipping on the Jayhawks not seen in the rivalry since 1955. The 36-7 K-State victory was thorough and provided the Wildcats with momentum as they pushed for the school's first bowl berth.

WILDCAT QUIZ

33. What was the last K-State varsity program to win a team title in the Big Eight Conference?

FINAL CHANCE K-State blew its chance to wrap up an Independence Bowl berth when it lost 24-16 to Oklahoma State at KSU Stadium in the second-to-last game of the regular season. Now 5-4-1, the Cats faced only one more chance to earn the sixth win necessary to get the bid when it played host to Colorado.

The Wildcats took a 17-10 lead into halftime and then dominated the Buffaloes in the second half. The 33-10 victory gave the Wildcats their Independence from their previously bowl-free past.

AND THEN IT RAINED The joy at being invited to play in a postseason bowl game was washed away by kickoff time. K-State fans converged on Shreveport, La., for the Independence Bowl in large numbers, but they would have to endure a cold rain as the Cats met Wisconsin.

After a scoreless first quarter, K-State took a 3-0 lead on kicker Steve Willis' 29-yard field goal with 7:10 left in the first half. Wisconsin took a 7-3 lead before halftime

A win over Colorado clinched the Cats' trip to the Independence Bowl.

WILDCAT QUIZ

34. When was K-State's last men's team title in the Big Eight Conference?

with a 16-yard touchdown. Then, the Badgers backed that up with an 87-yard touchdown pass in the third quarter.

The score stayed at 14-3 the rest of the way as the rain turned the field into a mud pit and the downpour drenched the crowd of 49,523.

"I remember the difficulties we had in keeping our players focused due to their excitement and all the hoopla of the media," Coach Dickey said. "Then the game itself was played under miserable conditions: a driving rainstorm with temperatures in the 30s and the field a quagmire.

"We got behind early, and couldn't catch up when the weather got increasingly worse."

The loss ended K-State's 1982 season with a 6-5-1 record, not great by some schools' standards, but it was the best record at K-State since the Cats went 6-5 in 1970 under Vince Gibson.

RENEWED HOPE Coming off the 1982 "breakthrough" year, hopes ran high as the Wildcats entered the 1983 season. After all, 56 players returned to Manhattan who would be in either their third, fourth or fifth year at K-State.

"Our goal this season is to make progress and to be a better team than we were in the past year," Coach Dickey said, "but to do that will be quite a challenge. Last year winning was very important to us and we might have slipped up on a few teams because we wanted to win more than they did.

"We must keep that kind of feeling this year."

While the numbers were good for K-State, some of the top players who led the drive to the Independence Bowl were gone.

"Even though we lost some big name starters, I think we'll be able to replace them with players who are just as good, only you might not recognize their names."

WILDCAT QUIZ

35. What varsity program at Kansas State has won four of the last six conference team titles in Wildcat athletics?

SLIPPED UP K-State carried those high expectations into the 1983 season-opener with Long Beach State at KSU Stadium. The two teams traded the lead in the game four times, but it was Long Beach State that walked away a 28-20 winner.

Things continued to slip the next week when the Cats lost 31-12 at Kentucky.

IT'S A WINNER An idea by equipment manager Jim Kleinau may have helped the Wildcats pick up their first victory of the 1983 season. Frustrated by the team's lackluster performance in the season's first two games, Kleinau approached Coach Dickey about "punishing" the team by replacing their new jerseys with those worn by the 1978 version of the Wildcats. Dickey liked the idea, so the old jerseys came out of storage and the Cats came to life.

Playing host to Texas Christian in the season's third game, K-State fell behind 3-0 but then sprang back to take a 20-3 victory. TCU outgained the K-State offense 296-209, but the Cats limited TCU's option attack with a special six-man front.

Equipment manager Jim "Shorty" Kleinau devised a way for Coach Dickey to inspire the Cats after a sluggish start to the 1983 season.

WHILE IT LASTED So what if the Cats were 2-5 as they prepared to host Nebraska? That didn't mean the team and fans weren't optimistic.

K-State kicked off to the Huskers and Mike Rozier settled under the ball in the end zone. Rozier caught the ball, started to bring it out and then knelt down for the touchback. However, the officials said Rozier had come out of the end zone and then stepped back in. It was ruled a safety, and K-State led 2-0.

The party was on at KSU Stadium. However, it didn't last long. Nebraska scored the next 38 points and took a 38-5 lead at halftime. The Huskers won 51-25.

WILD ONE Here's the scene: K-State trails the Oklahoma State Cowboys 20-14 with 2:23 left in the game when the Wildcats take possession at their own 23. Quarterback Stan Weber opens the drive with two short passes to Darrel Wild, a little-used wide receiver who drew the start when All-Big Eight performer Mike Wallace came down with the flu.

Quarterback Stan Weber rallied the Cats to a win over Oklahoma State in 1983. Weber is now the color commentator for Wildcat football radio broadcasts.

The two march the Cats down the field. Things look bleak momentarily when K-State faces a fourth-and-10 at the OSU 31, but again Weber and Wild hook up for 11 yards and a first down. Weber is sacked for a 7-yard loss on the next play, but goes to Wild on the next play for a 24-yard gain to the OSU 3.

K-State calls a time-out with 15 seconds to play and no time-outs remaining. Everyone expects the Cats to pass into the end zone, but they roll the dice.

Coach Dickey calls a pitch to tailback Greg Dageforde out of a passing formation, and Dageforde plunges into the end zone for the tie. Placekicker Steve Willis drills the extra point to put K-State up 21-20.

The game isn't over, though. With only seconds remaining, Oklahoma State kicker Larry Roach tries a 58-yard field goal. Roach's attempt is straight but short.

The win was K-State's only Big Eight victory during the 3-8 season and the school's first victory in Stillwater since 1971.

WEBER WATCH The fans were restless as the Wildcats carried a 1-4 record into their 1984 clash with Kansas, but thanks to the outstanding play of quarterback Stan Weber, the Wildcats whipped KU, 24-7.

Weber rushed for 63 yards and passed for another 85 as the Cats bounced back from a 7-0 hole to cruise to victory.

"The coaches have been taking a lot of heat," Weber said. "As players, we still believe in (Coach Dickey). ... He's the head coach and if he's going to take the blame when we lose, he should take the credit when we win."

The victory seemed to mollify some the hostility being directed toward Dickey. "Obviously, this probably ranks up with one of the greatest wins I've experienced as a head coach or as an assistant," Dickey said. "You just don't know how important this game was to us."

Tim MacDonald was K-State's only healthy linebacker when they played at Nebraska in 1984.

BUSTED K-State must have been in a hurry to get to Nebraska two weeks later. The Wildcats' bus driver got a speeding ticket on its way to Lincoln, and the 62-14 trouncing that awaited the Cats there.

On top of that, K-State played a strange 6-1 defense because injuries had limited the Cats to Tim MacDonald as their lone healthy linebacker. "We tried to compensate for that," Dickey said, "but today proves that Nebraska is the best team in the league until somebody proves differently."

K-State proved out-manned most of the 1984 season, going 3-7-1.

SUNFLOWER SHOWDOWN The 1985 season opened with a match-up of two struggling programs. Kansas State and Wichita State met before a crowd of 21,399 at KSU Stadium.

The Shockers won the contest 16-10 as K-State managed only 225 yards of offense. Wichita State held the ball for more than 38 minutes of the 60-minute contest. K-State had just lost to a poor team and in front of its home crowd to start the season. To say the least, the natives were very restless.

Free safety Barton Hundley intercepted nine passes during his K-State career.

HUNDLEY A HERO Even during the losing, K-State had its stars. During the 1985 season, free safety Barton Hundley, a senior from Clay Center, Kans., stood out. Hundley intercepted six passes during the season, ending his K-State career with a total of nine. The hard-hitting Hundley was named to the All-Big Eight team in both the 1984 and '85 seasons.

THE GRIM REAPER The next week, Northern Iowa came to Manhattan. The game will always be best remembered for Athletic Director Larry Travis' pacing back-and-forth in front of the K-State locker room as the final minutes expired. He was waiting to put an end to Coach Jim Dickey's tenure at K-State.

Coach Dickey announced his resignation two games into the 1985 season.

When K-State's 10-6 loss to the Division I-AA opponent was in the books, Dickey was gone.

MOON RISING The next day, Assistant Athletic Director Lee Moon took over the K-State program on an interim basis. Moon's first game was a 24-22 loss to Texas Christian, and it was followed by losses to North Texas State, Oklahoma, and Kansas before the Wildcats stunned Missouri 20-17 in Columbia, Mo. It would be K-State's only victory of the 1985 season.

STAN PARRISH: 1986-88

"I'll never us the word rebuild; you'll never hear it here," were some of Stan Parrish's first words when he was introduced as Kansas State's 25th football coach on December 2, 1985. "I didn't come here to rebuild this program, I came here to win. I came here to win next fall."

And win Parrish did the following fall. Twice, beating Western Illinois in his first game and spanking Kansas in his first game against K-State's bitter rival.

After that, Parrish stopped winning — for the final 27 games of his tenure. The only respite was a 17-17 tie against Kansas in 1987.

Stan Parrish never spoke the word rebuild at K-State, and his inability to build a program led to his firing following the 1988 season. Parrish, who had come to K-State following two mediocre seasons at Marshall University, compiled a three-year mark of 2-30-1. The K-State football program had hit rock bottom by the end off the 1988 season. There were only two places to go: up or out of college football.

Stan Parrish led his program into its first spring game in 1986 full of promises for immediate victories.

THE FIRST WIN Parrish made a successful debut by routing Western Illinois 35-7. Quarterback Randy Williams directed the Wildcats, and the Air Parrish offensive attack, to five touchdowns. Williams' completed 9 of 18 pass attempts, with one interception, two touchdowns, and 168 yards.

THE FINAL WIN K-State's defense helped the Wildcats build a 16-0 lead at halftime during Parrish's first meeting against Kansas. Only 27,352 fans showed up at KSU Stadium to watch two of college football's worst programs play.

Led by outside linebacker Grady Newton, the Wildcats forced Kansas into four turnovers and stifled the Hawks in the 29-12 victory. Safety Erick Harper returned an interception 39 yards for a touchdown in the fourth quarter.

Parrish would remain at Manhattan for two and one-half years, but his teams wouldn't win again.

WILDCAT QUIZ

36. What tie does Tiger Woods, a two-time United States junior national golf champion, have to K-State?

A RECORD Even during the Parrish years, K-State teams were known for the players who rose above the mediocrity. One of those players was tailback Tony Jordan, who ended up carrying much of the offensive load once it became obvious the coach's Air Parrish offense was better dubbed Error Parrish.

Jordan, however, shined, setting a single-game rushing record at K-State during the Wildcats' 1986 loss to Iowa State in Ames. Jordan rushed 35 times for 218 yards in the 48-19 loss to the Cyclones.

By the time the Rochester, N.Y., native was done at K-State, he would be third on the school's all-time rushing list with 427 carries for 1,593 yards and nine touchdowns.

A BAD START Parrish's team had won two games in 1986, and fans were optimistic as the 1987 season opened. The optimism quickly died. The Wildcats opened the season against lightly regarded Austin Peay State, a Division I-AA team.

The Governors built a 16-0 lead, but back-up quarterback Gary Swim came in and led the Wildcats back. It looked as if the Wildcats would win after Swim hooked up for his third touchdown pass to John Williams. The 48-yard pass put the Wildcats up 22-19 in the fourth quarter. The TD set off a rowdy celebration amongst the 23,350 fans on hand, (many of whom had come to see the free Willie Nelson concert scheduled after the game).

But the game was not over. Austin Peay began to drive, with the march's progress stalling at the K-State 35 with less than 30 seconds remaining. The Governors decided to rely on the arm of quarterback Dale Edwards. Receiver Rico Ransom ran a deep route, burning the Wildcat defense, but Edwards' throw to Ransom was too long.

So, what do you do if you're the Austin Peay coaching

Tony Jordan stood out during the bleak Parrish years.

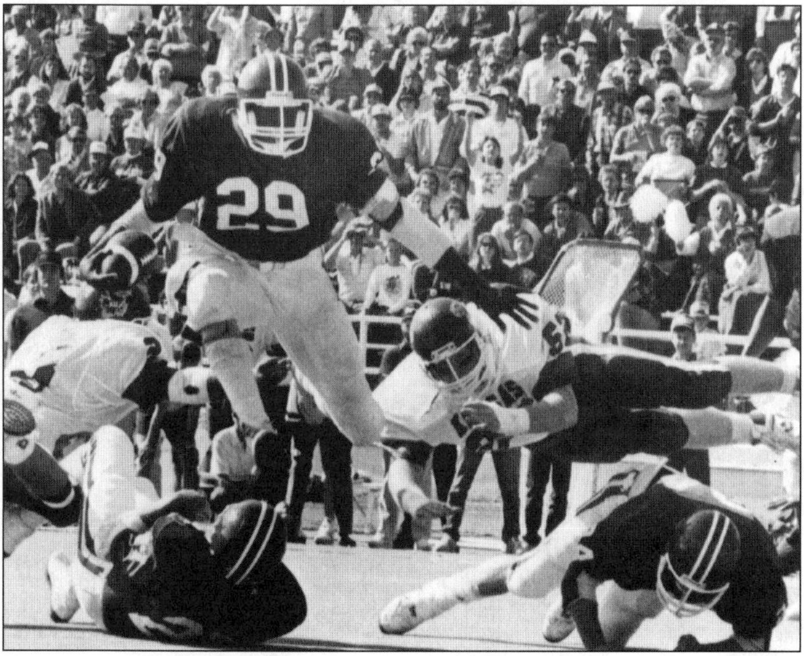

staff? You run the same play. Looking as if they had never seen the formation before or didn't know what Ransom would do, the K-State coaches misread the offense a second time. Once again, Ransom broke wide open down the east sideline, but this time Edwards delivered the pass on target.

The touchdown with 10 seconds remaining gave the Governors a 26-22 victory and set off an even more rowdy celebration by their players. After the clock had expired, many K-State fans remained to watch the free concert, so some of the Governor players put on a show. A handful of Austin Peay players went to mid-field and danced wildly on the Wildcat painted at the 50-yard-line. Then, they started to extend their middle fingers to the booing fans. An Austin Peay assistant coach raced to mid-field, but once he arrived, he too began to dance and flip off the crowd.

In Austin Peay's next game, Edwards broke his leg. The Governors' victory over the Cats would be their last of the season.

INFAMOUS AGONY When Kansas and Kansas State met on November 7, 1987, at KSU Stadium, football in the Sunflower State was at an all-time low.

It looked as if the Wildcats would win, but KU scored a late touchdown to tie the score at 17. On the game's final play, a field goal attempt by K-State's Mark Porter was blocked. The game ended with the two teams groping for a loose ball squirting across the turf. That image summed up the haplessness of the Parrish years.

PATCHING IT TOGETHER The 1988 season marked the 125th anniversary of Kansas State University, so the football team wore a commemorative patch on its uniforms. The patch, designed by Coach Parrish and equipment manager Jim "Shorty" Kleinau featured a Wildcat head and the words, "125 Years, K-State."

With his program in total disarray, Parrish resigned after the 1988 season.

A GLIMPSE OF THE FUTURE K-State lost its 1988 season opener at Tulsa, 35-9, and then kicked off its home slate by hosting Iowa, only the second Big Ten opponent to play in Manhattan. The Hawkeyes won the game 45-10 behind 377 yards of passing. Directing the Iowa attack up in the KSU Stadium press box was Iowa's scholarly offensive coordinator, Bill Snyder.

BAD BEYOND BELIEF The next week, the Wildcats traveled to New Orleans to take on Tulane at the Superdome. K-State came painfully close to victory, but the reason for the loss represented the chaos within Parrish's program.

K-State surged into the lead with 1:47 remaining in the

contest when quarterback Carl Straw connected with Greg Washington for a 16-yard touchdown to make it 16-13. In their excitement to celebrate the victory, the K-State coaches left the press box and headed for the field.

Tulane took over possession of the ball and began to march up the field. Parrish called up to the press box for defensive signals but got no response. Then he saw his coaches joyfully dancing toward him on the sidelines. Tulane, greatly benefiting from consecutive penalties on K-State for having 12 men on the field, scored the winning touchdown with 14 seconds remaining. The final score: Tulane 20, K-State 16.

WILDCAT QUIZ

37. How many times has the men's basketball team won Newcomer-of-the-Year honors starting back in 1969?

BAYOU REVISITED The next week the Cats played host to another Louisiana school, Louisiana Tech. Led by a school-record four touchdown passes by Paul Watson, the Wildcats raced out to a 28-7 halftime lead. It appeared the losing was over. But then the Wildcats fell apart. Tech scored 24 unanswered points in the second half, including 17 in the fourth quarter, to win 31-28.

IT WAS OVER 56-14. That's the final score of the final game of the Stan Parrish era. The loss to Colorado brought to a close perhaps the sorriest chapter in major college football history.

During his three-year stay in Manhattan, Parrish's program quickly disintegrated from the two wins in his first season. Thanks only to the ineptitude of Kansas during the same time frame, Parrish didn't lose all 21 of his Big Eight games. As it was, his conference record was 1-19-1. His team lost non-conference games to the likes of Northern Iowa, Austin Peay State, Army, Tulsa (twice), Tulane, and Louisiana Tech.

The school decided against dropping football and leaving the Big Eight Conference. Instead, it hired little-known offensive coordinator Bill Snyder from Iowa to piece together the wreckage and begin the rebuilding process Parrish never undertook.

Basketball: 1903-96

Jack Gardner, 1939-42, 1946-53; 147-81

Tex Winter, 1954-68, 262-117

Jack Hartman, 1970-86; 295-169

The first "official" basketball game played at Kansas State Agricultural College took place in 1903, but the game actually arrived in Manhattan in 1901 when an intramural contest pitting two women's teams took place. Two years later, the men adopted the sport in spirit, even though they were less than skilled in the fundamentals of basketball.

On January 6, 1903, a KSAC team accepted the challenge of a squad from Haskell Institute. This is how the Student Herald recounted the contest: "... with our boys, breath was at a premium, and they exhibited neither the speed nor the skill of their dusky competitors." In other words, the Native Americans whipped the Aggies, 60-7.

That first season's 0-5 record was so demoralizing that the school elected not to field a team for two years. In 1905, C.W. Melick led his team to a 7-9 record, setting the stage for the legendary Mike Ahearn to take over the program the next season. Ahearn coached the team for the five years, while also coaching the football program during the same time frame. During the 1906-07 season, Ahearn led KSAC to a 29-25 victory over the University of Kansas in the first basketball showdown between the two schools.

Kansas State basketball hummed along with only marginal success until the 1916-17 season arrived under new coach Z.G. Clevenger. That fall, Clevenger led the school's football team to a 6-1-1 record, and he continued that excellence during the winter's basketball campaign. The Aggies went 15-2, winning their first Missouri Valley championship since joining the conference in 1912.

Clevenger's team brought home the MVC crown again after the 1918-19 season with a 17-2 record, going a perfect 10-0 in league games. Clevenger coached one more season in Manhattan before stepping down.

Over the next 19 seasons, K-State had four coaches, with Charles Corsaut coaching from 1923-33 and Frank Root taking over until 1939. During those 19 seasons, K-State compiled a 148-190 record.

After Root's team went 5-13 in 1938-39, school officials turned the future of the program over to a man named Jack Gardner. Gardner would eventually be enshrined in the Naismith Basketball Hall of Fame, but he was far from that during his first three seasons at K-State, going 20-34. The start of World War II took Gardner away from K-State for four seasons, with the program going 27-62 in his absence.

Gardner returned from the war and to his old job in 1946. From that point on, Kansas State basketball started a remarkable run of achievement. The 1946-47 season provided the basketball program's first winning season in 15 years. Gardner's 14-10 campaign put his program on the path toward greatness.

That season, the Wildcats posted a winning record on their home court, something they have done every season since. The streak was pushed to 50 seasons with the conclusion of the 1995-96 season.

Gardner's second stint in Manhattan lasted seven seasons, with his team averaging 18 wins a year. The

NICHOLS GYM: THE FIRST HOME

Nichols Gymnasium was completed in June 1910, giving the school a home for its basketball program after years of playing games at various sites around Manhattan, including Commercial Hall, the Y.M.C.A., a closed skating rink, and the Ag Barn on campus.

The $84,190 that it cost to build Nichols (named for former school president Ernest Nichols, who served from 1899-1909) was paid by the state. At the time, Nichols was state of the art. The gym could seat 2,800 fans, and a swimming pool was located in the basement.

KSAC won the first game played in Nichols, a 40-20 decision against Bethany College, and then proceeded to win 63 percent of its games in the building over the next 40 seasons.

Nichols housed the Kansas State basketball program through World War II. When Coach Jack Gardner returned from the war, he immediately put the program on a winning course. Crowds began to overflow the gym.

Nichols Gymnasium opened in June 1910.

popularity of the program grew so dramatically that the state saw fit to build a new basketball arena to replace the aging Nichols Gymnasium.

The 1950-51 Wildcats opened Ahearn Field House in fitting fashion. In what may have been the greatest basketball season in school history, Gardner directed a talented team to a 25-4 mark, losing in the finals of the NCAA Tournament to Kentucky, 68-58. Led by Ernie Barrett, a sharp-shooting forward from Wellington, Kans., the Wildcats were an offensive powerhouse.

Lon Kruger, 1986-90; 81-47

The 1951-52 season saw Dick Knostman set a new scoring record for K-State, but the 19-5 season was best remembered for an epic 90-88 overtime loss to ultimate national champion Kansas and Clyde Lovellette. The next year, Knostman topped his own scoring record, and the Cats finished 17-4. Following the 1952-53 season, Gardner accepted the head coaching position at the University of Utah, and the reins of the K-State program were turned over to Assistant Coach Tex Winter.

A rebuilding process highlighted Winter's first two seasons at the K-State helm, but the expectations of the fans were now unreasonably high. Winter's young teams struggled through some of the toughest schedules in school history, finishing the 1953-54 and 1954-55 seasons with 11-10 records.

The slow start to the Winter era led to the appearance of signs around Manhattan proclaiming, "Spring is here. Winter must go." As it turned out, two seasons simply weren't enough for Tex Winter to grow into the challenge.

WILDCAT QUIZ

38. What player scored the first basket in Ahearn Field House?

In 1956, the Wildcats went 17-8 and captured the Big Eight crown. Winter coached 12 more seasons in Manhattan, leading the Wildcats to the league title seven more times.

Winter also directed the Cats to two Final Four appearances. Bob Boozer starred for the Wildcats during the 1958-59 season when the Cats went to the Final Four, where they finished fourth. That remarkable 25-2 season came on the heels of a 22-5 campaign. Winter's Cats put up a 22-3 mark in the 1961-62 season, and then went back to the Final Four in 1964. The 22-7 season ended with a fourth-place finish in the NCAA Tournament.

After Winter directed the Wildcats to another Big Eight title in 1968, he decided to move on and the controls of the program were once again turned over to an assistant coach. Lowell "Cotton" Fitzsimmons gained prominence in Manhattan by leading the Cats to a 34-20 record in his two seasons before moving on to the NBA's Kansas City Kings.

With Fitzsimmons' departure, Athletic Director Ernie

Barrett, the same man who was an All-American in 1951, found a young coach at Southern Illinois. Jack Hartman arrived in Manhattan in 1970 and settled in for 16 seasons.

Like Gardner and Winter, Hartman got off to a rocky start. His first edition of the Wildcats went 11-15, but by the time he was done, Hartman's teams had won 20 or more games seven times and had captured three Big Eight titles. The most memorable win during Hartman's tenure was a 50-48 NCAA Tournament second-round victory over Oregon State in 1981. Rolando Blackman's 17-foot baseline jumper as time expired not only lifted the Cats to victory, but landed Blackman on the cover of *Sports Illustrated.*

Heart problems eventually forced Hartman to retire, and one of his all-time great players took over the program. Lon Kruger returned to Manhattan from Texas-Pan American and promptly returned the Cats to the NCAA Tournament. Kruger stayed in Manhattan for four seasons, landing the program four NCAA bids. In 1988, Kruger's Mitch Richmond-led team went to the tournament's Elite Eight.

When Kruger departed for Florida in 1990, Dana Altman, a former assistant under Kruger, moved into the hot seat and went 68-54 over his four seasons. In 1993, Altman led the Cats back to the tournament, and the following season the team advanced to the NIT's semifinals in New York. However, the uneasy relationship between Altman and the fans came to an end following that season when he accepted the head coaching job at Creighton.

Enter Tom Asbury, who had gained a national reputation as both a coach and recruiter at Pepperdine. Asbury's first season in 1994-95 ended with a 12-15 record, but he backed that up with a 17-12 mark and another trip to NCAA tourney.

The program's 22nd trip to the NCAA Tournament continued K-State's rich history of basketball excellence. Those 22 bids rank the program ninth in the country in all-time NCAA tournament berths. Through the years, K-State has produced a collection of outstanding players and coaches matched by few college programs. Here's a look at the great names in Wildcat basketball:

JACK GARDNER The foundation for Kansas State's rich basketball tradition was laid by Gardner. After coaching at K-State from 1939 to 1942, he left for military service during World War II. Upon his return in 1946, Gardner put the Wildcats on the winning track they still ride.

A coach famed for his tactical abilities, Gardner took a program that had not experienced a winning season in

WILDCAT QUIZ

39. How many times has the K-State men's basketball team lost to the eventual National Champion at the NCAA tournament?

15 years and helped the school string together seven consecutive winning seasons. Gardner directed the Cats to the Final Four in 1951 and built a program with such a frenzied following that Ahearn Field House was constructed to allow more fans to see the team in action.

Gardner departed in 1953 to take over the head coaching position at the University of Utah, where he remained for 18 years. He is a member of the Naismith Hall of Fame, the sport's highest honor. Gardner is semiretired, working as a consultant for the NBA's Utah Jazz.

AHEARN FIELD HOUSE: THE OLD BARN

Mike Ahearn

A push for a new field house, which had begun before the war, kicked into high gear. Using money appropriated over the course of 10 years, the state completed construction of the $2 million building prior to the 1950-51 season.

A primary force behind the construction was Mike Ahearn, K-State's former athletic director. The native of Rotherman, England, had come to Manhattan in 1904 to oversee the school's greenhouses. A multisport star at Massachusetts State College, Ahearn began coaching the K-State football team in 1905 and took control of the basketball program the next year. Ahearn also coached KSU's track, tennis, and golf teams. Ahearn then served as K-State's athletic director from 1920-46.

The name of the new facility seemed obvious. Mike Ahearn Field House was born.

"The name of Mike Ahearn will be embossed in gold letters in the athletic history of Kansas State," wrote C.E. McBride, the sports editor of the Kansas City Star during the construction of K-State's new field house. "I see that Manhattan will build a monument in memory of Mike Ahearn and that is well … but knowledge of the life Mike lived, the job he did, the friends he made, the tradition that will ivy its way around his name in years to come will be the greatest monument."

The "Old Barn" carried the K-State basketball program through its glory years, hosting 465 games. The Wildcats won 378 of those contests for a winning percentage of .813.

The winning was in part a product of the great talent put on the court, but the fans and atmosphere also played a significant role. The largest crowd to see a game in Ahearn was 14,028 during the 1950 season. Changing fire codes eventually shrank the capacity of the building. A sellout crowd of 11,850 watched the last game in Ahearn, a 92-82 victory over Missouri on March 5, 1988.

In the midst of Ahearn's greatness, tragedy struck the K-State

RICK HARMAN When Gardner returned to K-State in 1946, one of his first recruits was Rick Harman, a 6-foot-3 guard from Hoisington, Kans. Harman led the Wildcats in scoring for three seasons, ending his K-State career in the 1949-50 season. That year he averaged 11.2 points a game, and earned All-America honors from a number of publications and wire services.

During the 1947-48 season, Harman helped the Wildcats win their first 16 games and move to the top of the national rankings. "We didn't even have team warm-ups, still wearing mismatched gray sweats while being ranked No. 1 in the nation," he said.

Rick Harman led the Cats in scoring for three seasons.

Ahearn Field House was home to great basketball teams and knowledgeable crowds from 1950 to 1988.

campus when an arsonist's fire gutted Nichols Gymnasium on December 13, 1968. The building remained a limestone shell until the state financed a complete renovation, transforming Nichols into classroom and theater space in the mid-1980s.

Through the years, Ahearn grew into one of the nation's most-feared courts. The acoustics inside the limestone and steel building reflected the noise back to the floor. When an Ahearn crowd was in full roar, a fan could not shout to the person standing next to him and be understood. The crowd often made it impossible for opposing coaches to communicate with their team even during time-outs. Ahearn crowds were also famed for their knowledge of the game, rising to their feet at the precise moment when the Cats sought an emotional lift or the opposition needed to be disrupted.

"This has to be the greatest basketball crowd in America," said Indiana Coach Bobby Knight.

Eventually, the "Old Barn" began to look more and more like an old barn. Locker room and office facilities were far behind the times, and an aging Ahearn when viewed without fans failed to impress many potential recruits.

Howie Shannon played basketball with a premium on athleticism.

HOWARD SHANNON During Harman's sophomore season, a lightning-quick guard from Munday, Texas, ruled the court at Nichols Gymnasium. "Howie" Shannon introduced Kansas State fans to a new type of basketball. Shannon played the sport with darting moves and dead-eye shooting.

With Shannon at the helm, the Wildcats won the Big Seven title in 1948 after finishing in last place the season before. The Wildcats finished fourth in the national tournament being held after that season, and Shannon was named an All-American by the Helms Foundation.

"He was one of the greatest players I ever had, no question about it," Coach Jack Gardner told the *Topeka Capital-Journal* when Shannon died of lung cancer in 1995. "He did things in those days that are comparable to the players of today. He'd take off from the top of the key and fly to the basket. ... He had tremendous skills."

"He could take off from the free-throw line, drive in and dunk it," remembered Ernie Barrett, a teammate with Shannon for a year. "And at 6-1, that was an amazing feat back then. He was just so smooth. We even called him 'Silent Smoothie.' "

Shannon was named the NBA's Rookie of the Year in 1949 while playing for the Providence Steamrollers. He averaged 10.8 points a game the next season for the Boston Celtics, but he retired from the professional game after that season to enter coaching.

Shannon coached at Topeka High School for four seasons before Tex Winter asked him to serve as an assistant coach at K-State. Shannon stayed in Manhattan through the 1963 season, even serving as head coach for Puerto Rico's national team during the 1960 Summer Olympics.

In 1963, Shannon became the head coach at Virginia Tech, stepping down in 1971. He led the Hokies to their first NCAA Tournament berth in 1967, and resigned to take over the school's intramural program even though he was a successful coach.

"One day, I just woke up and felt like doing something else," Shannon said at the time. "So I did."

Shannon retired from Virginia Tech in 1988 and moved back to Texas, living in Plano until his death.

WILDCAT QUIZ

40. What was unique about the Kansas vs. Kansas State match-up in the 1957 men's Big Eight Holiday Tournament championship game?

ERNIE BARRETT Of all the great players at K-State prior to the arrival of Coach Jack Hartman, Barrett's name stands out. His association with K-State as a player, coach, and administrator over the past 40 years has earned Barrett the nickname "Mr. K-State."

Barrett played three seasons for the Wildcats following his graduation from Wellington (Kans.) High School. During the 1950-51 campaign, his senior season,

Ernie Barrett was an All-American for the Cats in 1951 and later became K-State's athletic director.

Barrett and the Wildcats opened Ahearn Field House in style.

The Wildcats went to the Final Four with Barrett and a talented corps of players. With the national title within one victory, Barrett injured his shoulder, which limited the forward's famed outside shot. Barrett ended his senior season averaging just over 10 points a game, and was named an All-American.

Barrett played briefly for the Boston Celtics, and then returned to K-State as an assistant coach. In 1961, Barrett moved into athletic administration at K-State, becoming the school's athletic director in 1969.

"I made the decision that I'd probably be at Kansas State forever," Barrett said. "Nothing is forever. Little

Napoleon came along."

That's a reference to Duane Acker, the school president who fired Barrett in 1975. "We had a great deal of differences of opinion on how the athletic program should be run," Barrett said. "He's the only person I've known in my life I disliked."

That could have been the end of Barrett's relationship with K-State, but eventually Acker left K-State, and Jon Wefald became the school's president. With Wefald's arrival, Barrett rejoined the Athletic Department. Barrett

Dick Knostman stepped into the spotlight in 1952.

currently serves as the Athletic Department's Director of Major Gifts. Mr. K-State is now visible at most K-State functions, drumming up support and financing with his infectious enthusiasm and iron handshake.

DICK KNOSTMAN During the 1950-51 run to the national championship game, a sophomore forward was learning the game under Barrett. Dick Knostman averaged 7.5 points a game that season, but once Barrett and his classmates left, Knostman stepped into the scoring void. The next two seasons, the 6-foot-2 Wamego, Kans., product averaged 16.3 points and 13.3 rebounds, and 22.7 points and 11.9 rebounds. Those two seasons led to Knostman being named an All-American and All-Big Seven.

When Knostman left K-State in 1953, he was the school's all-time leading scorer. He currently ranks 12th on the list.

"All moments have been great for me at K-State," Knostman said in 1993, "but I would have to rank the '51 season as the best. It was great to be a part of it. It was just a great team with a bunch of good guys who really loved to play ball."

Six-foot-nine Jack Parr remains one of the great centers in K-State history.

TEX WINTER Frederick Morice Winter was a baby-faced assistant coach under Jack Gardner when he took over the K-State program in 1954 after Gardner left for Utah. After a slow start in his first two seasons, "Tex" Winter helped propel the Wildcats into the national spotlight. During his 15 years in Manhattan, Winter's Cats won the conference title eight times and appeared in two Final Fours.

Winter remained married to the school until 1968, earning a national reputation as a creative offensive coach. He left to become head coach at the University of Washington, eventually bouncing between assistant coaching jobs in the NBA and head and assistant jobs at the college level.

In 1985, Winter joined the coaching staff of the Chicago Bulls. It was there that Winter made famous "The Triple Post Offense," a creation that has helped the Bulls dominate the professional ranks in the 1990s.

JACK PARR One of Tex Winter's greatest recruiting steals was going into Richmond, Va., and convincing 6-foot-9 Jack Parr that he should attend K-State instead of the University of Virginia.

Parr was known as an aggressive rebounder and he

sported an assortment of shots, including a virtually unstoppable hook shot. During Parr's three-season career in Manhattan from 1955 to 1958, he averaged 16.9 points and 12.7 rebounds a contest.

In Parr's senior campaign, he blocked a lay-up attempt by Kansas' Wilt Chamberlain late in the game to help the Cats beat KU 79-75 in two overtimes, and thus win the Big Seven championship for the second time during his stay at K-State. The two-time All-American later went on to play professionally with the NBA's Cincinnati Royals before settling into private business in Salina, Kans.

BOB BOOZER Standing 6-foot-8, Boozer was a player ahead of his time when he first took the floor for K-State in 1956. The muscular forward possessed a finesse game and a light, outside touch. It became common knowledge that when K-State needed a hoop, the Wildcats would just

Bob Boozer possessed a smooth outside jump shot, and went on to star in the NBA.

clear one side of the floor, run Boozer across a couple of picks, and open him up for a 20-foot jump shot.

As one opposing coach said, "I knew he would shoot, my players knew he would shoot, the good Father above knew he was going to shoot, but we couldn't do anything about it."

Boozer averaged 21.9 points and 10.7 rebounds during his three seasons in Manhattan (1956-57, '57-58 and '58-59). He was named to the all-conference team each season and selected as an All-American following both his junior and senior seasons.

"We had such strong team unity," Boozer recalls. "You just don't see this much in college basketball anymore, and I think teams are missing the boat in this vital ingredient to success."

Boozer won a gold medal as part of the United States Olympic basketball team in 1960, and then played 11 seasons in the NBA before returning to his hometown of Omaha, Neb.

Mike Wroblewski blossomed during his senior season.

MIKE WROBLEWSKI During Wroblewski's first two seasons in Manhattan, he averaged about 7 points and 4 rebounds a game. Then in the 1961-62 season, Wroblewski exploded on the national scene. Averaging 19 points and 8.5 rebounds a game, the 6-foot-8 center from South Bend, Ind., was named second-team All-America by the Helms Foundation.

WILLIE MURRELL Kansas State has now become known as a college basketball program that offers opportunities for stardom to junior-college transfers. In the early 1960s, juco transfers weren't widely recognized.

Willie Murrell starred at K-State after transferring from a junior college in 1962.

In 1962, a 6-6 forward from Taft, Okla., transferred to K-State from Eastern Oklahoma A&M Junior College. By the time Willie Murrell was done, he had established himself as one of the most prolific scorers in school history. He racked up impressive numbers with his slashing moves to the basket and his soft touch around the hoop. He also won legions of fans at K-State and around the league because of his infectious grin and good nature.

Murrell averaged 20.6 points and 10.7 rebounds during his two years for the Wildcats, leading the Cats to the Final Four in 1964. His career average places him fourth on K-State's all-time list behind Bob Boozer, Norris Coleman, and Mitch Richmond. Murrell went on to play four seasons in the American Basketball Association before retiring.

COTTON FITZSIMMONS When Coach Tex Winter departed, K-State once again looked within for its new coach.

Cotton Fitzsimmons coached at K-State before becoming a coach and executive in the NBA.

Lowell Fitzsimmons had served under Winter and was promoted to the head position in 1968. Fitzsimmons' 34-20 record in his two seasons caught the interest of the NBA's Kansas City Kings, who promptly hired him away in 1970.

Fitzsimmons was named the NBA's Coach of the Year in 1979 while with the Kings He eventually moved to the Phoenix Suns, where he has served as both head coach and senior vice president of the franchise.

JACK HARTMAN Fitzsimmons' quick departure left Athletic Director Ernie Barrett with a sudden job opening. This time, Barrett looked outside of K-State for its 16th head basketball coach. Jack Hartman had made a name for himself at Southern Illinois, coaching the likes of NBA superstar Walt Frazier.

Hartman came to Manhattan in 1970 and led the Wildcats to an 11-15 record in his first season. He then compiled 11 straight winning seasons. Hartman made himself at home for 16 seasons at Ahearn Field House. His record of 295-169 makes him the winningest basketball coach in school history. Hartman's overall collegiate record is 589-279 (a record of 3-4 can be added in from his service as interim women's coach at the end of the 1995-96 season).

"Nobody coaches a team as well as Jack Hartman," Coach Eddie Sutton said while he was at Arkansas.

After that slow start in the 1970-71 season, Hartman's Cats surged to the Big Eight title in 1971-72 with a 19-9 mark. His Cats also went to the final eight of the NCAA tournament. That trip was the first of nine for the Wildcats under Hartman, and the first of four trips to the Elite Eight.

With heart problems threatening his well-being — and a dislike for the way college basketball was evolving — Hartman retired in 1986 after going 56-59 in his final four seasons.

STEVE MITCHELL Known to K-Staters as the "Big Kid," 6-foot-10 Steve Mitchell is one of the greatest centers in the history of Wildcat basketball. Mitchell made an immediate impact after taking the court his sophomore season. Averaging 14.3 points and 8.1 rebounds during the 1970-71 campaign, Mitchell starred for a young team that struggled to an 11-15 record.

Center Steve Mitchell shined from the first day he took the court at Ahearn Field House.

While Mitchell's averages dropped the next two seasons, he played a large role in the Cats' capturing back-to-back Big Eight championships in 1972 and 1973. The Oklahoma City native developed into a bull around the basket, while perfecting his soft shooting touch. He finished his K-State career averaging 13.1 points and 7.9 rebounds. For his career, Mitchell shot 52 percent from the field.

"(Coach Jack) Hartman keeps stressing the importance of being a complete ball player," Mitchell said during his playing days in Manhattan, "like screening off the boards, reading defenses, outlet pass execution, and overall game concentration. He wants you to have a good reason for everything you do."

Mitchell did develop into a complete player, and went on to star in the European professional ranks. In 1978, five years after leaving K-State, Mitchell was found dead in a friend's apartment in Pesaro, Italy.

WILDCAT QUIZ

41. Who did K-State beat in 1984 to record the school's 1,000th basketball victory?

LON KRUGER He was too small, too slow, and too inexperienced to ever make an impact in big-time college basketball. Or, at least that's what many "experts" said of Lon Kruger when he arrived at K-State from Silver Lake (Kans.) High School. By the time Kruger's three years of playing were exhausted in 1974, he had been named the Big Eight's top player twice.

With Kruger serving as floor general, the Wildcats won Big Eight titles in 1972 and 1973. After the 1971-72 season, Kruger was named the Big Eight Sophomore of the Year. After his junior and senior campaigns, Kruger was named the league's Player of the Year.

"When I first got there," Washburn Coach Bob Chipman, a former KSU teammate of Kruger's, told the *Topeka Capital-Journal* in 1986, "we often had two-hour pickup games before the coaches came out. When they were over I'd go back to the dorm just dead tired, but Lonnie would go out and run six miles. No one ever out-worked him."

Known mostly as a point guard — assists weren't recorded during Kruger's playing days — he also developed into an explosive scorer. Kruger scored 1,063 in his three years, averaging 17.6 points a contest his senior year. Kruger remains third on K-State's career free- throw percentage chart with an .826 average.

Kruger, who was also drafted to play professional baseball, went on to serve as an assistant coach under Hartman before becoming the head basketball coach and athletic director at Texas-Pan American.

On March 17, 1986, Kruger was named the 17th head basketball coach in K-State history. He stayed in Manhattan four seasons, compiling an 81-47 record and taking the Cats to four straight NCAA Tournaments. Kruger left K-State after the 1989-90 season to take over the program at the University of Florida, and directed the Gators to the 1994 Final Four. Two years later, he accepted the head coaching job at the University of Illinois.

WILDCAT QUIZ

42. How many men's basketball conference championships have the Wildcats won in history, and what coach has led the K-State to the most league titles?

CHUCKIE WILLIAMS There's no telling what kind of damage Williams could have done to record books if the 3-point line had been in place when the pure-shooting guard played in the mid-1970s.

Williams played sparingly his sophomore season, but during his final two seasons (1974-75, 1975-76), he averaged 21.5 points and hit 48 percent of his shots. Considering many of those shots were taken from long range, Williams' numbers are remarkable. His total of 1,364 points places him sixth on K-State's all-time scoring list.

Coach Jack Hartman simply described Williams this way: "Chuckie is just an outstanding shooter. The best I've ever been around."

Williams held the school record for most points in a game for 19 years with a 47-point outburst against Holy Cross in 1975. Also that season, Williams grabbed the national spotlight with his performance in the NCAA East Regional. The 6-foot-3 guard from Columbus, Ohio, poured in 87 points in three NCAA games, taking the Cats to the regional final against Syracuse. Williams scored 35 in K-State's dramatic overtime loss to the Orange. Despite playing for the losing team in the game, Williams was easily voted the regional's most valuable player.

Williams' skills as a scorer were learned playing endless hours on an elementary school playground in Columbus.

"I used to spend every free minute on that court

WILDCAT QUIZ

43. Only one time in the history of Kansas State — 1982 — have three players been drafted in the same year to the NBA, who were they?

shooting baskets ... except when the older kids would run me off," Williams remembered prior to the 1975-76 season. "In the summers we'd play 11-12 hours a day. We wore out a lot of sneakers, and scuffed up a lot of basketballs. In the winter my fingers would crack and split."

Williams closed his K-State career in 1976 by being a unanimous selection to the All-Big Eight team.

Chuckie Williams poured it in from long range.

Dean Harris was a rising star at K-State, but died in a car accident after his freshman season in 1974.

DEAN HARRIS In September 1973, a lanky freshman from East St. Louis, Ill., arrived at K-State. Dean Harris slid right into the starting lineup next to four veterans. Harris proved himself to be a fascinating mixture of youthful exuberance and remarkable maturity. His warm smile and high energy made him a fan favorite.

After averaging 7.4 points and 6.5 rebounds a game during the 1973-74 season for the 19-8 Wildcats, Harris went home on summer vacation. On May 17, 1974, he suffered multiple injuries in a head-on collision during a driving rainstorm. Three days later, Dean Harris died at age 19.

"Dean was extremely popular with his teammates and the student body," Coach Jack Hartman said after Harris' passing. "He was one of the finest men I had the privilege to coach. And above all, Dean Harris was a refreshingly open, honest young man. He scored high in intangibles."

The next fall, Hartman dedicated the program's "Freshman of the Year" award in Harris' name. The first winner of the "Dean Harris Freshman of the Year" award was Mike Evans. Others receiving the honor have included Rolando Blackman, Ed Nealy, Norris Coleman, Steve Henson, and Askia Jones.

WILDCAT QUIZ

44. Who was the first K-State basketball player to represent the United States in the Olympics?

MIKE EVANS What made K-State particularly dangerous during the days of Chuckie Williams was the fact he wasn't alone in his long-range exploits. Williams was one half of a duo that came to be known as the "Purple Pop Guns." The other half was a 6-1 guard from Goldsboro, N.C., named Mike Evans.

Evans was two years behind Williams in school, but the NCAA made freshmen eligible to play by the time Evans had arrived. As a freshman, Evans averaged 17 points a game on the team that lost to Syracuse in the 1975 East Regional finals. Throughout the course of his four years of action in Manhattan, the pure-shooting Evans steadily built his scoring average — 17.0, 17.9, 18.3, 19.1.

By the time Evans was done, he had established a new career-scoring record at K-State with 2,115 points, a record he still owns. Despite taking most of his shots from the perimeter, Evans finished his career with a 49 percent field goal percentage. He was named to the All-Big Eight team both his junior (1976-77) and senior ('77-78) seasons, earning some All-America mentions in 1978.

Evans posted many memorable performances while wearing K-State's vintage two-tone purple uniforms. He connected on 12-of-13 field goals in a game against Missouri, poured in 40 at Colorado, and had a 19-point performance in the second half of a game

Mike Evans, along with Chuckie Williams, comprised the "Purple Pop Guns."

against Nebraska.

Evans went on to play in the NBA with Kansas City, San Antonio, Milwaukee, Cleveland, and finally for six years with Denver. Evans served as an assistant coach with the Nuggets and is now the franchise's Director of Player Personnel.

ROLANDO BLACKMAN All great college basketball programs have their legendary players whose exploits seem to grow with each passing year. Topping the list of K-State legends is Blackman, a player who helped revolutionize the big guard position.

Blackman came to K-State in 1977 from Brooklyn, N.Y. He remains second on the school's all-time scoring list with 1,844 points. He's third on the all-time assist

Rolando Blackman always rose to the occasion for the Cats.

list, and his name covers the log of category leaders kept each season. However, it isn't his scoring averages (which peaked at 17.8 in his junior season) that astound. It was Blackman's knack for making the big play that keeps him close to K-Staters' hearts.

Blackman scored, rebounded, passed precisely, played stifling defense, and hit the big shots. No shot was bigger than the 17-footer he sank in March 1981 to knock off second-ranked Oregon State in the second round of the NCAA Tournament. Blackman was a three-time unanimous All-Big Eight selection, and named the league's top player after his junior season. He was selected as an All-American after both his junior and senior campaigns.

"Nobody means more to his team than Rolando means to ours," Coach Hartman said during Blackman's playing days. "Whatever the situation, he normally rises to the occasion."

Blackman was a starter on the 1980 U.S. Olympic team, and after leaving K-State in 1981 was drafted by the Dallas Mavericks as the ninth overall pick in the NBA draft. Blackman played 12 seasons for the Mavericks, being selected to play in the NBA All-Star Game four times. He averaged no less than 17 points a game during his days in Dallas, and was traded to the New York Knicks after the 1992 season. He closed out his NBA career in 1994, and then moved on to play professionally in Europe.

WILDCAT QUIZ

45. Besides Jack Hartman, who is the only other K-State men's basketball coach to be named Big Eight Coach of the Year?

ED NEALY Blue collar. That sums up the play of Ed Nealy, the owner of the school's all-time rebounding record with 1,071. Few gave Nealy a chance to succeed at the college level when he graduated from Bonner Springs (Kans.) High School. One recruiting service said Nealy was just a big white kid from Kansas.

That he was, but Ed Nealy could also play basketball. A tenacious rebounder and fiery competitor, the 6-foot-7 Nealy always found ways to score and make his teammates better. The "experts" always said Nealy couldn't shoot from the outside, but K-State fans remember him differently.

Simply put, the Wildcats were a great team with Nealy on the floor. The Cats went 85-38 during his four years. He closed his playing days in Manhattan in 1982 with career averages of 10.6 points and 8.7 rebounds. Nealy was named to the first-team All-Big Eight team in '82, and he was also named to the Big Eight's All-Academic team three times.

With the critics bringing up the same minuses he heard coming out of high school, Nealy wasn't selected in the NBA draft until the Kansas City Kings picked him in the eighth round. Nealy spent 12 years in the NBA, winning NBA championship rings in 1991 and 1993 as a reserve for the Chicago Bulls.

NORRIS COLEMAN The only way to describe Coleman's two years in Manhattan is as a saga. He came to K-State in 1985 as a 22-year-old freshman. That was the first bit of information about Coleman that wasn't quite factual. He was actually 24 and had spent six years in the Army, not four as thought.

Coleman played much of his first season and was

Norris Coleman's two-year stay at K-State featured some great basketball and even more controversy.

named *Sports Illustrated* National Player of the Week after scoring 71 points, grabbing 27 rebounds, and blocking five shots in his first two Big Eight games. Eventually, a long string of discrepancies surfaced concerning Coleman's background. He was immediately suspended, because some of the new information indicated Coleman should have never been eligible to play at K-State.

WILDCAT QUIZ

46. What is the highest K-State has ever finished in the Associated Press rankings?

Coleman's skills were never in question. The 6-8 forward could flat play, using his bony body to score at will and rebound ferociously. Even though Coleman indicated on the questionnaire he filled out for the K-State Sports Information Department that he had been a standout basketball and track performer during his high school days in Jacksonville, Fla., it became known that Coleman was a below-average basketball player and never ran track.

He had developed his basketball skills while playing on U.S. military teams in Germany. All the time he played, spread over two stints in the Army, Coleman's NCAA eligibility was expiring.

Also, Coleman's high-school grade-point average came into question. K-State had used an eight-semester GPA to determine that he was eligible, but the NCAA ruled a six-semester GPA should have been used. At one point, the NCAA ruled Coleman would have to sit out a year if he stayed in Manhattan, but he could transfer and play immediately. Basketball powerhouses came out of the woodwork in an attempt to woo Coleman. Eventually, Coleman was given one additional year of eligibility at K-State that he could use the next year.

Norris Coleman performed for KSU two seasons, playing in Jack Hartman's final season as coach and starring for Coach Lon Kruger's first team in 1986-87. Coleman scored 1,003 points in 47 games, placing him 18th on K-State's all-time list. In 1987, he was named to the Big Eight's first team.

WILDCAT QUIZ

47. What freshman has the highest scoring average in K-State men's basketball history?

Coleman never played in the NBA, but has become a vagabond of professional basketball, playing in the Continental Basketball League and United States Basketball League, as well as a variety of foreign professional leagues.

MITCH RICHMOND The story goes that Mitch Richmond was from such a poor background in Fort Lauderdale, Fla., that his home wasn't much more than a shack. And when he arrived at Moberly (Mo.) Community College, he didn't have and couldn't afford a winter jacket. Since those humble beginnings, Richmond has become one of the greatest players in school history and an elite player in the NBA.

During his two years at K-State, Mitch Richmond reminded people of Rolando Blackman, because of his knack for delivering in the clutch.

Richmond was recruited to Moberly by Coach Dana Altman, who was hired by Lon Kruger when Kruger returned to K-State in 1986. Altman persuaded Richmond and teammate Charles Bledsoe to also come to Manhattan, and they made immediate contributions.

Richmond, playing much of his junior season wearing a cast on his right shooting wrist, played alongside Norris Coleman in the Wildcats' 20-11 season in 1986-87. Despite being hampered by the cast, Richmond averaged 18.6 points a game during his junior season.

It was as a senior that Richmond burst onto the national scene, eventually being named an All-American. He poured in 22.6 points a game for the Cats, reminding K-State fans of Rolando Blackman. Like Blackman, Richmond possessed a remarkable skill for hitting clutch shots.

"You look at Rolando when he was here," Coach Kruger said at the time, "and they are very similar because Mitch does a lot of the same things Rolando did."

Former K-State coach Jack Hartman saw similarities

WILDCAT QUIZ

48. What remains the highest point total scored by a Wildcat in Big Eight action?

between Richmond and a legendary player Hartman coached at Southern Illinois.

"He has got some of the same qualities that Walt Frazier had," Hartman said. "A big guard, strong quick hands. He's in that same category. ... Just his completeness. He has no weaknesses."

WILDCAT QUIZ

49. What year did the K-State men's basketball team play the powerful Soviet Union team in Ahearn Field House?

Richmond played a significant role in leading the Cats to the Elite Eight of the NCAA Tournament during his senior season. The 25-9 record under Kruger in the 1987-88 season was the school's best in 10 years. Richmond's two-year stop at K-State earned him the seventh spot on the school's all-time scoring list with 1,327 points.

After playing on the 1988 Olympic team, Richmond was selected fifth in the first round of the 1988 NBA draft, going to the Golden State Warriors. He played with the Warriors for three seasons before being traded to the Sacramento Kings. He has developed into one of the league's finest shooting guards, and was named Most Valuable Player of the 1995 NBA All-Star Game.

STEVE HENSON Coach Lon Kruger's top priority upon arriving in Manhattan was to convince a point guard from McPherson, Kans., that he belonged at K-State. Kruger was successful in his attempt to attract Steve Henson to Manhattan, and the 6-1 guard grew into what one media member called, "K-State's stick of dynamite."

During his freshman season, Henson was thrown into the fire, looking overmatched at times in the Big Eight Conference. During his sophomore season, Henson had grown into the type of floor leader capable of leading his team to the final eight of the NCAA Tournament. However, during both seasons he wasn't asked to score many points, averaging 8.4 points a contest.

WILDCAT QUIZ

50. What is the record for most rebounds by a Wildcat in Bramlage Coliseum?

When Mitch Richmond graduated, Henson took over the scoring responsibilities. He averaged 18.5 points a game as a junior and 17.4 as a senior. Plus, Henson wasn't a score-first point guard. He holds the school's all-time assist record with 582.

"He's hard-nosed, self-disciplined, self-motivated, and skilled," Coach Kruger said. "And that's a very good combination for a basketball player." In other words, Henson reminded a lot of K-State fans of Kruger in his playing days.

Henson developed into a pure shooter. He also holds the school record for most 3-point shots made with 240. If the shot clock was winding down, opponents couldn't cover Henson far enough away from the basket. Numerous times, Henson hit shots of over 30 feet just seconds before the shot clock expired. Henson also holds the school record for free-throw percentage, hitting 90 percent of his attempts in his four years (361-401).

The bottom line, though, was K-State won during Henson's stay in Manhattan. Playing all four years of Kruger's tenure at the school, the Cats went 81-47. The guard was named to the Big Eight's first team in 1989, and was twice an honorable mention All-American.

Point guard Steve Henson led the Wildcats during each of Coach Lon Kruger's four years in Manhattan.

Henson was selected in the second round of the 1990 NBA draft by the Milwaukee Bucks, where he played two years. Since then, Henson has bounced around the league, filling teams' needs for a gritty, consistent back-up point guard.

Coach Dana Altman led the Cats from 1990-94.

DANA ALTMAN So obvious was the selection as K-State's coach to succeed Lon Kruger when he took the job at Florida, that Altman was announced as KSU's 18th coach before Kruger had been introduced to Florida fans. Altman had served as an assistant under Kruger for three years before being selected as the head coach at Marshall. Altman stayed just one year in West Virginia before K-State called and asked him to come home.

Altman's four-year record in Manhattan was 68-54, but his teams were best known for winning close games. Under Altman, the program won 28 of 35 games decided by six points or fewer. During the 1992-93 season, Altman's "Cardiac Cats" won 11 games in the final minutes, went 19-11, broke into The Associated Press

BRAMLAGE COLISEUM: THE PURPLE PALACE

Just as with the building of Ahearn Field House, a movement for a new facility stirred to life about 10 years before the building would be opened. A donation of $2.8 million from Junction City, Kans., businessman Fred Bramlage led the charge in the fund raising for the $17.5 million facility. Unlike Nichols and Ahearn, no state funds were used to build Bramlage Coliseum. The student body paid $7 million towards its construction, with the alumni matching that total.

"What we begin here today will add to the glory and reputation of KSU," Bramlage said at the ground-breaking ceremony on October 18, 1986. "My hope is that this coliseum will inspire people to come together around teams in the spirit of cooperation." Bramlage died March 17, 1992, at age 81.

In its first eight seasons, K-State's record is 89-32 in Bramlage for a .736 winning percentage. Included in the win total is an 81-77 roller-coaster victory over Purdue in the building's debut on November 26, 1988.

Fred Bramlage

Some people think that crowds are far smaller since the Wildcats moved to 13,500-seat Bramlage. But the average attendance during the 1994-95 season, when the Cats went 12-15, was almost identical to the average of 9,856 in 1980-81, Rolando Blackman's final season.

What has been lost in the move from Ahearn to Bramlage is much of the crowd's basketball savvy, something K-State Coach Tom Asbury thinks can be born again.

Top 25 poll, and put K-State into the NCAA Tournament for the 21st time.

The next season, Altman's team went to Lawrence and upset the then-No. 1 ranked Kansas Jayhawks on national television. The 1993-94 Cats finished the year 20-14, and advanced to the semifinals of the National Invitation Tournament in New York.

Despite Altman's winning record and postseason appearances, his stay in Manhattan was rocky. Many of the same fans who clamored for his return never felt comfortable with Altman as coach. It seemed obvious that Altman would eventually leave KSU, and he departed on his terms the day following the conclusion of the 1994 postseason NIT, returning to his home state of Nebraska to coach at Creighton University in Omaha.

WILDCAT QUIZ

51. Who scored the first basket in the first game ever played in Bramlage Coliseum?

ASKIA JONES Those who were there will never forget the performance "Ski" Jones turned in on March 24, 1994. Playing in the quarterfinals of the NIT at Bramlage Coliseum against Fresno State, Jones set the all-time Big

"I know a lot of purists wish we were still (in Ahearn) and never moved," Asbury said, "but I love Bramlage. It's a great arena to play in. The facilities are nice and new. The locker rooms and all the amenities are excellent. I think it's a terrific place to play in — one of the best in college basketball."

Bramlage Coliseum opened in November 1988.

Eight scoring record with a 62-point explosion. Jones' 17 points at halftime seemed impressive, but the senior then poured in 45 points in the second half.

Shooters talk about being in "the zone." All on hand could clearly see Jones was there. He hit 14 of 18 3-point attempts, roaming the floor from well behind the 19-foot, 9-inch arc and setting the ball on a course that led straight through the net.

Most amazingly, Jones did this in only 28 minutes of playing time. Each time the K-State coaching staff would pull him out, they would be alerted of another NCAA, NIT, Big Eight, or school record Jones was nearing, and in he would go. If Jones had played an entire 40 minutes scoring at the clip he was scoring, he would have tallied 89 points.

This senior season was made possible by an unfortunate break in 1990. Coming off a solid freshman season, Jones broke his foot and missed the entire 1990-91 season. That redshirt season gave Jones

Ski Jones destroyed numerous records when he scored 62 points against Fresno State, in the process hitting 14 of his 18 3-point attempts.

additional time to mature, and his stats grew from 7.9 points a game as a freshman to 22.1 in his senior year if 1993-94.

Despite never making an All-Big Eight first team, Jones sits in third on K-State's all-time scoring list with 1,834 points. He played 10 games with the NBA's Minnesota Timberwolves in the 1994-95 season.

Tom Asbury took over the program in 1994 and led the Wildcats to the NCAA Tournament in just his second season.

TOM ASBURY When Altman abruptly left K-State after the 1994 season, a national search for K-State coach No. 19 began. It didn't take long before the name Tom Asbury moved to the top of the list. Asbury came to Manhattan after six seasons at Pepperdine.

Not much was expected from the Cats in Asbury's season, and the team went 12-15. Expectations remained low heading into the 1995-96 season. Most polls tabbed K-State to finish seventh or eighth in the Big Eight, but Asbury's club tied for fourth and finished the season with a 17-12 mark. A team loaded with youth, the Wildcats also made their 22nd visit to the NCAA Tournament.

"Considering where we were picked and the expectations for this team," Asbury said, "then I would say we've had a pretty nice year."

The Best of the Rest

Throughout the history of Kansas State University, the school has been known as a national championship contender in men's basketball. More recently it has become a rising football power. However, that does not mean all K-State's star athletes and coaches are found in those two sports. Legends reside all across the athletic board in Wildcat Land. Here's a look at the best of the rest:

ATHLETIC DEPARTMENT

DeLoss Dodds was K-State's athletic director for three years before moving on to the University of Texas.

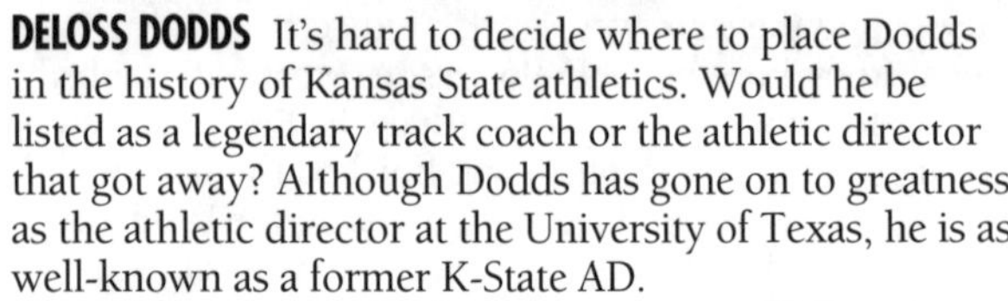

DELOSS DODDS It's hard to decide where to place Dodds in the history of Kansas State athletics. Would he be listed as a legendary track coach or the athletic director that got away? Although Dodds has gone on to greatness as the athletic director at the University of Texas, he is as well-known as a former K-State AD.

Dodds, a native of Riley, Kans., came to K-State in 1957 to run track. In 1958, he won a Big Eight championship in the 440-yard dash and also anchored K-State's Big Eight champion relay team. After completing his eligibility, Dodds served two years in the Army.

In 1961, he returned to Manhattan as assistant track coach under Ward Haylett. When Haylett retired in 1963, Dodds became only the second track coach in school history. During the next 14 years, Dodds led the Wildcats to two Big Eight indoor titles and three runner-up finishes. Outdoors, Dodds' team finished second in the conference five consecutive years.

In 1976, Dodds resigned to become an assistant commissioner of the Big Eight Conference, only to return to Manhattan two years later as the new athletic director. Dodds stayed in Manhattan for three more years before being hired by Texas, where he remains.

WILDCAT QUIZ

52. Who is the only Wildcat golfer to win medalist honors at the Big Eight golf championships?

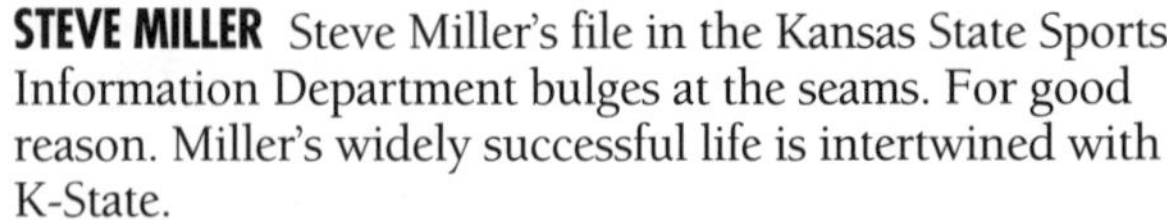

STEVE MILLER Steve Miller's file in the Kansas State Sports Information Department bulges at the seams. For good reason. Miller's widely successful life is intertwined with K-State.

Miller arrived in Manhattan as the school's track and field coach in 1981 after leading California State Poly-San Luis Obispo to three straight NCAA Division II track championships. Miller led the track and cross-country programs for five years before being named assistant athletic director by Larry Travis. During the 1985-86 school year, Miller worked as both an administrator and as the track coach. He moved up to associate AD the next year, overseeing the school's fund-raising efforts for

Steve Miller made his name as a track coach before becoming athletic director. Miller now works for Nike, Inc.

the Mike Ahearn Scholarship Fund and leading the athletic department's marketing efforts.

After that year, Miller left K-State to become the chief executive officer of the Pennsylvania Special Olympics. He served in that capacity for 15 months before Travis was fired as K-State's AD, and Miller took over the job.

In June 1991, Miller resigned his post to accept the job of Director of Athletics for Nike, Inc. Miller's move not only offered him an enormous financial package, but put him in charge of the track and field program at the world's largest sports and fitness company.

This is "a once-in-a-lifetime opportunity to have a major impact on the sport which has been the dominant focus of my professional career," Miller said at the time of his resignation.

Miller left K-State's Athletic Department on the rise, but also at least $3 million in debt. His aggressive promotion of the school energized fans, but left a legacy of financial troubles for the department.

PORKY MORGAN Rarely does the name of an athletic trainer become so entwined with the athletic history of a school. After serving in World War II, Morgan returned from overseas to earn his college degree and briefly work as a trainer for a professional basketball team. Morgan came to K-State in 1951, serving as the school's head trainer for the next 30 years, focusing on basketball.

Morgan is best remembered for his gruff exterior. "He was a no-nonsense guy who ran a tough, disciplined

Trainer Porky Morgan oversaw K-State athletes' health for 30 years.

WILDCAT QUIZ

53. Who is second to Mike Clark in all-time coaching victories for the baseball team?

ship," former head basketball coach Tex Winter said. "There were actually times I was scared to go into the training room myself." That doesn't mean, though, that Morgan was not loved. He remains one of the most respected men in K-State sports history.

Morgan fell ill prior to a basketball game with Colorado in 1980 and died a few days later. After that season, the basketball program's award for the team's "most inspirational player" was renamed in his honor. The "Porky Morgan Most Inspirational Player" award is the basketball program's most-treasured honor.

THE VANIERS The success of any school's athletic program hinges on the ongoing financial support of alumni. K-State is no different in that respect, but Jack and Donna Vanier stand out among the many loyal supporters of the Wildcats.

The husband and wife from Brookville, Kans., have been involved in almost every aspect of the school's athletic department but are best known for their contributions to football and basketball. They have made substantial contributions toward the construction of Bramlage Coliseum, the press box at KSU Stadium, the indoor practice facility, the expansion of the football weight rooms, and the renovation of the football offices that now carry their name. In 1995, the couple was enshrined in the Kansas State University Sports Hall of Fame.

A rancher, Jack Vanier gained his love for K-State from his father, J.J. And, Jack and Donna have now passed that legacy to their three children, all K-State graduates. Without their financial support and tireless work on behalf of the athletic department, much of what has occurred in Manhattan in recent years would not be possible.

BASEBALL

WILDCAT QUIZ

54. How many conference baseball championships has Kansas State won in 67 years of competition?

ELDEN AUKER Among the great names in K-State sports history, Elden Auker can lay claim to the title of "greatest of them all." At one time while at K-State, Auker was named an All-American in football, baseball, and basketball. This from a man who did not intend on playing sports when he arrived in Manhattan from Norcatur, Kans.

"I came to Manhattan to get an education," Auker said in 1994. "I loved school, and I wanted to study medicine. I played sports throughout high school, but I didn't plan on playing in college."

When football coach A.N. McMillin saw Auker kicking a football one day, he asked him to try out. Auker did and made the team. That began Auker's remarkable athletic journey. While playing at the collegiate level from 1930 to 1932, Auker stood out in all

Elden Aucker lettered in three sports at K-State before becoming a Major League baseball star.

sports, most notably as a quarterback for the football team and a pitcher on the baseball field.

When he graduated with a degree in pre-medical training, he had to choose between professional contract offers from football's Chicago Bears and baseball's Detroit Tigers. At the time, the money was much better in baseball, so he was off to Detroit.

"The Chicago Bears, who were dominating the league at the time, offered me $500 a game with a 12-game guarantee," Auker recalls. "But when the Detroit Tigers made me choose between football and baseball, I chose baseball for the money."

Auker played with the Tigers, Red Sox, and the St. Louis Browns over the next 10 years. It was with Detroit, though, that Auker got his taste of big-time success. When he joined the team in 1933, the Tigers weren't a great organization. One year later, Detroit won the American League pennant. The Tigers lost the 1934 World Series to the St. Louis Cardinals, but in 1935 the

WILDCAT QUIZ

55. Kansas State has had a total of three players on the Big Eight baseball all-tournament team in 1995 and 1996. Who is the only other player in Wildcat baseball history to make the all-tournament team?

WILDCAT QUIZ

56. Who was the first baseball player to win the Player-of-the-Week honors starting in 1984?

Tigers beat the Chicago Cubs in the World Series.

"Winning the pennant and then the World Series was just a great thrill. It brought so much joy to the city of Detroit, which had been devastated by the Depression. It was just like Christmas."

Auker stayed with Detroit until he was traded to Boston in 1939. He spent one season there before being traded to the Browns. Auker, and his unique submarine pitching style, retired after the 1942 season.

Auker matched his athletic success with success in the world of business. He worked his way up through the corporate ranks, becoming the chief executive officer of Bay Street Abrasive in Massachusetts in 1969. He retired in 1975, moving with his wife, Mildred, to Vero Beach, Fla.

Mike Clark is the winningest baseball coach in school history.

MIKE CLARK In his 10 years as baseball coach at Kansas State, Mike Clark has probably done more with less than any other coach in the Big Eight. Clark has fashioned a 268-282 record, making him the winningest coach in school history.

Skewing Clark's numbers at K-State were lean years in 1993 and 1994, when he fielded a young team while rebuilding. "I'm proud of the fact that I been able to put together a winning season for eight of the 10 years," he said. "I think it shows a tradition building."

During a game in April 1996 against Missouri, Clark posted his 600th career victory, dating back to his nine years in the high-school and junior-college ranks.

Ted Power pitched at K-State before moving on to the pros.

TED POWER When Power pitched for K-State from 1974 to 1976, he didn't exactly make a mark in Wildcat baseball history. A solid pitcher during his collegiate days, Power holds the school record for strikeouts in a game with 19. Other than that, there was little to indicate that Power would go on to play professional baseball for more than 20 years.

Power made a name for himself as a relief pitcher in 1984 for the Los Angeles Dodgers. Since then, the Abilene, Kans., native has played for six other major-league franchises.

BOBBY RANDALL An anchor at second base for the Minnesota Twins over four seasons, Randall was an All-Big Eight shortstop at K-State in 1969. He coached for 11 seasons at Iowa State before taking over the head job at Kansas in 1995.

ANDY REPLOGLE A two-time All-Big Eight pitcher while playing at K-State from 1973-75, Replogle was 25-9 at KSU and still tops KSU's career win chart. As a senior, he was a second-team All-America choice. Replogle was signed by the St. Louis Cardinals, but reached the major leagues in 1978 with the Milwaukee Brewers.

CRAIG WILSON Someday the name Craig Wilson may show up in a major-league box score, but for now Wilson is paying his dues in the minor leagues. A native of Phoenix, Ariz., the shortstop may have been the most dominating player in K-State history. Wilson was named the Big Eight's Player of the Year in 1992, and was the conference's first-team shortstop two years in a row.

Wilson was the only Big Eight player selected to try out for the 1992 U.S. Olympic team, and made the squad. Drafted in the 13th round by the Chicago White Sox, Wilson ranks in almost every offensive category with his career and single-season marks at K-State. He hit .349 with the Cats — including .416 in 1992 — and drove in 176 runs during his four years of play.

Craig Wilson played for the United States' team in the 1992 Summer Olympics.

GOLF

JIM COLBERT Many former K-Staters have competed in the professional ranks, but few athletes can claim as much pro success as Colbert. The Overland Park, Kans., native has become a great golfer with outstanding play on the PGA Senior Tour.

Colbert came to K-State in 1960 to play football but soon switched his full attention to golf. As a junior in 1963, he was the Big Eight runner-up, and the next year he finished second at the NCAA Championships. From there, Colbert went on to the pro ranks. His first PGA Tour win came in 1969 at the Monsanto Open. In 1983, he won three tournaments and finished 15th on the PGA money list.

Jim Colbert is now one of the greatest players on the PGA Senior Tour.

However, in 1987 a bad back forced him to retire from the PGA Tour. Colbert spent the next three years as a television golf analyst for ESPN. Once he turned 50, and with three years of rest for his back, Colbert joined the PGA Senior Tour in 1991 and proceeded to win the Southwestern Bell Classic in Kansas City. Since then, he has been the most dominant player on the Senior Tour.

In addition to his success as a pro golfer, Colbert has remained active in K-State sports. Since 1974, Colbert has helped raise money to help fund Olympic sports, and most notably the golf program, at K-State with his benefit golf tournament.

TRACK AND FIELD (MEN)

THANE BAKER An athlete from Elkhart, Kans., Baker went on to star on the world stage. Between his junior and senior years at K-State, Baker competed for the United

Thane Baker won four Olympic medals in two Summer Games.

States at the 1952 Summer Olympics in Helsinki, Finland, winning a silver medal in the 220-yard dash. Four years later while serving in the Air Force, Baker went to the Summer Games in Melbourne, Australia, and won three more medals. Baker earned a gold as a member of the U.S. 400-meter relay team, a silver in the 100-meter dash, and a bronze in the 200.

While at K-State, Baker won the NCAA title in the 220-yard dash during his senior year in 1953. Before that, he captured 10 Big Eight crowns, including three consecutive golds in both the 100- and 220-yard dashes from 1951-53. All of this from a man who never earned a full scholarship at K-State and had arrived as a walk-on.

Baker is retired from the Mobil Oil Company, and lives with his wife, Sally, in Granbury, Texas.

ED BROXTERMAN He entered the 1996 United States Olympic Trials as a longshot to make the team in the high jump, but Broxterman turned in a career performance and earned a trip to Atlanta. Broxterman, a native of Baileyville, Kan., had a career-best jump of 7-4 1/2 heading to the Trials, but leapt 7-6 1/2 and placed second in the event to become the only current K-State athlete to win a spot on the 1996 Olympic team.

Steve Fritz represented the U.S. in the decathlon at the 1996 Summer Olympics.

STEVE FRITZ Gypsum, Kan., has a population of less than 400, but it claims among its former citizens Steve Fritz. Fritz grew up in the small central Kansas town, eventually developing into one of the world's finest decathletes. Fritz first attended Hutchinson (Kan.) Community College before coming to K-State in 1988. He first played for the Wildcat basketball team, but once he focused on his tracks skills, he quickly developed into one of the nation's best decathletes.

Fritz's scores steadily climbed, and he fought through a series of small, nagging injuries, before establishing himself on the world stage in 1993 by wining the final major international decathlon competition of the year being held in Talance, France. The next year, Fritz took second in the Goodwill Games, and placed second at the USA Mobil Track and Field Championships in Knoxville, Tenn. His score of 8,548 represented his career best at the time, and trailed gold medalist Dan O'Brien by just 159 points.

At the U.S. Olympic Trials in June of 1996, Fritz put up a career-best score of 8,636, and finished just 90 points behind O'Brien to take second. Even though the score was his best ever, Fritz said he was disappointed with his performance in seven of the 10 events. Heading toward the 1996 Summer Olympics in Atlanta, Fritz was considered not only one of the USA's best decathletes, but a contender for an Olympic medal. Fritz, however, finished fourth in Atlanta with 8,644 points, another career best. He finished just 20 points out of the bronze medal, the equivalent of three seconds in the 1,500 meter run.

"His strength is there are no weaknesses," said Fritz's coach, Cliff Rovelto, the head track and field coach at K-State. "That's the goal of a multi-eventer. That's what we've worked on for the last eight years. He's become remarkably consistent and has developed a remarkable average in how he derives his scores."

As Fritz prepared for the Olympics, he remained at K-State, serving as an assistant coach under Rovelto.

WILDCAT QUIZ

57. Can you name the two K-State baseball players to receive first-team All-America honors?

KENNY HARRISON While at K-State, Harrison earned All-America accolades 11 times. Harrison competed at K-State from 1984-88, and still holds the school records for the indoor long jump (26-feet, 9 3/4-inches), and the outdoor long jump (26-feet, 11-inches) and triple jump (56-feet). It was in the triple jump that Harrison excelled internationally, eventually capturing the gold medal at the 1996 Summer Olympics in Atlanta.

In 1990, Harrison was named the winner of the Jim Thorpe Award, given each year to the United States' best male athlete in the field event/decathlon category. That year, Harrison had the best triple jump in the world (58-feet, 10-inches), as well as winning the U.S. championships and the gold medal in the Goodwill Games.

Kenny Harrison won the gold medal in the triple jump at the 1996 Summer Olympics.

WILDCAT QUIZ

58. Out of the six no-hitters in Wildcat baseball history, name the man who threw one against a conference opponent in 1976?

The next year, Harrison leapt 58-feet, 4-inches to win the gold medal at the World Track and Field Championships in Tokyo, Japan. As the 1992 Olympics neared, Harrison was considered a contender for a spot on the U.S. team, but a nagging knee injury prevented him from qualifying. Redemption came in 1996 when Harrison won the U.S. Olympic Trials with a leap of 59-feet, 1 1/4-inches, and then took first in the Olympics with a mark of 59-4 1/4.

WARD HAYLETT As an athlete, few were more talented than Haylett. While attending Doane College in Crete, Nebr., in the mid-1910s, Haylett was the center on the basketball team, the quarterback on the football team, a pitcher in baseball, and ran the quarter- and half-mile during track season. He lettered in all four sports, and was considered a cinch to make the U.S. Olympic team as a decathlete in 1916 before World War I canceled the competition.

Despite all of his success as an athlete, Haylett became better known as a track coach. After serving in World War I, and coaching at the high school and small-college levels, Haylett came to K-State in 1928 to establish the school's track program. He spent the next 35 years in that position, finding time to teach classes at K-State and even coaching the K-State football team from 1942-44.

Ward Haylett started the K-State track program in 1928 and retired in 1963.

Haylett retired in 1963.

Haylett built the K-State program into a factory of fine athletes. He also became known around the world as one of the finest track coaches anywhere and served on the United States Olympic Track and Field Committee three times.

"The chief reward I get out of coaching and working with the young men is having some effect on lives," Haylett once said. Born in 1895, Haylett stayed in Manhattan after retirement.

WILDCAT QUIZ

59. Who is the only Wildcat player to throw a perfect game?

RAY HILL Hill competed just one year at Kansas State, but in 1986 the sprinter rewrote the school's records after amazing performances at both the Big Eight indoor and outdoor meets. Indoors, Hill owns the school's records for the 55-meter (6.15) and 200-meter (21.29) dashes. Outdoors, Hill holds the school record in the 100 meters after running at 10.49, and he also owns the outdoor record in the 200 with a 20.76.

KEN SWENSON Swenson may be the greatest K-State athlete you've never heard about. From 1967 to 1970, Swenson was a key component of a K-State track team that ran off an impressive streak of Big Eight titles and national championships. Specializing in the 880-yard run

Ken Swenson specialized in the 880-yard run and the two-mile relay during a sterling K-State career.

After losing his right hand in a childhood accident, Ray Watson turned his athletic attention to track.

and the two-mile relay, Swenson was a two-time All-American, won four NCAA championships, and won a trio of Big Eight championships. Swenson also anchored 21 K-State relay teams to first-place finishes.

After leaving K-State, Swenson anchored four different world indoor two-mile relay teams that set world records, and another that set an American record. He also set the American record in the 880-yard run with a time of 1:44.8.

RAY WATSON Not only K-State's first national champion in track — capturing the one-mile race in 1921 — Watson also set the standard for K-Staters in the Olympics. Watson not only earned a spot in the 1920 Summer Games in Antwerp, Belgium, (taking seventh in the steeplechase), but he returned to the Olympics in 1924 and 1928.

Watson grew up in Wichita with a bright athletic future, then he lost his right hand in a shotgun accident. From then on, Watson concentrated on competing on the track, arriving at Kansas State Agricultural College in 1918 to run cross-country. After retiring from competition, Watson taught and coached at Quincy (Ill.) High School until retiring in 1964. Watson died in August 1974.

TRACK AND FIELD (WOMEN)

NICOLE GREEN From the first day Green started running track at K-State, she made an impact. Competing in the 200-meter dash and the 400-meter run, Green qualified for the NCAA Championships six out of her eight opportunities (indoor and outdoor). The Springfield, Ill., product saved her best for last, winning the NCAA women's 400-meter outdoor title in 1995 with a time of 52.01 seconds.

DEB PIHL When Deb Pihl graduated from Lindsborg (Kans.) High School in 1979, she weighed less than 100 pounds. The fact that she might blow away in a Kansas wind surely scared away major-college recruiters, even though Pihl had proved herself as the state's top middle-distance runner in high school.

So, Pihl walked on at K-State and proved her worth. Amazingly, Pihl owns three K-State indoor records: the 800-meter run (2:09.14), the 1,000-meter run (2:46.80), and the one-mile (4:39.06). Outdoors, Pihl also claims the 1,500-meter run (4:12.94) and the 3,000-meter run (9:09.60) records.

Nicole Green, left, proved herself to be one of the nation's best 400-meter competitors.

Deb Pihl, middle, owns three K-State indoor records and two school outdoor records.

Jacque Struckhoff's, right, name appears in the KSU records indoors, outdoors and in cross country.

JACQUE STRUCKHOFF No matter where you look in the Kansas State track records, you find the name Jacque Struckhoff. Indoor, outdoor, or cross-country, Struckhoff has earned her spot in K-State sports history.

A product of tiny Grinnell, in far western Kansas, Struckhoff competed at K-State from 1984-88. Indoors, Struckhoff still owns the school record in the two-mile (9:52.75). Outdoors, Struckhoff tops the charts in the 5,000-meter run (15:54.12) and the 10,000-meter run (33:22.64). In cross-country, Struckhoff is K-State's only woman to be named a two-time All-American (1984 and '85). She was also a three-time Academic All-American at K-State.

Pinkie Suggs set the standard in the shot put for Wildcat athletes.

PINKIE SUGGS To say Pinkie Suggs had presence would be an understatement. The Manhattan native stayed in town to put the shot and throw the discus, arriving at K-State as a 260-pound freshman in 1983. Soon, she had trimmed down and began conquering the K-State record books.

Suggs competed most of her collegiate career under her high school weight, and still developed into the finest women's weight competitor in school history. Suggs owns the indoor record in the shot put (54-feet, 11 1/4-inches), as well as the outdoor record in the shot (55-feet, 6 1/2-inches) and discus (194-feet, 1-inch). During her five-year run for the Cats, Suggs earned All-American status three times.

CONNIE TEABERRY By the time Teaberry had exhausted her eligibility at K-State in 1992, she had established herself as one of the great high jumpers in school history. However, her career high leap in college was just 6-2 1/4, below what it would take to compete at the international level. When the 1996 Olympic Trials arrived, she leapt into the world league with a jump of 6-4 1/4, earning her second place at the Trials and a spot on the U.S. Olympic team.

GWEN WENTLAND Wentland is one of those great all-around athletes who has to be seen to be believed. She can do a little of everything, competing in the pentathlon

Gwen Wentland developed herself into one of the nation's top high jumpers in the mid-1990s.

while at K-State. Her specialty, however, is the high jump, and by the time she was done competing for the Wildcats in 1995, she had established herself as one of the nation's best.

Wentland owns the world pentathlon high jump record (6-4 1/4), as well as four K-State records: indoor (6-5), outdoor (6-4 1/4), pentathlon (4,115) and heptathlon (5,063). The native of Grand Blanc, Mich., won the 1995 U.S. indoor title, three Big Eight crowns and was a four-time All-American.

VOLLEYBALL

SHAWNEE CALL In the late 1980s, Shawnee Call established herself as possibly the best volleyball player in school history. A great all-around athlete at Ellsworth (Kans.) High School, Call developed into a dominating hitter during her playing days at K-State. In 1986, 1987

VOICE OF THE WILDCATS: A LASTING LEGACY

Many young Kansas State fans grew up wishing they could shoot a basketball like Mike Evans or pass a football like Lynn Dickey. Other young Wildcats-to-be had entirely different dreams.

"As a kid, I wanted to be the next Dev Nelson," Mitch Holthus said.

Dev Nelson. A name that will forever be the "Voice of the Wildcats." The unofficial title is hung on the Wildcat Network's radio play-by-play announcer. From 1954 to 1979, Nelson broadcast Wildcat football and basketball games to fans throughout the Midwest.

One of those fans was a young man in Smith Center, Kans., who hung on every word by the legendary Nelson. Holthus listened to not only what Nelson said, but how he said it. He dreamed of some day being the "Voice of the Wildcats," and reached that goal when he was named the K-State announcer in 1984. For 12 school years, Holthus stood in the shoes of greatness.

"The school's been good for me, and I think I've been good for the school," Holthus said.

Mitch Holthus

When Nelson retired his post, many said no one could ever live up to his legend.

Nelson's voice not only became recognizable, but so did his face. The radio announcer became a celebrity of sorts in Wildcat Land.

Nelson's trademark call for K-State thrillers — "Rip-snorting hootenanny double-barreled deep-dish dilly" — is legendary in the state. But it's not as legendary as the man himself.

"People identify me with the school because of my long association with it. I feel like an ambassador in a small way," said Nelson in 1984.

Months after Nelson said those

and 1988, Call was named to the All-Big Eight team. She remains the school's only player to ever receive the honor three times.

Call remains atop K-State's career list for kills (1,337) and attacks (3,372) and is second in attack percentage (.265). "Shawnee is just one of the real unique athletes we have at Kansas State," head coach Scott Nelson said during her playing days. "I think she has a lot of talents that are God-given, yet she's a real team player."

Shawnee Call translated her all-around athletic ability into volleyball stardom at K-State.

SCOTT NELSON It would have been easy for Nelson to wonder what might have been. As a player, he was an All-American at Ball State, and later a member of the U.S. national team. In 1976, he was slated to be part of the team that would compete in the Summer Olympics before President Jimmy Carter announced the United States' boycott of the games.

Instead of continuing his playing career, Nelson

Dev Nelson

words, a young sideline announcer for the Wildcat Network was promoted to the play-by-play job. Years later, Holthus would emerge from Nelson's sizable shadow.

Holthus eventually also grew larger-than-life, a man who could be recognized by his voice or his face. And he came with his own unique call. Holthus rated significant K-State victories on his "big" scale. Six bigs were saved for the run-of-the-mill notable victories — as in, "It's a big, big, big, big, big, big Wildcat victory" — leading up to a high of 13 bigs for the most significant wins.

In between the two men, a string of talented announcers sat in the "Voice of the Wildcats" seat. Kansas City Royals announcer Fred White and Steve Physioc, who can be seen on cable telecasts nationwide, were two who announced K-State sporting events in the interim.

But Nelson and Holthus will forever be known as the men who brought the most distinction to the title. Nelson, who died in January 1993 at age 66, would surely be proud of the way Holthus followed in his footsteps.

Holthus stepped down following the 1995-96 basketball season at age 38 to concentrate on his duties as the lead radio announcer for Kansas City Chiefs football broadcasts and to meet the growing demand for him as a television play-by-play announcer. Holthus was succeeded by Greg Sharpe.

"The job has tremendous tradition," Holthus said. "Any great program is able to hand the baton from great person to great person."

And because of that, the tradition of K-State's "Voice of the Wildcats" will live on.

Scott Nelson remains K-State's all-time winningest volleyball coach.

decided to go into coaching. In 1980, Nelson took over the K-State women's program and became the winningest coach in the program's history. After resigning in January of 1991, Nelson had complied a record of 168-176-1 at K-State.

WOMEN'S BASKETBALL

JUDY AKERS When K-State started a women's basketball team to compete on the intercollegiate level beginning in 1968, it turned to Judy Akers to establish the program. Akers proved to be up to the task.

Her team, playing a limited scheduled that first season, finished 11-3. Four seasons later, in the 1972-73 campaign, Akers' Wildcats went 20-6. Six more 20-win seasons followed, ending with a 20-11 record in 1978-79. After that season, Akers decided to step down from coaching, but she had established a legacy of winning. In her 11 seasons, Akers went 206-94, winning 69 percent of her games. Her Wildcats won two Big Eight titles, and went to five of the eight AIAW national tournaments that were held during her tenure (prior to the women's NCAA Tournament).

Judy Akers started the school's women's basketball program.

"Her efforts the past 11 years have been a tribute to her and a positive plus for Kansas State University and the athletic department," Athletic Director DeLoss Dodds said at the time of her resignation. "She leaves the university with a basketball program that is in tremendous shape."

Akers currently lives in Brookville, Kans., where she operates a bed and breakfast.

EILEEN FEENEY When discussing the all-time top scorers in K-State women's basketball history, Feeney's name might not pop up right away. But, with 1,670 career points, Feeney is tied for second on the scoring list. The native of East Hanover, N.J., accomplished this with amazing consistency, starting with her first year as a Wildcat.

Eileen Feeney sits in second on K-State's scoring and rebounding lists.

Feeney scored 330 points during the 1976-77 season, averaging 9.4 points a game as a freshman. Over her next three seasons, Feeney never averaged more than 13.6 points a game, scoring between 419 and 462 points a season. The 5-foot-11 forward still ranks second on K-State's all-time rebounding list with 783 boards.

After her playing days were over, Feeney joined the K-State staff as an assistant coach and went to Texas A&M with Coach Lynn Hickey.

PRISCILLA GARY In the history of K-State women's basketball, only once has a player been named a first-team All-American. In 1982, Priscilla Gary arrived in

Manhattan after being named a junior-college All-American at Shelby State Community College in Memphis, Tenn. The 5-foot-5 guard was known as a jumping jack, using her 40-inch vertical leap to allow her to wrap her fingers around the rim.

"She's an outstanding guard and will be a tremendous help immediately," Coach Lynn Hickey said when the signing was announced. Hickey was right. Gary averaged 18.2 points a game as a junior, and then backed that up with an 18.3 average as a senior in the 1982-83 season.

"Once I'm on the court, I'm going full blast," Gary told the Manhattan Mercury. "I'll do whatever it takes to win. I hate to lose."

During Gary's two years at KSU, the Wildcats went 51-13. During her 64 games with the Cats, Gary put together a 37-game string during which she scored in double figures. It was after her senior season that Gary was named to the 10-member Kodak All-America team.

Priscilla Gary is K-State's only women's basketball All-American.

NADIRA HAZIM When Hazim came to K-State from Topeka West High School, she didn't mess around. The 5-foot-7 guard made an immediate impact for the Cats, although she was still learning the game. Hazim averaged 11.4 points a game in 1988, setting her on track to become only one of two players to average double figures at K-State all four years. Hazim finished her career in 1991 by being named an honorable mention All-American. She is tied for second on the school's all-time scoring list (1,670 points) and averaged 14.9 points a game throughout her career.

Nadira Hazim started immediately after arriving from Topeka West High School.

LYNN HICKEY If you're going to hire an assistant coach from the University of Oklahoma to take over a program at K-State, then the coach better prove his or her worth darn fast. That's exactly what Lynn Hickey did at K-State.

Taking over for the legendary Judy Akers at just 28 years of age, Hickey led her first group of Cats to a 26-9 record in the 1979-80 season. She stayed at KSU for five seasons, compiling a 125-39 record (a .762 winning percentage). Following the 1983-84 season, Hickey accepted the head coaching job at Texas A&M, and with husband Bill, K-State's baseball coach for one year, left for College Station.

"I'm proud that we proved ourselves," she told the Manhattan Mercury just days after resigning. "We became an entertaining commodity for the community."

Lynn Hickey won 125 games in her five years as head coach of the women's program.

DIANA MILLER The only other player besides Nadira Hazim to average double figures in points all four years of playing at K-State is Miller, the school's all-time leading scorer with 1,705 points. With Hazim at guard all four years, the 5-10 Hutchinson (Kans.) High School product held down one of the school's forward spots from the 1987-88 season through 1991. As a freshman, she averaged 10.1 points a game. By the time she was a junior, she was averaging 17.3 points — which earned her honorable mention All-America honors. She improved to 19.2 points a contest during her senior season.

Tammie Romstad fought through a series a knee injuries to star for the Cats.

TAMMIE ROMSTAD During some of the best years of K-State women's basketball, Romstad stood out. "Tammie Romstad is the best center I've ever coached," Coach Lynn Hickey said in 1982. "I've seen very few centers that have any better moves or quickness. When she's on, she's unstoppable."

The 6-foot-2 center from Independence, Mo., sits fourth on K-State's all-time scoring list with 1,548 points. After scoring just 113 points her freshman season, Romstad erupted to average 19.6 points a game during her sophomore campaign. Her 686 points in 1979-80 are a single-season school record. She then leveled out to average 16.7 and 16.1 points her junior and senior years. Romstad also owns the school's single-season rebounding mark with 337 boards in 1979-80.

"I'm not the type of player who gets caught up in stats," Romstad said during her senior season. "The only goal I have set is to be the best player I possibly can. I feel the numbers will come if I do that."

Romstad, who accomplished all of her impressive statistics despite a series of painful knee injuries, entered high school coaching after graduating from K-State in 1982. She returned to her alma mater in 1993 as an assistant coach on Brian Agler's staff. She left K-State in 1995 to become the head coach at Wichita Southeast High School.

Shanele Stires first came to K-State as a shot putter, but went on to star in basketball.

SHANELE STIRES Upon graduating from Salina (Kans.) Central High School in 1990, Stires packed up and moved to Manhattan on an athletic scholarship. In track. Stires was a multiple state champion in the shot put in high school, and had the makings of a great field performer at the Big Eight level.

But Stires couldn't shake her basketball dreams. She was cut from her eighth-grade team but developed into a second-team all-state performer by the time she was senior. An enigma as a high-school player, Stires stood 5-foot-11 and had the body of shot putter, but she could handle the ball like a point guard and shoot 3-pointers.

After one season at K-State, she left to play basketball at Cloud County (Kans.) Community College in Concordia. During that season, Stires not only proved herself as a basketball player, but transformed her body from the bulk needed to throw the shot to a much more athletic build. In 1992, Stires returned to K-State on a basketball scholarship.

During her three remaining years of basketball eligibility, Stires averaged 13.4, 17.1, and 19.3 points a game. Stires' total of 1,344 point ranks fifth on K-State's all-time list. Playing guard, forward, and center during her career, Stires was a versatile overachiever who was named an All-Big Eight performer following her senior season in 1995.

"Her ability to be so versatile has helped her scoring," Coach Brian Agler said during Stires' junior season. "She can score with her back to the basket, flash across the lane and catch, or hit from the 3-point line. ... Shanele has a good work ethic. She gives 110 percent all the time and never lets up."

WILDCAT QUIZ

60. Who are the only two people in the history of cross country as a individual to finish in the top 10 of the NCAA Tournament meet?

CARLISA THOMAS It just takes a glance at the K-State women's record books to get an idea of how exciting it was to watch Thomas, who played from 1983 to 1987. Thomas' name appears on numerous lists, but the most striking are her marks for most rebounds in a game (20) and most assists in a game (13). Thomas had two triple-doubles while at K-State (recording double digits in rebounds, assists, and points in a game), a feat nearly unheard of in women's basketball.

Carlisa Thomas recorded two triple-doubles during her career.

Thomas could also score. The 5-foot-9 forward netted 1,116 points in her career, averaging between 10.5 and 11.6 points a game from her sophomore to senior seasons. Not only did the Jacksonville, Fla., product do a little of everything, she always did it with style. Thomas was known for her fancy behind-the-back passes and wizard-like ball-handling.

"Carlisa is a great, great athlete," Coach Matilda Mossman told the Topeka Capital-Journal in 1986. "She is capable of dominating a basketball game, of completely turning a basketball game around. Carlisa is one of those players that a team looks up to. People wait for Carlisa to make things happen and then everyone else kind of falls in."

By the Numbers

The statistics found here are provided by the Kansas State Sports Information department and are updated through the 1995-96 school year.

FOOTBALL SEASON-BY-SEASON

Year	Coach	W	L	T
1896	Ira Pratt	0	1	1
1897	A.W. Ehrsam	1	3	1
1898	W.P. Williamson	1	1	2
1899	Albert Hanson	2	3	0
1900	F.G. Moulton	2	4	0
1901	Wade Moore	3	4	1
1902	C.E. Dietz	2	6	0
1903	G.O. Dietz	3	4	1
1904	A.A. Booth	1	6	0
1905	Mike Ahearn	6	2	0
1906	Mike Ahearn	5	2	0
1907	Mike Ahearn	5	3	0
1908	Mike Ahearn	6	2	0
1909	Mike Ahearn	7	2	0
1910	Mike Ahearn	10	1	0
1911	Guy Lowman	5	4	1
1912	Guy Lowman	8	2	0
1913	Guy Lowman	3	4	1
1914	Guy Lowman	1	5	1
1915	John R. Bender	3	4	1
1916	Z.G. Clevenger	6	1	1
1917	Z.G. Clevenger	6	2	0
1918	Z.G. Clevenger	4	1	0
1919	Z.G. Clevenger	3	5	1
1920	Charles Bachman	3	3	3
1921	Charles Bachman	5	3	0
1922	Charles Bachman	5	1	2
1923	Charles Bachman	4	2	2
1924	Charles Bachman	3	4	1
1925	Charles Bachman	5	2	1
1926	Charles Bachman	5	3	0
1927	Charles Bachman	3	5	0
1928	A.N. McMillin	3	5	0
1929	A.N. McMillin	3	5	0
1930	A.N. McMillin	5	3	0
1931	A.N. McMillin	8	2	0
1932	A.N. McMillin	4	4	0
1933	A.N. McMillin	6	2	1
1934	Lynn Waldorf	7	2	1
1935	Wes Fry	2	4	3
1936	Wes Fry	4	3	2
1937	Wes Fry	4	5	0
1938	Wes Fry	4	4	1
1939	Wes Fry	4	5	0
1940	Hobbs Adams	2	7	0
1941	Hobbs Adams	2	5	2
1942	Ward Haylett	3	8	0
1943	Ward Haylett	1	7	0
1944	Ward Haylett	2	5	2
1945	Lud Fiser	1	7	0
1946	Hobbs Adams	0	9	0
1947	Sam Francis	0	10	0
1948	Ralph Graham	1	9	0
1949	Ralph Graham	2	8	0
1950	Ralph Graham	1	9	1
1951	Bill Meek	0	9	0
1952	Bill Meek	1	9	0
1953	Bill Meek	6	3	1
1954	Bill Meek	7	3	0
1955	Bus Mertes	4	6	0
1956	Bus Mertes	3	7	0
1957	Bus Mertes	3	6	1
1958	Bus Mertes	3	7	0
1959	Bus Mertes	2	8	0
1960	Doug Weaver	1	9	0
1961	Doug Weaver	2	8	0
1962	Doug Weaver	0	10	0
1963	Doug Weaver	2	7	0
1964	Doug Weaver	3	7	0
1965	Doug Weaver	0	10	0
1966	Doug Weaver	0	9	1
1967	Vince Gibson	1	9	0
1968	Vince Gibson	4	6	0
1969	Vince Gibson	5	5	0
1970	Vince Gibson	6	5	0
1971	Vince Gibson	5	6	0
1972	Vince Gibson	3	8	0
1973	Vince Gibson	5	6	0
1974	Vince Gibson	4	7	0
1975	Ellis Rainsberger	3	8	0
1976	Ellis Rainsberger	1	10	0
1977	Ellis Rainsberger	2	9	0
1978	Jim Dickey	4	7	0
1979	Jim Dickey	3	8	0
1980	Jim Dickey	4	7	0
1981	Jim Dickey	2	9	0
1982	Jim Dickey	6	5	1
1983	Jim Dickey	3	8	0
1984	Jim Dickey	3	7	1
1985	Jim Dickey	1	10	0
1986	Stan Parrish	2	9	0
1987	Stan Parrish	0	10	1
1988	Stan Parrish	0	11	0
1989	Bill Snyder	1	10	0
1990	Bill Snyder	5	6	0
1991	Bill Snyder	7	4	0
1992	Bill Snyder	5	6	0
1993	Bill Snyder	9	2	1
1994	Bill Snyder	9	3	0
1995	Bill Snyder	10	2	0

FOOTBALL COACHING RECORDS

Years	Coach (Seasons)	W	L	T	Pct.
1896	Ira Pratt (1)	0	1	1	.000
1897	A.W. Ehrsam (1)	1	3	1	.200
1898	W.P. Williamson (1)	1	1	2	.250
1899	Albert Hanson (1)	2	3	0	.400
1900	F.G. Moulton (1)	2	4	0	.333
1901	Wade Moore (1)	3	4	1	.375
1902	C.E. Dietz (1)	2	6	0	.250
1903	G.O. Dietz (1)	3	4	1	.375
1904	A.A. Booth (1)	1	6	0	.143
1905-10	Mike Ahearn (6)	39	12	0	.765
1911-14	Guy Lowman (4)	17	15	3	.486
1915	John R. Bender (1)	3	4	1	.375
1916-19	Z.G. Clevenger (4)	19	9	2	.633
1920-27	Charles Bachman (8)	33	23	9	.508
1928-33	A.N. McMillin (6)	29	21	1	.569
1934	Lynn Waldorf (1)	7	2	1	.700
1935-39	Wes Fry (5)	18	21	6	.400
1940-41	Hobbs Adams (2)	4	12	2	.222
1942-44	Ward Haylett (3)	6	20	2	.214
1945	Lud Fiser (1)	1	7	0	.143
1946	Hobbs Adams (1)	0	9	0	.000
1947	Sam Francis (1)	0	10	0	.000
1948-50	Ralph Graham (3)	4	26	1	.129
1951-54	Bill Meek (4)	14	24	1	.359
1955-59	Bus Mertes (5)	15	34	1	.300
1960-66	Doug Weaver (7)	8	60	1	.116
1967-74	Vince Gibson (8)	33	52	0	.388
1975-77	Ellis Rainsberger (3)	6	27	0	.222
1978-85	Jim Dickey (8)	26	61	2	.292
1986-88	Stan Parrish (3)	2	30	1	.061
1989-95	Bill Snyder (7)	46	33	1	.575

INDIVIDUAL RECORDS

MOST POINTS SCORED

Game: 24, Mack Herron vs. Missouri, 1969; Bill Butler vs. Oklahoma, 1971; Pat Jackson vs. New Mexico State, 1990

Season: 126, Mack Herron, 1969

Career: 196, Ralph Graham, 1931-33; Tate Wright, 1990-93

MOST TOUCHDOWNS

Game: 4, Mack Herron vs. Missouri, 1969; Bill Butler vs. Oklahoma, 1971; Pat Jackson vs. New Mexico State, 1990

Season: 21, Mack Herron, 1969

Career: 31, Mack Herron, 1968-69

MOST EXTRA POINTS KICKED

Game:7, Ross Estes vs. Fort Hays State, 1949 and vs. Baker, 1950

7, Martin Gramatica vs Oklahoma, 1995; and vs Iowa State, 1995

Season: 43, Martin Gramatica 1995

Career:103, Tate Wright, 1990-93

MOST CONSECUTIVE EXTRA POINTS KICKED

Career: 69, Steve Willis, 1981-1984

MOST FIELD GOALS

Game: 3, Keith Brumley vs. Kansas, 1973; Steve Willis vs. Kentucky, '82 and Iowa State, 1982; Mark Porter vs. TCU, 1986, vs. Kansas, 1986 and Tulane, 1988; Tate Wright vs. Oklahoma State, 1991

Season: 13, Steve Willis, 1982

Career: 37, Steve Willis, 1981-1984

MOST RUSHING ATTEMPTS

Game: 41, Bill Butler vs BYU, 1971

Season: 232, J.J. Smith, 1994

Career: 506, Cornelius Davis, 1966-68

MOST RUSHING YARDS GAINED

Game: 227, J.J. Smith at UNLV, 1994

Season: 1,137, Isaac Jackson, 1973

Career: 2,210, J.J. Smith, 1991-94

MOST RUSHING TOUCHDOWN

Game: 4, Pat Jackson vs. New Mexico State, 1990

Season: 14, Bill Butler, 1971

Career: 22, J.J. Smith 1991-94

MOST 100-YARD RUSHING GAMES

Season: 6, Isaac Jackson, 1971

Career: 10, J.J. Smith, 1991-94

MOST PASSING ATTEMPTS

Game: 61, Lynn Dickey vs. Colorado, '69

Season: 372, Lynn Dickey, 1969

Career: 994, Lynn Dickey, 1968-70

MOST PASS COMPLETIONS

Game: 33, Chad May at Kansas, 1994

Season: 200, Chad May, 1994

Career: 501, Lynn Dickey, 1968-70

MOST PASSING YARDS GAINED

Game: 489, Chad May at Nebraska, 1993

Season: 2,682, Chad May, 1993

Career: 6,208, Lynn Dickey, 1968-1970

MOST TOUCHDOWN PASSES

Game: 4, Paul Watson vs. La Tech, 1988; Chad May vs. Iowa State, 1994; Brian Kavanagh vs Colorado State, 1995
Season: 22, Matt Miller, 1995
Career: 34, Chad May, 1993-94

PASSING YARDS PER ATTEMPT

Game (Min. 25): 10.92, Matt Miller, vs. Oklahoma (20-of-25, 273 yards), 1995
Season (Min. 250): 7.66, Chad May, 1993
Career (Min. 500): 7.65, Chad May, 1993-94

PASSING YARDS PER COMPLETION

Game (Min. 18): 20.1, Paul Watson, vs. La. Tech, 1988 (18-of-42, 362 yards)
Season (Min. 100): 14.8, Dan Manucci, 1978
Career (Min. 250): 13.2, Paul Wtason, 1988-91

MOST TDS PASSING/RUSHING COMBINED

Season: 30, Matt Miller, 1995 (22 pass/8 r ush)
Career: 44, Chad May, 1993-94 (34 pass/10 rush)

CONSECUTIVE PASSES WITHOUT INTERCEPTION

Game: 44, Chad May at Kansas, 1994
Season: 148, Chad May, 1994
Career: 158, Chad May, 1993-94

LOWEST INTERCEPTION PERCENTAGE

Season: 1.78, Chad May, 1994 (6 in 337 att.)
Career: 2.33, Chad May, 1993-94 (16 in 687 att.)

CONSECUTIVE GAMES WITH TD PASS

Season: 11, Chad May, 1993
Career: 16, Chad May, 1993-94

HIGHEST PASSING EFFICIENCY

Season: 157.3, Matt Miller, 1995
Career: 131.9, Chad May, 1993-94

HIGHEST PASS COMPLETION PERCENTAGE

Season: 64.2, Matt Miller, 1995
Career: 62.3, Matt Miller, 1994-95

HIGHEST AVERAGE PASSING YARDS PER GAME

Season: 247.6, Lynn Dickey, 1969
Career: 238.7, Chad May, 1993-94

MOST 300-YARD PASSING GAMES

Season: 3, Lynn Dickey, 1969; Chad May, 1994
Career: 4, Lynn Dickey, 1968-70; Carl Straw, 1987-90; Chad May, 1993-94.

MOST PASS RECEPTIONS

Game: 13, Michael Smith, vs. Missouri, '89
Season: 70, Michael Smith, vs. Missouri, 1989
Career: 179, Michael Smith, 1988-91

MOST ??RECEIVING?? YARDS GAINED

Game: 188, Dave Jones vs. Nebraska, '66
Season: 928, Greg Washington, 1988
Career: 2,457, Michael Smith, 1988-91
Most 100-Yard Games: 9, Michael Smith, 1988-91

MOST TOUCHDOWN RECEPTIONS

Game: 3, John Williams vs. Austin Peay State, 1987; Michael Smith vs. ISU '91
Season: 13, Kevin Lockett, 1995
Career: 20, Kevin Lockett, 1993-present

YARDS PER RECEPTION

Game (Min. 3): 43.3, Gerald Alphin vs. Missouri, 1984 (3 for 130)
Season (Min. 25): 18.1, Andre Coleman, 1993 (42 for 761)
Career (Min. 50): 17.2, Russ Campbell, 1988-91 (67 for 1,150)

MOST TOTAL OFFENSE YARDS GAINED

Game: 461, Chad May at Nebraska, 1993
Season: 2,492, Chad May, 1993
Career: 5,779, Lynn Dickey, 1968-70

MOST TOTAL PLAYS

Game: 67, Lynn Dickey vs. Colorado, '69
Season: 424, Lynn Dickey, 1969; Chad May, 1993
Career: 1,104, Lynn Dickey, 1968-70

ALL-PURPOSE YARDS

Most Yards Gained
Game: 301, J.J. Smith vs. Rice, 1994
Season: 1,648, Henry Hawthorne, 1970
Career: 3,443, Andre Coleman, 1990-93

YARDS PER TOUCH

Game (Min. 10): 27.0, Andre Coleman vs. Missouri, 1993 (10-270)
Season (Min. 50): 22.0, Eugene Goodlow, 1978 (55-1208)
Career (Min. 175): 18.2, Andre Coleman, 1990-93 (189-3443)

MOST PUNTS

Game:12, George Carter vs. Missouri, 1951; John Drew vs. Missouri, 1961; Bob Coble vs. Missouri, 1968
Season: 83, Don Birdsey, 1977
Career: 283, Don Birdsey, 1977-80

HIGHEST PUNT AVERAGE

Game: 52.8, Doug Dusenbury vs. New Mexico, 1964; Sean Snyder vs. CU, 1992
Season: 44.7, Sean Snyder, 1992
Career: 43.0, Sean Snyder, 1991-92

MOST PUNT RETURNS

Game: 7, Henry Hawthorne vs. OU, 1969
Season: 32, Gerald Benton, 1992
Career: 59, Michael Smith, 1988-91

MOST PUNT YARDS RETURNED

Game: 122, Andre Coleman vs. MU, 1993
Season: 362, Andre Coleman, 1993
Career: 596, Veryl Switzer, 1951-53

MOST KICKOFF RETURNS

Game: 7, Don Calhoun vs. Nebraska, 1972; Gerald Benton vs. Washington, 91
Season: 30, Ivan Pearl, 1983
Career: 67, Dimitrie Scott, 1985-89

MOST KICKOFF YARDS RETURNED

Game: 155, Andre Coleman at Minnesota, 1993
Season: 632, Henry Hawthorne, 1970
Career: 1,458, Andre Coleman, 1990-93

MOST PASSES INTERCEPTED

Game: 4, Jaime Mendez vs. Temple, 1992
Season: 8, Chris Canty, 1995
Career: 15, Jaime Mendez, 1990-93

MOST YARDS RETURNED FROM INTERCEPTION

Game: 85, Dana Atkins vs. Kansas, 1944
Season: 154, Jaime Mendez, 1990
Career: 298, Jaime Mendez, 1990-93

TACKLES FOR LOSS

Season:28, Reggie Singletary, 1981
Career: 60, Reggie Singletary, 1981-83

TEAM OFFENSE

MOST POINTS
Game: 67, vs Akron, 1995
Season: 402, 1995 (11 games)

FEWEST POINTS
Season: 39, 1962 (10 games)

MOST TOUCHDOWNS
Game: 9, vs Akron, 1995
Season: 53, 1995 (11 games)

FEWEST TOUCHDOWNS
Season: 5, 1965 (10 games)

MOST EXTRA POINTS KICKED
Game: 8, vs Akron, 1995
Season: 45, 1995 (11 games)

FEWEST EXTRA POINTS KICKED
Season: 1, 1962 (10 games)

MOST FIELD GOALS
Game: 3, vs. Kansas, 1973; vs. Kentucky and Iowa State, 1982; vs. TCU and Kansas, 1986; vs. Tulane, 1988
Season: 13, 1982 (11 games)

FEWEST FIELD GOALS
Season: 0, several years

MOST RUSHING ATTEMPTS
Game: 78, vs. Missouri, 1957
Season: 641, 1973 (11 games)

FEWEST RUSHING ATTEMPTS
Game: 13, vs. Colorado, 1951
Season: 298, 1947 (10 games)

MOST RUSHING YARDS
Game: 439, vs. Drake, 1954
Season: 2,443, 1973 (11 games)

FEWEST RUSHING YARDS
Game: -93, vs. Kentucky, 1970
Season: 563, 1967 (10 games)

MOST PASS ATTEMPTS
Game: 63, vs. Colorado, 1969
Season: 443, 1988 (11 games)

FEWEST PASS ATTEMPTS
Season: 66, 1953 (10 games)

MOST PASS COMPLETIONS
Game: 33 at Kansas, 1994
Season: 227, 1988 (11 games)

FEWEST PASS COMPLETIONS
Season: 26, 1953 (10 games)

MOST PASSING YARDS
Game: 489 at Nebraska, 1993
Season: 2,698, 1993 (11 games)

FEWEST PASSING YARDS
Game : -3, vs. Oklahoma State, 1955
Season : 378, 1955 (10 games)

MOST TOUCHDOWN PASSES
Game: 4, vs. Louisiana Tech, 1988; vs. Iowa State, 1994; vs. Akron, 1995; vs. Kansas, 1995; vs Iowa State, 1995
Season: 18, 1994 (11 games)

FEWEST TOUCHDOWN PASSES
Season: 1, several years

MOST TOTAL PLAYS
Game : 100, vs. Kansas, 1970
Season: 894, 1971 (11 games)

FEWEST TOTAL PLAYS
Game: 34, vs. Iowa State, 1947
Season: 462, 1947 (10 games)

MOST TOTAL OFFENSE
Game: 590, vs. Akron, 1995
Season: 4,231, 1991 (11 games)

LOWEST TOTAL OFFENSE
Game: 16, vs. Colorado, 1992
Season: 1,329, 1961 (10 games)

MOST FIRST DOWNS
Game: 32, vs. Oklahoma, 1971; vs. Akron, 1995
Season: 277, 1995 (11 games)

FEWEST FIRST DOWNS
Game: 3, vs. several opponents
Season: 69, 1947 (10 games)

MOST PUNTS
Game: 16, vs. several opponents
Season: 84, 1975, 1992

HIGHEST PUNTING AVERAGE
Game: 52.8, vs. New Mexico, 1964 (6 punts); 52.8 vs. Colorado, 1992 (10)
Season: 43.6, 1992 (11 games)

MOST PUNT RETURNS
Game: 8, vs. Colorado, 1939
Season:40, 1969 (10 games)

FEWEST PUNT RETURNS
Season:10, 1987 (11 games)

MOST PUNT RETURN YARDAGE
Game: 122 vs. Missouri, 1993
Season: 447, 1947 (10 games)

FEWEST PUNT RETURN YARDAGE
Season: 54, 1972 (11 games)

MOST KICKOFF RETURNS
Game: 11, vs. Oklahoma, 1956
Season: 64, 1950 (10 games)

FEWEST KICKOFF RETURNS
Season: 2, 1953 (10 games)

MOST KICKOFF RETURN YARDAGE
Game: 211, vs. Iowa State, 1951
Season: 1,150, 1950 (10 games)

FEWEST KICKOFF RETURN YARDAGE
Season: 411, 1957 (10 games)

TEAM DEFENSE

FEWEST POINTS YIELDED
Season: 84, 1937 (10 games)

FEWEST TOUCHDOWNS YIELDED
Season: 12, 1937 (10 games)

FEWEST RUSHING ATTEMPTS YIELDED
Game: 18, by Kansas 1939
Season: 465, 1954 (10 games)

FEWEST RUSHING YARDS YIELDED
Game: -18, by Arizona, 1969
Season: 1,182, 1969 (10 games)

FEWEST PASS ATTEMPTS YIELDED
Game: 1, by Missouri, 1964
Season: 105, 1960 (10 games)

FEWEST PASS COMPLETIONS YIELDED
Season:66, 1953 (10 games)

FEWEST PASSING YARDS YIELDED
Season: 515, 1954 (10 games)

FEWEST TOUCHDOWN PASSES YIELDED
Season: 1, 1960 (10 games)

FEWEST FIRST DOWNS YIELDED
Game: 1, by Colorado, 1939
Season: 129, 1954 (10 games)

FEWEST TOTAL PLAYS YIELDED
Game: 33, by Colorado, 1939
Season: 576, 1954 (10 games)

FEWEST TOTAL OFFENSE YIELDED
Game: -13, by Colorado, 1939
Season: 2,476, 1954 (10 games)

MOST PASSES INTERCEPTED
Game: 7, vs. Missouri 1938 and 1951
Season: 21, 1992 (11 games)

FEWEST PASSES INTERCEPTED
Season: 6, 1960

MOST PASS INTERCEPTION YARDAGE
Game: 95, vs. Colorado, 1959
Season: 305, 1984 (11 games)

FEWEST PASS INTERCEPTION YARDAGE
Season: 29, 1983 (11 games)

MISCELLANEOUS FOOTBALL RECORDS

Most Penalties
Game: 17, vs. Western Illinois, 1990
Season: 85, 1952
Fewest Penalties
Season: 32, 1962
Most Yards Penalized
Game: 135, vs. Baker, 1950
Season: 766, 1970
Fewest Yards Penalized
Season: 310, 1960
Most Fumbles
Game: 12, vs. several oppponents
Season: 51, 1954
Most Fumbles Lost
Game: 6, vs. Iowa State, 1954; vs. Wyoming, 1955; vs. Colorado, 1983
Season: 29, 1976
Fewest Fumbles Lost
Season: 6, 1961
Most Consecutive Victories
13 (4th game, 1909-7th game, 1910)
Modern Era
8 (9th game, 1993-4th game, 1994)
Most Consecutive Defeats
28 (2nd game, 1945-2nd game, 1948)
Most Consecutive Conference Victories
8 (1934-35)
Most Consecutive Conference Defeats
26 (1960-63)
Longest Consecutive Scoring Streak
42 (5th game, 1967-5th game, 1971)
Longest Consecutive Game Scoring Steak by Opp.
184 (2nd game, 1975-10th game, 1991)
Longest Consecutive Scoreless Streak
5 (Last game, 1961-4th game, 1962)
Longest Cons. Game Scoreless Streak by Opp.
4 (1933)
Most Consecutive Quarters Held Opponent Without a Touchdown
14 (1995; 1st Q vs Akron - 3rd Q vs Okla. St)
Most Consecutive Quarters w/o Trailing
24 (9th game of 1991-3rd game of 1992)
Greatest Winning Margin
(Modern Era) 67, vs Akron (67-0), 1995
Greatest Losing Margin
(Modern Era) 76 - vs. Oklahoma (76-0), 1942

FOOTBALL LETTERMEN

A Abramowitz, Alan 1984; Acker, Delton W. 1971-72; Acker, John L. 1968-69-70; Adams, Carlos 1982-83; Adams, Troy 1985; Addeo, Anthony G. 1954-55-56; Agnew, Merrill 1912-13-14; Akin, Delmar 1896; Albacker, Carl 1952; Alexander, David L. 1965-66; Alexander, Donald R. 1969-70-71; Alexander, Elijah, 1988-89-90-91; Alexander, H.E. 1915; Allen, Dennis 1982-83; Allen, Martin W. 1966-67; Allen, Richard D. 1955; Allison, Jeff 1988; Alphin, Gerald 1983-84-85; Anderson, Andre 1994; Anderson, C. 1900; Anderson, Don 1987; Anderson, Gary 1979-80; Anderson, Joseph M. 1924-27; Anderson, John L. 1966; Anderson, Kenneth 1984; Anderson, Larry R. 1964-65; Anderson, Marvin 1952; Anderson, W.M. 1897; Anding, Larry C. 1970-71; Andrews, John 1974-75-76; Argo, Matt 1991; Armstrong, Richard 1934; Arreguin, Max M. 1968-69-70; Art, Oren 1943; Ashbrook, W.H. 1897; Ast, David 1983-84-85; Atkins, Dana Mac 1944-47-48-49; Atterberry, DeDe 1979; Aubuchon, Martin W. 1963-65; Auker, Elden L. 1929-30-31; Austin, Lon D. 1966-67-68; Austin, Mark 1987-88; Avery, H.P. 1896-98; Axline, A.A. 1920-22-23; Aye, J.M. 1917; Ayers, Leo 1934-35-36.

B Bagshaw, Craig 1989; Bailey, Arthur 1974; Bailey, Eric R. 1982-83-83; Bailey, Gregory F. 1970; Baird, C.O. 1898; Baird, H.E. 1915; Balderston, Robert E. 1951-53; Balducci, Richard K. 1965-66-67; Ballard, Charles R. 1962-65; Ballard,

J.W. 1923-24-25; Bandy, Alva 1945; Banks, Oree V. 1958; Barber, Adrian 1983; Barger, Phillip G. 1961; Barlow, Ronald L. 1963-64; Barnes, Benjamin F. 1914; Barnes, J. Bert 1914-15-16; Barnes, Thomas K. 1966; Barnett, R.J. 1898; Barnhart, Frank 1939-40-41; Barr, Kenneth 1950-51-52; Barre, H.J. 1928; Barrera, Manuel T. 1968-69; Barta, Brooks 1989-90-91-92; Bartley, Derrill 1946; Bascom, George S. 1945; Bassetti, Eugene L. 1959; Bastian, Bob 1977; Batdorf, Harold G. 1973; Bates, Harry P. 1907-08-09-10; Bates, L. 1909; Bates, Roman 1979-80; Batten, Clifford 1943; Bauman, K.C. 1927-28-29; Bayer, Henry B. 1914-15-16; Baziel, Dewayne 1986-87; Beach, Ira 1901; Bean, Geo. F. 1901; Becker, Robert H. 1961-63-64; Beeler, Don 1934-36-37; Beezley, Bill 1937-38-39; Beffa, Robert N. 1964-65; Bennett, Monte 1977-78-79-80; Bentley, Arthur 1910; Bentley, Hal 1981; Benton, Gerald 1991-92; Benton, Kerry 1979-80; Berger, Zeno 1941; Bernard, Lawrence 1914; Berry, Joel H. 1949; Berry, Robert J. 1942-46-47; Bertrand, Robert 1951; Bessert, Bob 1983-84-85-86; Best, Greg L. 1978-80-81-82; Best, Keith A. 1969-70-71; Beyrle, Steve J. 1969-70-71; Biggs, J. 1901; Birdsey, Donald 1977-78-79-80; Black, Darryl 1977-78-79-80; Blackbourne, Doug 1987-88; Blackwell, Denby L. 1962-63-64; Blackwell, Reggie 1989-90-91-92; Blades, Eric 1986-87; Blaine, Dan 1931-32-33; Blake, Cool 1905-07; Blanchard, Joseph E. 1947-48-49; Blanke, Jack 1937-38; Blaylock, Ronald D. 1959-60; Bletscher, Rudolph 1955-56; Bliss, Charles D. 1949; Bogina, August 1944-45; Bogue, Doug A. 1980-82-83; Bogue, Gary 1975-76; Bogue, J.A. 1917-18-19; Bogue, Richard J. 1946-47-49-50; Bokenkroger, William 1928; Bolick, Mark P. 1965; Bonds, Rondell 1988; Boone, Joe 1989-90-91; Borota, Milan J. 1965-66-67; Borre, LeRoy B. 1963; Bortka, John 1941-42; Bowen, Ronald L. 1967-68; Bowlby, R. 1908; Bowling, Chuck 1978-79; Bowman, David 1988; Bowman, Phillip B. 1943; Boyd, Richard 1989-90; Boyd, Richard D. 1957-58; Bradford, Emmett 1987-88; Branch, Clarence 1947; Brandley, C.A. 1922; Brandt, Joseph R. 1971-72; Brandt, Robert G. 1973-74; Branson, Carl E. 1965; Branson, Richard L. 1962-63-64; Breen, Emmett 1931-32; Brettschneider, Thomas H. 1959-60-62; Bridges, William A. 1969; Briggs, Robert A. 1937-38; Brinery, Earl B. 1914; Brion, C.W. 1925-26; Brittain, Billy A. 1971-72-73; Brock, James 1937-38-39; Brodman, Wayne E. 1970; Brookover, Paul E. 1930; Brooks, Barrett 1991-92-93-94; Brooks, David 1988; Brouhard, Leo P. 1969-70-71; Brown, Antonio J.(Toney) 1982; Brown, Carl J. 1961-62-64; Brown, Clark 1986; Brown, David J. 1971-72-73; Brown, Ernest Lane 1950-51-52; Brown, Gordon 1994-95; Brown, H.L. 1921; Brown, I.E. 1904-05-06-07; Brown, Ira 1905-06-07; Brown, John 1922; Brown, Lawrence 1967-68; Brown, L.J. 1978-79-80; Brown, Pete 1980-82; Brown, Ron 1994; Brown, Terry D. 1971-72-73; Brown, Tony 1976-77-78; Brown, William E. 1922; Bruhin, Michael J. 1967-68; Brumley, Keith 1972-73; Bryan, Harold L. 1946-47-48; Bryan, Lewis J. 1921; Bryant, Theopilis 1973-74-75-76; Buchanan, Tim 1978-79; Burkholder, Arthur L. 1911-12-13; Burns, Oran 1934-36; Burris, Lynn E. 1949-50; Burtin, Hartzell 1918-19-20-21; Bush, Rick 1995; Bushby, Tom B. 1931-32-33; Bussey, Malcom 1976-77; Butcher, Archie W. 1923-24; Butler, John 1990-91-92-93; Butler, Ray 1977-78; Butler, William E. 1969-70-71; Byers, Henry 1914; Byers, Tom 1990-91-92-93.

C Cafferty, Danny M. 1971; Cain, Osmond 1965-66-67; Cairl, John F. 1963-64-65; Calhoun, Donald C. 1971-72-73; Campbell, Bryan 1993; Campbell, Donnie E. 1982-83-84; Campbell, Russ 1988-89-90-91; Canty, Chris 1994-95; Carbone, Ronald E. 1959-60; Cardarelli, Augustus C. 1934-35; Carlson, John W. 1955-56-57; Carrington, William C. 1954-55-56; Carter, George 1951; Carson, Alton 1974-75; Carver, James M. 1968-69-70; Case, Glenn I. 1937-38; Cashman, Gerald 1951-52-53; Castille, Dwayne 1984-85-86; Castillo, Victor C. 1965-66; Cataldo, Nunzio A. 1958; Cave, Russell 1905-06; Cave, W.B. 1907; Chambliss, Dave 1974-75-76; Chambliss, Gordon A. 1972-73-74; Chandler, John A. 1980-82-83; Chandler, Vic 1974-75-76; Channell, Glen L. 1949-50; Chapin, Christopher H. 1971; Chase, L.E. 1901; Chaves, Leslie S. 1973; Cherry, John 1975-76-77; Cheves, David 1974; Childs, Henry 1971-72-73; Christensen, John L. 1963-64; Christenson, Dennis 1976; Christian, Robert V. 1906-07-08-10; Christiansen, Galen 1947-49; Christlieb, Craig 1985-86; Christopolus, Thomas 1947; Churchill, Ralph 1933-34-35; Claassen, Warren 1990-91-92-93; Clabaugh, Oscar 1950-51; Clair, Ronald K. 1952-53; Clarington, Charles 1970-72-73; Clark, John Allen 1916-17; Clark, S.P. 1907; Clark, Steve 1978-79-80; Clarke, C.H. 1901; Clarke, John A. 1916-17; Clary, William J. 1944; Clawson, Kyle W. 1982-83-84; Clay, Keith 1979; Clayton, Eric 1990, 1991, 1993; Cleland, R.E. 1919-20-21; Clelland, G. Lynn 1913; Clements, Joe Bob 1995; Clements, Verne 1922; Clerihan, Patrick J. 1973-74; Cleveland, Howard W. 1935-36-37; Clifford, Kerry F. 1955-56; Cliggett, Don 1984-85; Clowers, Richard 1944; Cobb, Chris 1988-89-90; Coble, Robert J. 1966-67-68; Cochrane, Owen L. 1924-25-26; Cochrun, Benny K. 1960-61-62; Coffman, Paul 1975-76-77; Cokeley, Will H. 1980-82; Cole, (Bud) Roy Everett 1948-49; Cole, Tim 1979-80; Coleman, Andre 1990-91-92-93; Coleman, Ernie 1980-81; Colley, A.R. 1904; Collins, 1899; Collins, Charles 1968-69; Collins, Richard V. 1943; Collins, Scott 1994-95; Colquitt, Joe H. 1969-70-71; Colston, Tim 1992-93-94-95; Compton, Steve 1986; Condit, Gerald L. 1962-63-64; Condit, Lawrence E. 1962-63-64; Conley, David 1995; Conley, John F. 1946-47-48; Converse, Verne 1946-47-48; Conwell, Herman H. 1906; Conwell, Kenneth 1935; Cook, Jerry L. 1963-64-65; Cook, William F. 1941; Cooley, A. Ralph 1904-05-10; Cooper, James K. 1961-63; Cooper, Thomas A. 1961; Coppenbarger, Ronnie 1970-71-72; Copping, Farley D. 1898; Corbin, Richard W. 1955-56-57; Cordelli, Anthony M. (Tito) 1954-56; Corrigan, Lawrence T. 1961-62-63; Corrigan, Richard E. 1959-60-61; Cottle, Charles F. 1963-64-65; Cotton, Brent 1985-86-87; Couch, James 1974-76; Cowan, Dale 1943-44-45-46; Cowell, E.R. 1919-20; Cowell, Warren C. 1919-20-21; Cowings, Todd 1986-87; Cox, Kerwin 1975-76; Cox, Michael 1980-81-82; Coxen, Harry H. 1912-14; Crandell, Paul H. 1953; Crawford, Charles G. 1981-82-83-85; Crawford, John 1988-89; Crawley, John C. 1936-37; Creed, Lloyd Michael 1969-70-71; Crenshaw, Willis C. 1960-62-63; Creswell, David M. 1971; Creviston, Elmer G. 1949-50-52; Crews, Tyrone 1976-77-78-79; Crim, George 1946; Crist, Gwinn 1943; Cromleigh, James 1976-77; Cronkite, Henry O. 1929-30-31; Crosby, William E. 1973; Croyle, George S. 1907-08-09-10; Crumbaker, Don 1937-38-39; Cullars, Willie 1972-73; Culver, Chuck 1991-92; Cunningham, J.C. 1901-04; Cunningham, James 1972; Cunningham, Sol Whitney 1904-05-06-07; Curry, Brian 1985; Curry, Robert 1947; Cusic, W.D. 1912-13.

D Dabney, Sean 1990, 1991, 1993; Dageforde, Greg L. 1982-83; Dahnke, Robert E. 1952-53-54; Dalton, Lloyd H. 1931-32; Damiani, Richard 1951; Damon, David 1995; Danieley, Edward L. 1963-64-65; Daniels, Robert M. 1981-82-83-84; Daniels, William 1928-29-30; Darland, Kirk 1974-75-76; Darnell, Lawrence A. 1933; Darter, Don A. 1959; Davenport, Clinton 1977; Davenport, Ramon 1989; Davidson, Jamie 1975-77-78; Davis, Cornelius G. 1966-67-68; Davis, Shirley 1937-38; Dawson, LeRoy M. 1946-47; Dayhoff, Harold J. 1924-25-27; Dean, Jimmy 1995; Dean, Kent 1984-85-86-87; DeArmond, Will 1899-1900; DeBitetto, George, L. 1954-55; DeBord, Joe W. 1938-39; DeLaHunt, Tom 1975-76; Demby, Reggie 1985; Dern, H.L. 1899; Dettmer, Arlan W. 1956; Dial, F.V. 1896; Dickerson, Ronald L. 1968-69-70; Dickerson, W.E. 1971; Dickey, Clifford Lynn 1968-69-70; Dickey, Darrell Ray 1979-80-81-82; Dillon, Tom 1987-88; Dimel, Dana 1985-86; Dimmitt, H.A. 1928; Dirk, Duane 1976-77-79; Dodrill, J.M. 1915-16; Doll, Raymond 1931-33; Donaldson, Amos R. 1978-79-80-82; Doolen, Arthur H. 1922-24; Dorsey, Floyd 1974-75-76-77; Douglas, James M. 1925-26-27; Douglass, Robert 1936; Dowell, Russell T. 1960-61-62; Draper, Terry M. 1968-69-70; Dresser, Henry D. 1913; Drew, John A. 1961; Drouillard, Jeff 1986; Drown, James 1944; Dubois, Norman P. 1969-70-71; Duckers, John W. 1969-70; Dudley, Bernard C. 1951-52-53-54; Dukelow, James D. 1968-69-70; Dulan, Antoine 1988-89; Duncan, James M. 1966-67; Duncan, Lawrence 1940-41-42; Duncan, Roosevelt 1976-77-78-79; Dunlap, C.E. 1926; Durant, Edwin Irwin 1899; Dusenbury, Douglas K. 1962-63-64; Duwe, Kent 1939-40-41; Dvorak, Rockey 1985-86.

E Eagle, Ray 1994-95; Easterwood, Robert 1986-87-88; Eaton, Stephan L. 1971-72; Ebert, Thomas E. 1951-54; Eckardt, Kenneth A. 1966-67-68; Edwards, Albert R. 1925-26-27; Edwards, E.J. 1909; Edwards, Jim B. 1934-35; Edwards, L.T. 1974-75; Edwards, Leon 1992-93-94; Edwards, Lewis Sidney 1899; Ehret, Delbert 1948; Ehrlick, Al 1926; Ehrsam, A.W. 1897; Eisenhauer, Terry 1983; Ekeler, Mike 1991-92-93-94; Elder, Darrell K. 1960-61-62; Elder, Maurice L. 1934-35-36; Elder, Todd 1984-85-86; Elliott, Earl 1944; Elliot, George R. 1909-10; Elliott, Larry A. 1954; Ellis, Donald J. 1961; Ellis, Harlan 1943; Ellis, Ray 1936-37; Engelland, William 1941-42; Enin-Okut, James 1987-88-89-90; Enlow, Charles R. 1916-17-19; Enns, Karl C. 1925-26-27; Enns, Nicholas 1913-14; Epps, Frederick Wm. 1898; Epps, Jack 1983-84-85; Erickson, Oscar Jr. 1941-46; Erickson, William 1942; Errington, C. Hugh 1928-29; Estes, Lloyd D. 1949; Estes, Ross O. 1945-48-49-50; Eteuini, Malo

1978; Eubanks, Willone E. 1972-73; Evans, H. 1904; Evans, Jay Dale 1958-59-60; Evans, T. Marion 1927-28-29; Evans, Robert 1977-78.

F Faerber, Tom 1978-79; Fagler, Paul 1937-38; Fair, Eugene 1939-40; Fairbank, Paul E. 1930-31; Fairman, Charles 1938-40; Fairman, H. 1917; Falk, Max C. 1958-59; Fanning, Paul K. 1934-35-36; Fanshier, Robert 1942-46-47; Faraimo, Iosefatu 1981-82; Farinella, Charles 1952; Faubion, Hiram Henry 1949-50-51; Faubion, J. William 1943-44; Faubus, C.L. 1970; Faulkner, Chad 1986-87-88-89; Faunce, Troy 1985-86; Feather, Elwin E. 1924-25-26; Feldman, Joe 1988; Felps, Clemens I. 1911-12; Fergerson, Rick B. 1970-72; Ferguson, Clayton Jr. 1971-72; Finfrock, John R. 1960; Finley, John L. 1948; Fiser, Doug 1984; Fiser, Lud 1929-30; Fisher, William 1977-78; Fitzgerald, L.D. 1954; Fleck, Theodore 1925-26-27; Fleming, Jack K. 1935-36; Fleming, Shawn 1988-89; Flenthorpe, Don 1933-34-35; Fogle, DeShawn 1993-94-95; Foote, Mitch 1980; Forbes, Blair C. 1933; Forst, Dart 1994; Fowler, George G. 1981-84-85; Fox, Phil 1896; Frankenhoff, C.A. 1917; Franks, 1899; Franz, John E. 1922; Frazee, Dennis 1974-75-76; Freeland, James R. 1933-34; Freeman, A.H. 1927-28-29; Freeman, Gary L. 1972-73-74; French, John R. 1958-59; Frick, Forris 1944; Friedrich, Alan 1987-88-89; Frigon, Blake 1995; Fulhage, Scott A. 1981-82-83-84; Fulner, Brad 1985; Furey, James A. 1953-54-55.

G Gale, J. Darren 1980-81-82; Gallagher, Cliff 1918-19; Gallagher, William J. 1958-59-61; Gallon, Eric 1989-91-92; Garber, Matt 1990-91-92; Garner, Laird 1990-91; Garcia, James 1995; Garst, Kyle 1992; Garver, Matt 1986-87; Gaskins, Percell 1993-94-95; Gatz, Ike F. 1917-18-19-20; Gehlbach, Walter R. 1948-49-50; Gentry, Austin P. 1951-52-53; George, Chester A. 1958; Gibson, Oscar J. 1968-69-70; Gill, Howard Eugene 1948-50; Gilles, Fred N. 1899-1900; Gingery, Howard L. 1916-19; Gingery, J.B. 1907-08-09; Ginther, Jim 1978-79; Givens, Hoyt 1950; Glatz, Gary F. 1970-71-72; Glaze, Raymond C. 1955-56-57; Gleue, David 1990-91; Godfrey, Gary L. 1968; Godinet, Randall 1985; Goerger, John M. 1970-71-72; Goerke, D.A. 1920; Goff, John H. 1948-49-50; Goforth, John 1944; Goldner, Dan 1986-87; Gonzalez, Tony 1990-91; Goode, Rob 1985-86-87-88; Goodpasture, Donald T. 1959-61-62; Goolsby, Brian 1995; Gordon, Joe 1993-94-95; Gordon, Ira C. 1968-69; Gowdy, Kenneth K. 1951-52-53; Gowing, Tommy L. 1955; Goyne, Richard M. 1965-66-67; Gragg, Dennis L. 1973-74; Graham, Ralph M. 1931-32-33; Gramatica, Martin 1994-95; Graves, Roy R. 1906; Gray, Rickey E. 1973-74-75; Gray, Ty 1988; Grechus, James W. 1963-64-65; Green, Charlie 1976-77-78; Green, Mack 1977-78; Green, Mont 1904; Green, Rogerick 1988-89-90-91; Greene, Kelly 1991-92-93-94; Greenwood, Ross 1993-94-95; Greve, William B. 1965-66-67; Griffing, O. Dean 1933-34; Griffith, Ekwensi 1989-90-91-92; Grimes, James Theodore 1945-46-47; Grogan, Steven J. 1972-73-74; Grosdidier, Jarrett 1994-95; Grosse, Ben E. 1956-57-58; Grush, Doug 1990-91; Guice, Gracen 1975; Gump, Robert H. 1930; Gwinn, Francis 1942.

H Hagg, Chris 1975-76; Haas, Harvey W. 1944-45; Habiger, Frank J. 1898; Hackl, Frank 1913; Hackney, Elmer 1937-38-39; Hackney, Gerald E. 1948-49; Hafferty, John 1976-77-78; Hageman, 1901; Haggman, E.A. 1905-06; Hahn, Isaac 1911; Hahn, Ray 1918-20-21-22; Hall, Pat 1983-84-85; Halliburton, Willie 1986-87; Hamler, R.E. 1926-27; Hamlin, Howard E. 1942-45; Hamlin, Kenneth 1939-40; Hammond, A.L. 1909-10; Hammond, Lee 1926-27; Hancock, John 1939-41; Hanks, Steve 1993-94-95; Hannah, Paul 1938-39; Hanney, Paul W. 1967-68-69; Hanson, Homer P. 1931-32-33; Hanson, Tim 1986-87; Harbert, Darrell 1991-92-93-94; Hardin, Russell 1944-45; Harding, Andrew L. 1981-83-84-85; Hardwick, Conrad E. 1960-61-62; Hardy, Eric 1994; Haresnape, David 1990; Harper, Erick 1986-87-88-89; Harris, Richard 1945; Harrison, John 1935-36; Harrison, Russell 1968-69-70; Harsh, Glen 1930-31; Harshberger, Gary 1985-86; Harter, Bernard C. 1922-23-24; Harter, Kenneth W. 1932-33; Hartshorn, Larry L. 1951-52-53-54; Hartwig, Charles 1911; Hartwig, Fred 1913-14-15; Harvey, Max 1944; Harvey, Robert 1943; Harwood, Nathan D. 1915-16-17; Haskard, Richard E. 1925; Hasler, Harry 1930-31-32; Hatcher, Joe 1975; Haun, Harold L. 1960; Haury, Earl 1943-44; Havley, Chester 1924; Hawthorne, Henry E. 1969-70; Hayes, Edward M. 1937; Hayes, Jerry L. 1955-56; Haymaker, H.H. 1913-14; Haynes, 1912; Hays, Barney A. 1934-35-36; Haywood, R. 1909; Heath, Clarence "Huck" 1941-42-46-47; Heath, Richard M. 1969-70-71; Heaton, Carl 1937; Hedberg, Axel 1974; Hedges, Donald E. 1954; Heinrichs, M.A. 1906-08-09; Heinz, Gary J. 1960-61-62; Hemmerling, Dwight F. 1968; Hemphill, Matt 1991-92-93-94; Hemphill, William 1935-36; Henderson, Shelby 1974-75; Hennesy, Matt 1989; Henrikson, Wendell 1976-77; Henry, Maurice 1986-87-88-89; Herds, Tyreese 1986-87-88-89; Hernandez, David C. 1971-73-74; Hernandez, Frank 1988-89-90-91; Herrick, Eric 1989; Herron, Mack W. 1968-69; Hess, Chris 1995; Heter, Richard 1979; Heun, Scott 1994-95; Hickson, Eric 1994-95; Hilgendorf, Harold Lyster 1945; Hill, Rusty 1981; Hill, T.N. 1896-97; Hilliard, Don 1990; Hilliard, Robert G. 1953-54; Hinds, George W. 1917-18-19; Hitch, Ken 1977-78-79; Hite, Don 1946; Hixson, R.W. 1918-19; Hlasney, Todd 1994-95; Hmielewski, Jim 1991-92-93-94; Hocutt, Kirby 1991-92-93-94; Hoffman, Russell 1896; Hoffman, Russell A. 1924-26; Hokanson, Dean T. 1966; Holland, Rolla B. 1934-35-36; Hollinger, Robert Deane 1945; Holman, William M. 1971-72-73; Holmbeck, John M. 1971; Holmes, Jacob C. 1910-11; Holsinger, Joe F. 1925-26-27; Hood, Richard 1945; Hooper, Frank G. 1950; Hopkins, Larry P. 1971-72; Hoppas, Dean 1945; Hopper, George 1911; Hoppock, Douglas G. 1978-79-80-82; Horchem, Brad 1976-77-78-79; Houchin, Rob 1976-77-78-79; Householder, Dee J. 1926-27; Howard, 1899; Howard, Duane 1976; Howard, Henry S. 1964-65-66; Howenstine, L.L. 1911; Hraba, Adolph R. 1929-30-31; Hubbell, Rob 1989; Hudson, Paul 1970; Huff, Edward 1939-40-41; Huffman, Ralph 1938-39; Huggins, Guy 1985; Hughes, Curtis 1983-84-85; Hughes, Dan 1986-87; Hughes, Glen 1979-80; Hull, William Adam 1948; Hull, William T. 1961-62; Humbarger, Mark D. 1981; Humphrey, Kevin 1985-86; Hundley, Barton N. 1981-82-84-85; Hundley, Mark W. 1980-81-82-83; Hunter, Earl S. 1941; Hunter, O.W. 1907-08; Hurd, Jeffery 1983-84-85-86; Hurd, Oliver 1986; Husted, A. 1918; Husted, H. 1916; Huston, G.D. 1918-19-20, 1926; Hutchins, Alfred 1985; Hutto, C.E. 1919; Hutton, Ronald V. 1922-23-24.

I Isernhagen, Glenn A. 1961; Ives, Robert 1946.

J Jackson, Ed 1896-97; Jackson, Issac W. 1971-72-73; Jackson, Jim 1980; Jackson, Pat 1989-90; Jackson, Tim 1985; Jacobs, Matt 1985; Jacobs, Wesley A. 1972; Jacox, Kendyl 1994-95; James, Lemuel 1983-84; Jeffery, Chester 1976-77-78; Johndrow, Edward J. 1973; Johnson, Damian 1981-82-83-84; Johnson, David 1936; Johnson, D.L. 1978-79-81; Johnson, Douglas 1982-83; Johnson, Clyde 1994-95; Johnson, Jason 1993-94-95; Johnson, Lauren Richard 1948-49-50; Johnson, Rod 1987; Johnston, Kenneth K. 1948-49-50; Jolley, Alvin 1918; Jones, Al 1988-89-90-91; Jones, Daniel C. 1956-57-58; Jones, David R. 1966-67-68; Jones, Gregory E. 1971-72-73; Jones, Kevin S. 1971-72; Jones, Larry C. 1959; Jones, Lee 1941; Jones, Marion J. 1945; Jones, Nate 1977; Jones, Oliver 1975; Jones, Sonny Ray 1988; Jones, Victor 1946-47; Jones, Willie Lee 1963-64-65; Jordan, Tony 1984-85-86-87; Julian, Robert E. 1949-50.

K Kane, Dennis F. 1949-52; Karetski, Alvin J. 1952-53-54; Kavanagh, Brian 1994-95; Keady, Lloyd E. (Gene) 1956-57; Keefer, Leland E. 1923-24; Keelan, John E. 1955-56-57; Keeler, William 1952; Keeley, Bill J. 1982-83; Keller, August 1951-52; Keller, Larry F. 1969-70; Kelly, Dederick 1993-94-95; Kelly, Howard 1948; Kemp, Lloyd Paul 1959; Kendrick, John 1984-85; Kennedy, Jim 1980-81-82; Kennedy, William H. 1966-67-68; Kerr, Bob 1981-82-83; Kershner, Gary J. 1959; Key, Clyde C. 1917; Kientz, Emile F. 1937-38; Kier, Charles 1940-41; Kilgore, Charles W. 1973-74-75; Kilian, Jody 1989-90-91-92; Killough, Robert 1942-43; Kimball, Ronald D. 1972; Kinard, Harold 1944; King, Derek 1995; King, Jackie Joe 1961-62; King, Lawrence 1942-46-47; King, Manzy 1975-76-77; King, Phillip A. 1963-64-65; King, Robert K. 1944-45; Kirk, Arthur 1938-39-40; Kirk, Clarence B. 1904-05; Kirk, Donald P. 1982; Kirk, Henry 1934; Kirk, Robert W. 1934-35-36; Klaassen, Matt 1978; Klawiter, Warren D. 1963-64-65; Klimek, Ed 1936-37; Knoll, John 1950; Knowles, Brandon 1995; Koch, Randy 1986-87-88; Kochera, Richard L. 1964; Koenning, Victor E. 1978-79-80-82; Kolb, Josh 1990-91-92; Kolich, Michael J. 1968-69-70; Koontz, Lyle 1948-49; Kopsky, Mike A. 1979-80-81-82; Kouneski, Alfred C. 1959-60-61; Kovar, Ray E. 1959-60; Koyl, Jeff S. 1981-83-84; Kozak, Mark 1975-76; Kraft, Vernon A. 1966-67; Kramer, Karl 1945-46; Krebs, Donald E. 1962-63; Krizan, Robert L. 1957; Krueger, Anthony F. 1935-36-37; Kruger, David 1987-89; Krull, Jon 1987-88-89-90; Krull, Leslie E. 1957-58; Krysl, Jerry 1924-25-26; Kuhn, Michael J. 1968-69-70; Kuklenski, Dave 1976-77-78.

L Lacy, Ronald F. 1961-62; Laddish, George P. 1955-56-57; Lafferty, Gary Lee 1959-60; Laflin, R.D. 1910; Lambert,

Brad 1984-85-86-87; Lambing, Ralph M. 1957-58-59; Lander, Jim E. 1935; Landry, Ben 1978-79; Lane, Phillip 1942-43; Langford, David J. 1964-65-66; Langvardt, Chris 1938-39-40; Lankas, Daniel J. 1965-66-67; Lareau, Donald E. 1972-73-74; Larson, Lyndon A. 1968-69; Larson, Paul 1943; Larzarlere, R.G. 1908; Lasswell, Tull 1922; Latimore, Marion L. 1970-71; Latiolais, Bobby 1994-95; Lauridsen, Kent 1983-84; Lauridsen, Scott 1981-82-83; Laurie, David R. 1960; Lawrence, Bobby 1987-88; Lawrence, Mike 1994-95; Lawrence, Toby 1989-90-91-92; Lawson, Gerald W. 1967-68-69; Lee, Terry E. 1958; LeGault, Leonard A. 1954-55; Lehman, Gale L. 1947; Lembright, James A. 1973-74-75; Lesco, Harmon A. 1946; Letourneau, David J. 1982; Lewis, Rick R. 1980; Lewis, Rick L. 1984-86-87; Liebe, John 1976-77-79-80; Limes, James 1952; Limes, Joe 1926; Lindsey, Billy E. 1955; Lindsey, Fred R. 1904-05; Lindsey, Robert 1980; Lininger, James H. 1950-51; Linta, Edward 1952-53-54; Littlejohn, John B. 1959; Lockett, Kevin 1993-94-95; Logsdon, Richard J. 1954; Lojka, Brian 1992-93-94-95; Long, Kenneth D. 1953-54; Long, Robert A. 1968-69; Loomis, Fred H. 1911-12-13; Lorenz, Jack C. 1950-51; Lorenzen, Randall 1975-76-77; Lovely, Kenneth 1976-77; Lowe, Jeff 1986-87-88-89; Lummio, Al 1949-51; Luzinski, James P. 1956-57-58; Lyon, George C. 1926-27-28.

M MacDonald, Tim 1984-85-87; Machen, James 1943; Mack, Eric 1980-81-82-83; Mack, James 1975; Mackey, Mark 1981; Madden, Curtis 1988-89-90-91; Maddox, George 1932-33-34; Madison, L.E. 1980-81-82-83; Magrath, L.A. 1918; Majeski, Bob 1983; Makalous, Clifford 1942; Makalous, Kenneth 1939-40; Mallon, Carl 1904-05-06; Manges, Harry L. 1945; Manning, Rick 1981-82; Manucci, Dan 1977-78; Marble, A.L. 1912-13-14; Marciniak, Ronald J. 1951-52-53-54; Marcoline, John J. 1958-59; Margrove, 1901; Marlowe, Chuck 1993-94-95; Marn, Gregory A. 1966-67-68; Marshall, T. 1920; Martin, Don A. 1956-58; Martin, Jeremy 1995; Martin, Max F. 1963-64-65; Martin, Roy 1907; Martin, Tom 1943; Marxen, E. 1910; Massieon, Richard J. 1966; Masters, C.J. 1989-90-91-92; Masters, Claude 1897-98; Masters, Richard D. 1960-61; Matan, William D. 1963-64-65; Matney, Clayton 1936-37; Maughlin, 1910-11; Maupin, Theodore E. 1949-50-51; May, Chad 1993-94; Mayer, Robert C. 1950; McBride, Derrick 1992; McBurney, Ed C. 1927-28; McCain, Will 1987-88-89; McCarthy, John C. 1971-72-73; McConnell, Vernon K. 1958-59; McCutchen, Elvis 1938-39; McDonald, Harry E. 1968; McDonald, Ronald T. 1960-61-62; McEntyre, Kenny 1992-93; McEwen, Matt 1993-94-95; McFillen, Ralph W. 1961-62-63; McGalliard, E.R. 1915; McGee, H.L. 1924-25; McLane, Timothy P. 1969-70-71; McKinnis, Chad 1988; McKinnon, Stuart 1980-81; McMillin, Ray J. 1929-30-31; McMurray, Craig 1980-81; McNeely, Melvin 1982; McNeil, Edgar 1942-46-47-48; McNorton, Kent 1979-80; McShulski, John 1952; Mears, Rick 1988; Meek, Donald 1924-25-26; Mehner, David Lee 1961-62; Meier, Gene R. 1956-57-58; Meissenger, W.H. 1928-29; Melcher, Gary W. 1970-71-72; Melody, William 1947; Menas, Thomas 1980-81-82; Mendenhall, George 1942; Mendez, Jaime 1990-91-92-93; Menke, George G. 1896; Merrifield, Thomas 1974-75; Merrill, Fred L. 1971-73; Merriman, Harry 1942-46-47; Mersch, Ron 1975-76; Meschke, David G. 1966; Meyer, Earl H. 1951-52-53; Meyers, Alfred 1929; Meyers, Jeff 1979-80-81; Michael, Lloyd 1930-31-32; Michenko, Dave 1981; Mickens, Charlie 1986; Mildrexter, John L. 1923-24; Miles, Donald W. 1957; Miller, 1899; Miller, Jim 1977-78-79; Miller, J.J. 1977; Miller, L. 1918; Miller, Les 1983-84-85; Miller, Marcus 1986-87-88-89; Miller, Matt 1994-95; Miller, Rick 1986; Minis, J. 1900; Minter, Joseph R. 1968; Mitts, Robert I. 1962-63-64; Montgomery, James Michael 1968-69-70; Montgomery, Joseph S. 1904-05-06-07; Moody, Joe Bill 1954; Moody, Todd 1983-84-85-86; Mooney, Robert 1944; Moore, James M. 1967; Moore, Mike 1990; Moore, T.E. 1915; Morgan, John C. 1965; Morgan, Lee T. 1932-33; Morrill, Gary B. 1979-80-81-82; Morris, James Robert 1980-82; Morrison, Dennis C. 1971-72; Moten, Steve 1990-91-92; Mudge, Ben 1898-1900; Muhlheim, Wilson 1935-36-37; Munn, Lyle 1922-23-24; Munsell, E. 1904; Munzer, Don 1938-39-40; Murphy, D.D. 1921; Murray, Michael Joseph 1964-67; Murray, Tim 1980-81; Muscolino, Sam 1947.

N Nash, Kenneth H. 1960-61-62; Navarro, Ernie 1976-77-78; Nearhouse, John M. 1982-83; Needham, Danny 1988-89-90; Neely, Shelby M. 1927-31-32; Neill, Hobart 1942; Nelms, Keith 1976-77; Nery, Ronald D. 1953-54-55; Nesmith, Kenneth L. 1954-55-56; Neujahr, Quentin 1990-91-92-93; Nevius, Harold 1948; Newell, Jack 1944; Newton, Grady 1983-84-86-87; Newton, Mark K. 1981-82-83-84; Nichols, Ralph E. 1921-22-23; Nichols, Robert B. 1963-64-65; Nichols, William 1939-40; Nicholson, Rodney O. 1965; Nickerson, Nelson 1981-82-83-84; Nielson, H.T. 1897-1900-01; Nieman, Elmer 1938-39; Niemoller, Al 1939-40; Nigro, Alex 1928-29-30; Noblitt, David D. 1958-60-61; Noblitt, Robert L. 1961; Noel, Phillip 1976-77; Norby, Marvin 1944-45-46; Nordstrom, Kenneth 1936-37-38; Norman, Josef F. 1951; Norris, Charles L. 1956; Northcutt, Jim 1981-82-83; Norton, Lawrence H. 1929-30; Nossek, William L. 1966-67-68; Novosel, John M. 1965; Noyce, Richard 1945-46; Nutt, Grover P. 1946-47-48; Nutter, Douglas R. 1962-64-65; Nystrom, Amer B. 1905-06.

O O'Boyle, Thomas J. 1951-52-53; O'Brien, Daniel J. 1956-57; Ochs, Dirk 1992-93-94-95; Ochs, Kenneth C. 1968; Ochs, Travis 1995; O'Connor, Jon J. 1949; Oehm, Jim 1985-86-87-88; Oettmeier, Bert W. 1971-72-73; O'Hara, Larry Joe 1960; Olander, Morgan 1979; Oldham, Arthur Loy 1943; Oldham, Carvel C. 1950-51-52; Oliver, G.W. 1915; Oltmanns, Chris 1993-94-95; O'Neil, Brian 1994-95; O'Neill, John C. 1970-71-72; Orr, Mike 1989-90-91-92; Osborn, Patrick R. 1973-74-75; Osborn, Michael 1975-76-77; Osborne, Verlyn D. 1958-59; Ostlund, A.J. 1905-06-07-08; Otto, Jim 1978-79; Otto, Louis 1943; Overton, Steven P. 1965-67; Owen, Sam 1977-78-79; Owens, David H. 1968-69.

P Pacchioli, Bob 1988; Pace, Talton Eames 1948-49-50; Palmer, Robert 1946; Pangburn, C. 1898-99; Pangburn, E.S. 1900; Parham, Don 1974; Pankratz, Gary F. 1963-66; Paris, Sheldon 1978-79; Parks, F.T. 1909; Partner, Dan 1933-34-35; Patee, Ervin A. 1945; Patterson, Chris 1989-90-91-92; Patterson, Greg 1990-91-92; Patton, Pat V. 1965; Paulus, Timothy L. 1973; Payne, David A. 1968-69-70; Payne, Donald A. 1968-69; Payton, Jay 1944; Pearl, Ivan W. 1980-81-82-83; Pearson, M. Bert 1926-27-28; Pearson, Robert 1992; Pearson, Zerlindon 1925-26; Peck, Leslie Dean 1951-52-53; Peddicord, George 1944; Peluso, Ralph D. 1957-58-59; Pemberton, Greg 1981-82-83; Pence, Edward L. 1951-52-53; Pence, Royce 1946-47; Pennington, Carl 1973-74-75-76; Penrod, Michael D. 1962-63-64; Perry, James C. 1962-64-65; Peters, Chester 1942; Peters, Richard 1939-40-41; Peters, Stu 1982-84; Peterson, Gerald 1977; Peterson, George P. "Bud" 1972-73-74; Peterson, Richard 1942; Petrus, Arvyd P. 1968-69; Pfeifer, Ralph J. 1955-56-57; Pickard, Phil 1978-79; Pickett, Lee 1987-88; Pierce, Robert 1945; Piersol, Paul Du Challu 1898-99; Pierson, D.C. 1897; Pierson, Michael W. 1981-82; Pilcher, L.B. 1931; Pitts, Staley 1936-37-38; Plank, Gregg 1984; Platt, W.E. "Tad" 1928; Pollock, Wendell 1947; Pollom, Joe 1944; Pollom, Lester B. 1912; Poole, Jerry 1983-84-85; Porter, Mark 1985-86-87-88; Poston, Leonard 1896-97; Potoski, Robert J. 1957; Potter, Luther E. 1896; Potterf, A.J. 1896; Pouch, Shane 1987-88; Powell, Orson L. 1968; Powierza, Richard J. 1971; Prather, Raymond 1911-12; Prather, Rollin W. 1946-47-48-49; Pratt, Harold 1896-97; Prentup, Frank B. 1929; Price, Cedric L. 1958-59; Price, Charles L. 1972-73; Price, James 1925; Price, Leo 1909; Price, William 1988-89-90-91; Pritchard, William R. 1945; Provenzano, Joseph S. 1961-62-63; Ptacek, E.H. 1915-16-17; Ptacek, L.D. 1916-17-19; Pulford, William J. 1957; Puls, Spencer A. 1961-62-63.

Q Quick, William 1940-41-42; Quinlan, A.W. 1919.

R Raemer, Norbert 1939-40-41; Raemer, Wilfrid M. 1949-50; Rainman, Joseph 1951-52; Rainsberger, Ellis D. 1955-56-57; Randalls, C.E. 1907-08; Randels, H.M. 1918-19-20; Randels, Horace 1925 Randels, Lee W. 1915-16-17; Randolph, Thomas 1990-91-92-93; Rankin, George C. 1935-36-37; Rapp, James A. 1966; Ratliff, G.T. 1910; Rawlings, Kitt 1990-91-92-93; Ray, Martin E. 1959-60-61; Reed, Myron W. 1924-25-26; Reed, Renneth 1984-85; Rees, Brian 1991-92-93; Reid, Lawrence 1946; Repstine, Marvin 1942; Rasetar, Edward 1946; Rhoades, James A. 1953; Rhodes, Lodis 1965-66-67; Rice, Cedric E. 1966; Rich, Billy J. 1959-60; Richards, Edward C. 1907; Richards, James C. 1907; Richards, Terry 1989; Richardson, James O. 1976-77; Richardson, John W. 1959-60-61; Ricketts, James E. 1982-83-84; Riechers, Harold D. 1957; Riederer, Russell 1977; Riggs, Richard A. 1962-63-64; Robb, Jim 1948; Roberts, Mike 1974-75; Roberts, Thomas C. 1969-70; Robertson, Johnny M. 1969-70-71; Robinson, Harold A. 1949-50; Robinson, James 1978-79-81; Roda, Carl O. 1916-17-19; Roda, Daniel P. 1966-68; Rodell, E.N. 1927; Rodman, Ivan F.,Jr. 1954-55; Roether, Douglas D. 1953-54-55; Rogers, Cecil 1950; Rogers, Jim 1976; Rokey, Ned 1941-42; Rokey, Raymond 1940-41; Romano, Chad 1993-94-95; Romero, Ray R. 1947-48-49; Rons, Leo 1948; Root, Frank P. 1913; Roots, Harvey G. 1908-

09-10; Ross, Randall 1968-69; Ross, Stan 1974-75-76; Rossello, Ronald A. 1968; Rothwell, D. Fred 1971-72-73; Running, Mitch 1992-93-94-95; Rusher, James F. 1954-55; Russell, Dougal 1932-33; Russell, Mike 1983-84; Ruzich, Dan M. 1980-81-82; Ruzich, Mike 1979-80; Ryan, C.H. 1901.

S Saey, Tom 1980; Salat, Leo W. 1965-66-67; Salmans, Oliver 1991-92; Sand, Gerald A. 1956-57; Sander, Charles 1984-85; Sanders, Robert E. 1927; Sanders, R.F. 1930; Sanft, Vili 1990; Sanner, Monty R. 1972; Scanlon, W. J. 1913-14; Schiller, Rod 1990-92-93-94; Schindler, Ira 1921-22-23; Schirmer, David 1946-47; Schmidt, Burton W. 1953-54-55; Schmidt, Robert L. 1957; Schmitz, Elmer 1985; Schmitz, Henry W. 1920-21; Scholz, W.T. 1904-05-05; Schooley, Frank L. 1930; Schrag, Andy 1985-86; Schroeder, Loren 1945; Schuster, Steve 1978-79-80; Schuster, W.A. 1911-12; Schweiger, Tyson 1992-93-94-95; Schwerdt, John 1950; Scobey, Roscoe 1974-75-76; Sconce, Lloyd 1934; Scott, Clarence B. 1968-69-70; Scott, Dimitrie 1985-86-88-89; Scott, Fred E. 1959; Scott, Robert E. 1973; Scott, Robert L. 1969; Searles, Joseph L. 1961-62; Sears, Maurice 1920-21-22; Sebring, Harold 1920-21-22; Sechler, Phillip 1942; Secrest, Edmund R. 1901; Seib, Brad 1990-91-92-93; Seelye, Melvin 1938-39; Seng, Augustus W. 1906-07-08-09-10; Severino, Anthony F. 1968-69; Sewell, Ken 1985; Shaffer, Don 1941; Shaffer, Leland K. 1931-32-34; Shaffer, R.W. 1911-12-13; Sharp, Guy "Jack" 1946; Shaternick, Dean A. 1968-69-70; Shaw, Wilbert 1966-67; Shine, Roy 1974-75-76; Shockey, Richard 1951; Shull, Dave 1914; Sicks, Frank 1939; Sidorfsky, Frank 1911-12-13; Sidorfsky, Henry 1899-1900-01; Simeta, Mike 1980-82; Simms, G. 1911-12; Simms, Merle H. 1908-10; Simoneau, Jeff 1992; Simpson, 1901; Simpson, Clare L. 1951-54; Simpson, Evan 1990-91; Sims, Fred 1936-37; Singletary, Reggie L. 1981-82-83; Singletary, Vantz 1987-88; Sinisi, Matthew F. 1965; Sinovic, Bill 1975-76; Sirila, Paul A. 1958; Sjogren, Robert D. 1962-63-64; Skaer, Dean A. 1957-58; Skinner, Emmett W. 1914-15-16; Slattery, F.A. 1915-16; Slyter, Ray Kenneth 1960; Smargiasso, Jason 1990-91-92; Smedley, 1897; Smerchek, John F. 1926; Smith, Alan 1987-88; Smith, Billy Ray 1990; Smith, Chris 1986; Smith, David 1983-84; Smith, George Lee 1947-48-49; Smith, J.J. 1991-92-93-94; Smith, Jean 1944; Smith, Jeff 1992; Smith, Kenny 1980; Smith, Linus Burr 1921; Smith, Mario 1993-94-95; Smith, Michael 1988-89-90-91; Smith, Paul Robert 1972-73-74-75; Smith, Raymond 1924-25; Smith, Robert E. 1951-52-53; Smith, Scott 1990; Smith, Thomas Eugene 1948; Smith, Thomas F. 1952-53; Snyder, Eugene 1940-46; Snyder, John M. 1961; Snyder, Sean 1991-92; Socolofsky, Charles R. 1937; Socolofsky, Homer 1942; Solmos, John A. 1958-59-60; Solt, Ronald B. 1972-73-74; Spagnoletti, Pat C. 1954; Spani, Gary 1974-75-76-77; Spare, David R. 1973-74; Sparks, 1898-99; Sparks, Dan P. 1981-82-83; Specht, David W. 1972-73-74; Speer, W.G. 1908-09-10; Speer, W. George, Jr. 1937-38; Speight, James R. 1957-58; Spence, Neal B. 1961-62; Spencer, W.H. 1898-99-1900-01; Sperry, Bryan 1943; Sperry, Kenneth 1943; Spiller, Monty 1995; Springer, Don 1925-26-27; Sprinkle, Charles R. 1956; Squires, David 1993-94; Stahl, E.G. 1910-11-12; Stahura, Edward 1952; Staib, Harry J. 1922; Stange, Russ 1987-88; Stansell, Roderick 1986; Stark, Arthur R. 1921-22-23; Starns, Francis Warren 1949-50-51; Stauffer, Marion W. 1920-21; Stauffer, Maurice I. 1906; Stealey, Ted R. 1971-72; Steelman, Alan D. 1968-69-70; Stefan, Brock 1995; Stehley, Donald R. 1949; Stehley, Jim 1947-48-49; Steinbach, Ray E. 1945; Steiner, Carl Regan 1973-74-75; Steiner, John 1921-22-23; Steinhur, 1901; Steininger, Paul D. 1972; Stephenson, Alvin H. 1929-30-31; Stevens, Jeff 1980-81; Stevens, Ronald L. 1968-69; Steves, Ray R. 1945; Stewart, Andrew J. 1957; Stewart, David 1979; Sticher, Henry 1898; Stinson, Jaydee F. 1956-57; Stocks, Wilbur A. 1953-54-55; Stolte, John A. 1958-59; Stone, Tim 1983-84-85; Stoner, Oren P. 1933-34; Stonner, John 1983-84-85; Stover, Harold 1926-27; Strahm, Gregory P. 1981-83-84-85; Straten, George 1937; Straw, Carl 1988-89-90; Strozier, Arthur 1965-66-67; Stucky, John R. 1968-69; Stucky, Roger N. 1972-74; Stull, Robert W. 1965-66-67; Sublette, Chris 1991-92-94; Sullivan, G.J. 1915-17; Sundgren, Eugene 1933-34; Sura, Patrick 1980; Swanson, Wallace 1939-40; Swartz, M. Burdette 1921-22-23; Swartz, Price K. 1928-29-30; Swazer, Thad 1995; Swedberg, Tyler 1992; Swift, Justin 1995; Swim, Gary 1987-89; Switzer, Calvin S. 1981-82-83-84; Switzer, Marvin 1974-75-76; Switzer, Phil 1978-79-81-82; Switzer, Veryl A. 1951-52-53.

T Tackwell, C.O. 1927-28-29; Tanha, Reza 1989; Taylor, Cecil R. "Corky" 1951-52-53-54; Taylor, Doug 1979-80; Telford, Don M. 1928; Teter, Robert E. 1931; Thomas, Kim K. 1973-74; Thomas, Leroy G. 1972; Thompson, Bert 1900-04; Thompson, Chris 1988; Thompson, R. 1900; Thornborrow, Charles 1950; Tidwell, Ralph E. 1949; Timmons, Andrew 1992-93-95; Timmons, Max 1940-41; Tiro, Anthony 1957-58-59; Tolbert, Lawrence 1986-87-88; Tolin, Ernest D. 1945; Toluao, Kilisimasi 1981-82; Tombaugh, Simon J. 1924-25-26; Torbett, David 1949-50; Towers, Richard 1950-51-52 ; Towler, R.T. 1908-09-10; Towler, William G. 1927-28-29; Towne, N.L. 1901 ; Travis, Scott 1988; Trojovsky, Art 1946; Tucker, Allen 1929; Tullos, J.O. 1898; Tullos, W.G. 1898; Turner, Brad 1980-81; Turner, Lewis 1940-46; Tuttle, John R. 1973-74.

U Ulutu, Tiny 1995; Underwood, Alan K. 1961; Underwood, Todd 1983; Ungles, James 1944.

V Vader, Jay J. 1967-69; Vader, Joseph N. 1957-58-59; Vajnar, Jason 1989-90; Vale, Joe 1910; Vargon, Michael 1942-46; Vay, Allen R. 1971; Veatch, Laird 1990-91-93-94; Venables, Brent 1991-92; Viers, Perry 1974-75-76; Villarreal, Raul 1981-82; Voelker, Randall L. 1981-82-83; Vohoska, Kevin R. 1971-72-73; Vrooman, John L. 1965-66.

W Waddick, 1898; Wade, Alonzo 1974; Wade, Dewey 1951-52; Wade, Jay 1985; Wagner, George S. "Doc" 1896-97; Wagner, Bradley 1976-77; Wakefield, Mike 1975-76-77; Walczak, Alexander M. 1966-67; Walker, Carroll 1904-05-06; Walker, James 1977-78-79-80; Walker, Jonathon L. 1955; Walker, Ken 1930; Walker, Lance 1990-92 ; Wall, William 1950; Wallace, David 1983-85-86-87; Wallace, Jack P. 1949-50; Wallace, Mike K. 1981-82-83-84; Wallerstedt, Matt 1984-85-86-87; Walling, Thurman 1942; Walters, Ralph E. 1960; Warren, Dick 1983-84-85; Warren, Doug 1988-89-90-91; Warren, Kenneth W. 1934-35-36; Wasemiller, Timothy G. 1973-74-75; Washington, Greg 1988; Wassberg, Ivan 1934-35-36; Watkins, James 1940-41; Watkins, John W. 1967; Watson, John 1945; Watson, Paul 1988-89-90-91; Watts, Freddie 1961; Weatherby, David J. 1944; Webber, Henry G. 1922-23; Weber, Stanley J. 1980-83-84; Webster, Ronnie 1944-47; Wecker, Michael A. 1973; Wegerer, Louis W. 1973-74-75; Wehrle, L.P. 1911-12-13; Wehrman, Casey 1995; Weiler, William 1945; Weiner, Bernard 1938-39-40; Weiner, Todd 1995; Weinhold, Dennis G. 1972; Welch, John 1984-85-86; Weller, Harold R. 1928-29-33; Wells, Eddie D. 1916; Wells, Forrest N. 1968-69; Wells, John J. 1971-72-73; Wentling, Wade A. 1978-79-80-82; Wentzel, Mark 1985-86; Wentzel, Scott W. 1981-82-84-85; Wertzberger, Melvin H. 1931-32-33; Weybrew, Neil 1930-31-32; Whearty, Riley R. 1935-36; Whedon, Edwin F. 1916-17; Wheeler, Mike 1989; Whipple, C.E. 1905; Whipple, G.E. 1908-09-10; White, Lindbergh 1972; White, Michael D. 1965; White, Scott 1983-85-86; Whitehead, Robert T. 1953-54-55; Whitfield, Kerr 1924; Whitley, Eddy 1976-77-78-79; Whitlock, Merle 1938; Whitney, George C. 1957-58-59; Whittle, Loren 1987-88; Wiggins, George 1929-30-31; Wilbur, B.N. 1905-07; Wild, Darrel E. 1982-83; Wilder, Marshall P. 1914-15-16; Wilkins, Lysle 1939-40-41; Wilkinson, Richard K. 1964-65-66; Wilkinson, W.J. 1904; Williams, Anthony 1989-90; Williams, Dean 1973-74; Williams, Earl E. 1941-42-48; Williams, Jabbar 1995; Williams, John 1986-87; Williams, Lucillious 1970; Williams, Randy 1984-85; Williams, Robert E. 1906; Williams, Tony 1990-91-92; Williamson, Jack 1980-82; Willis, Larry 1983; Willis, Steve P. 1981-82-83-84; Wilson, Cletis L. 1952-53-54; Wilson, Ira A. 1907; Wilson, Keith 1955-56-57; Wilson, Kerry 1979-80; Wilson, Otis 1923-24-25; Wilson, Ray 1984-85-86-87; Winchell, Tom 1974; Winchester, John G. 1959-60; Winfrey, Dennis R. 1962-63; Winters, M.S. 1918-19-20; Wiren, Nyle 1993-94-95; Witherspoon, James 1982-83-84-85; Wolford, Eric 1990-91-92-93; Wolgast, Richard 1940; Woodward, Daniel F. 1963-64-65; Woody, Forrest 1923; Wright, 1899; Wright, Dale 1946; Wright, Tate 1990-91-92-93; Wright, W.W. 1914-15-16; Wunderly, Fred 1991; Wyatt, Darrell 1988; Wywadis, Walt 1977-78-79.

Y Yandell, Don 1922; Yandell, Kenneth 1924; Yankowski, Ronald W. 1969-70; Yarnell, Lloyd P. 1969-70-71; Yeager, James 1928-29-30; Yniguez, Paul 1987-88-89; Young, F. 1918; Young, George A. 1911; Young, Mark 1988; Young, Reggie 1977-78-79; Young, Ryan 1995.

Z Zabelin, Eric 1987-88-89; Zadnik, Donald E. 1955-56-57; Zeckser, Walter 1930-31-32; Zele, Scott 1988; Zeleznak, Michael 1941-42-46-47; Zellers, Eldon W. 1953; Zickefoose, Charles E. 1953-54-55; Zier, Mark B. 1973-74-75; Zitnik, Joseph 1935; Zollars, Eldon 1948; Zoller, C.L. 1907-08-09-10; Zumalt, Clifford Ray 1948.

BASKETBALL SEASON-BY-SEASON

Year	Coach	W	L
1902-03	No Head Coach	0	5
1903-04	No games scheduled		
1904-05	No games scheduled		
1905-06	C.W. Melick	7	9
1906-07	Mike Ahearn	3	6
1907-08	Mike Ahearn	2	10
1908-09	Mike Ahearn	6	2
1909-10	Mike Ahearn	10	3
1910-11	Mike Ahearn	5	3
1911-12	Guy Lowman	9	5
1912-13	Guy Lowman	11	4
1913-14	Guy Lowman	10	7
1914-15	Carl J. Merner	6	12
1915-16	Carl J. Merner	13	3
1916-17	Z.G. Clevenger	15	2
1917-18	Z.G. Clevenger	12	5
1918-19	Z.G. Clevenger	17	2
1919-20	Z.G. Clevenger	10	8
1920-21	E.A. Knoth	14	5
1921-22	E.C. Curtis	3	14
1922-23	E.C. Curtis	2	14
1923-24	Charles Corsaut	8	8
1924-25	Charles Corsaut	10	8
1925-26	Charles Corsaut	11	7
1926-27	Charles Corsaut	10	8
1927-28	Charles Corsaut	8	10
1928-29	Charles Corsaut	6	10
1929-30	Charles Corsaut	9	7
1930-31	Charles Corsaut	11	6
1931-32	Charles Corsaut	7	8
1932-33	Charles Corsaut	9	9
1933-34	Frank Root	3	15
1934-35	Frank Root	5	15
1935-36	Frank Root	9	9
1936-37	Frank Root	9	9
1937-38	Frank Root	7	11
1938-39	Frank Root	5	13
1939-40	Jack Gardner	6	12
1940-41	Jack Gardner	6	12
1941-42	Jack Gardner	8	10
1942-43	Chili Cochrane	6	14
1943-44	Cliff Rock	7	15
1944-45	Fritz Knorr	10	13
1945-46	Fritz Knorr	4	20
1946-47	Jack Gardner	14	10
1947-48	Jack Gardner	22	6
1948-49	Jack Gardner	13	11
1949-50	Jack Gardner	17	7
1950-51	Jack Gardner	25	4
1951-52	Jack Gardner	19	5
1952-53	Jack Gardner	17	4
1953-54	Tex Winter	11	10
1954-55	Tex Winter	11	10
1955-56	Tex Winter	17	8
1956-57	Tex Winter	15	8
1957-58	Tex Winter	22	5
1958-59	Tex Winter	25	2
1959-60	Tex Winter	16	10
1960-61	Tex Winter	23	4
1961-62	Tex Winter	22	3
1962-63	Tex Winter	16	9
1963-64	Tex Winter	22	7
1964-65	Tex Winter	12	13
1965-66	Tex Winter	14	11
1966-67	Tex Winter	17	8
1967-68	Tex Winter	19	9
1968-69	Cotton Fitzsimmons	14	12
1969-70	Cotton Fitzsimmons	20	8
1970-71	Jack Hartman	11	15
1971-72	Jack Hartman	19	9
1972-73	Jack Hartman	23	5
1973-74	Jack Hartman	19	8
1974-75	Jack Hartman	20	9
1975-76	Jack Hartman	20	8
1976-77	Jack Hartman	24	7
1977-78	Jack Hartman	18	11
1978-79	Jack Hartman	16	12
1979-80	Jack Hartman	22	9
1980-81	Jack Hartman	24	9
1981-82	Jack Hartman	23	8
1982-83	Jack Hartman	12	16
1983-84	Jack Hartman	14	15
1984-85	Jack Hartman	14	14
1985-86	Jack Hartman	16	14
1986-87	Lon Kruger	20	11
1987-88	Lon Kruger	25	9
1988-89	Lon Kruger	19	11
1989-90	Lon Kruger	17	15
1990-91	Dana Altman	13	15
1991-92	Dana Altman	16	14
1992-93	Dana Altman	19	11
1993-94	Dana Altman	20	14
1994-95	Tom Asbury	12	15
1995-96	Tom Asbury	17	12

BASKETBALL COACHING RECORDS

Years	Coach (Seasons)	W	L	Pct.
1905-06	C.W. Melick (1)	7	9	.438
1906-11	Mike Ahearn (5)	26	24	.520
1911-14	Guy Lowman (3)	30	16	.652
1914-16	Carl J. Merner (2)	19	15	.559
1916-20	Z.G. Clevenger (4)	54	17	.761
1920-21	E.A. Knoth (1)	14	5	.737
1921-22	E.C. Curtis (2)	5	28	.152
1923-33	Charles Corsaut (10)	89	81	.524
1933-39	Frank Root (6)	38	72	.345
1939-42	Jack Gardner (3)	20	34	.370
1942-43	Chili Cochrane (1)	6	14	.300
1943-44	Cliff Rock (1)	7	15	.318
1944-46	Fritz Knorr (2)	14	33	.298
1946-53	Jack Gardner (7)	127	47	.730
1953-68	Tex Winter (15)	262	117	.691
1968-70	Cotton Fitzsimmons (2)	34	20	.630
1970-86	Jack Hartman (16)	295	169	.636
1986-90	Lon Kruger (4)	81	47	.633
1990-94	Dana Altman (4)	68	54	.557
1994-96	Tom Asbury (2)	29	27	.518

THE 1,000-POINT CLUB

2115	Mike Evans	1974-78
1844	Rolando Blackman	1977-81
1834	Askia Jones	1989-94
1685	Bob Boozer	1956-59
1655	Steve Henson	1986-90
1364	Chuckie Williams	1973-76
1327	Mitch Richmond	1986-88
1304	Ed Nealy	1978-82
1251	Tyrone Adams	1978-82
1184	Jack Parr	1955-58
1112	Willie Murrell	1962-64
1093	Dick Knostman	1950-53
1079	Steve Mitchell	1970-73
1063	Lon Kruger	1971-74
1045	Ernie Kusnyer	1970-73
1030	Curtis Redding	1976-78
1007	David Hall	1968-72
1003	Norris Coleman	1985-87

MOST POINTS

Career: 2115, Mike Evans, 1974-78
Single-season: 768, Mitch Richmond, 1987-88
Single-game: 62, Askia Jones vs. Fresno State, Mar. 24, 1994

HIGHEST SCORING AVERAGE

Career: 21.9, Bob Boozer (77 games), 1956-59
Single-season: 25.6, Bob Boozer, 1958-59

MOST FIELD-GOALS

Career: 890, Mike Evans, 1974-78
Single-season: 290, Chuckie Williams, 1974-75
Single-game: 22, Chuckie Williams vs. Holy Cross, Dec. 5, 1975

MOST FIELD-GOAL ATTEMPTS

Career: 1810, Mike Evans, 1974-78
Single-season: 594, Chuckie Williams, 1974-75
Single-game: 42, Chuckie Williams vs. Holy Cross, Dec. 5, 1975

HIGHEST FIELD-GOAL PERCENTAGE

(Minimum 5 attempts per game)
Career: .588, Steve Soldner (255-430), 1975-79
Single-season: .600, Steve Soldner (108-180), 1977-78
Single-game: 11/11, Joe Wright vs. Oklahoma State, Jan. 23, 1985; Eddie Elder vs. Colorado, Feb. 23, 1985

MOST 3-POINT FIELD-GOALS

Career: 240, Steve Henson, 1986-90
Single-season: 110, Askia Jones, 1993-94
Single-game: 14, Askia Jones vs. Fresno State, Mar. 24, 1994

MOST 3-POINT FIELD-GOAL ATTEMPTS

Career: 624, Askia Jones, 1989-94
Single-season: 279, Askia Jones, 1993-94
Single-game: 18, Askia Jones vs. Fresno State, Mar. 24, 1994

HIGHEST 3-POINT FIELD-GOAL PERCENTAGE

Career: .513, Will Scott (142-277), 1986-88
Single-season: .529, Will Scott (72-136), 1986-87

MOST FREE THROWS

Career: 702, Bob Boozer, 1956-59
Single-season: 197, Bob Boozer, 1958-59
Single-game: 23, Bob Boozer vs. Purdue, Dec. 1, 1958

HIGHEST FREE THROW PERCENTAGE

(Minimum 2 Attempts per Game)
Career: .900, Steve Henson (361-401), 1986-90
Single-season: .925, Steve Henson (111-120), 1987-88
Single-game: Not available

MOST REBOUNDS

Career: 1071, Ed Nealy, 1978-82
Single-season: 340, Jack Parr, 1955-56
Single-game: 27, David Hall, vs. Oklahoma, Jan. 25, 1971

HIGHEST REBOUNDING AVERAGE

Career: 12.7, Jack Parr, 1955-58
Single-season: 14.5, Jack Parr, 1956-57

ASSISTS

(since 1976-77 season)
Career: 582, Steve Henson, 1986-90
Single-season: 186, Steve Henson, 1987-88
Single-game: 16, Keith Frazier vs. Central Mo. St., Dec. 18, 1976

BLOCKED SHOTS

(Since 1979-80)
Career: 101, Les Craft, 1979-83
Single-season: 59, Gerald Eaker, 1995-96
Single-game: 5, six times

STEALS (SINCE 1980-81)

Career: 190, Steve Henson, 1986-90
Single-season: 66, Jeff Wires, 1990-91
Single-game: 8, Lynn Smith vs. South Dakota, Nov. 29, 1986; Elliot Hatcher vs. Wichita State, Jan. 2, 1996

MISCELLANEOUS RECORDS

Most Consecutive Field Goals: 17 by Ed Nealy (Missouri, Iowa State, Nebraska, Kansas) 1979-80
Most Consecutive Free Throws: 48 by Steve Henson, 1987-88
Most Consecutive 3-Point Goals: 9, Askia Jones vs. Fresno State, Mar. 24, 1994 (Big 8 Record)
Most Consecutive FGs: 12, Mike Evans vs. Missouri, 1974
Most Points In A Half: 45, Askia Jones vs. Fresno State, Mar. 24, 1994 (Big 8 Record)
Most 3-pointers In A Half: 11 (of 14), Askia Jones vs. Fresno State, Mar. 24, 1994 (NCAA Record)

BASKETBALL LETTERMEN

A Abbott, James H. 1955-58, F; Adams, Nugent 1954-55, F; Adams, R.V. 1913-16; Adams, Tyrone 1978-82, G/F; Alfaro, Tom 1983-85, F/G; Amerson, Keith 1989-91, F; Armstrong, Richard 1934-35; Arnold, Frederick O. 1967-68, F; Atkins, Dana M. 1944-45; Auker, Eldon 1929-32.

B Baird, H.S. "Harry" 1908-09; Balding, Gary L. 1958-59; Ballard, Ross B. "Sonny" 1957-58, 1959-60, G; Barber, Michael 1967-70, C; Barnard, Richard L. 1963-66, G; Barrett, Ernie D. 1948-51, G; Barrett, Ralph 1945-46; Barton, Fred 1976-81, G; Baxter, James N. 1960-63, F; Baxter, Mark 1974-75, F; Beane, Anthony 1992-94, G; Beard, Danny M. 1971-74, G; Beaumont, Larry 1940-42; Bell, (unk.) 1909-10; Bell, Jack F. 1944-45, G; Bengston, A.E. 1914-15; Bergen, Gary 1952-53, F; Berkholtz, Dennis L. 1964-67, G; Bidnick, J.S. 1933-34; Black, Jerry 1975-78, C; Blackman, Rolando 1977-81, G/F; Blair, G.Y. 1918-19; Blair, Roscoe Eugene 1908-10; Blake, Cool 1905-07; Bledsoe, Charles 1986-88, F; Boes, Glenn H. 1938-39; Bohm, Mark 1983-85, G; Boozer, Robert L. 1956-59, F/C; Bortka, John 1941-43; Boyd, Francis W. 1931-34; Brannum, Clarence D. 1946-50, C; Breen, Emmet 1931-33; Britt, Reggie 1988-90, F; Brittian, Maurice 1990-91, F/C; Broberg, William 1910-11, 1912-14; Brockway, S.H. 1927-28, 1930-32; Brooks, R.V. 1927-28; Brown, Warren S. 1959-62, G; Bryan, L.J. "Rocky" 1920-21; Bunger, H.L. 1918-21; Bunker, K.R. 1923-25; Burns, Allen W. 1935-38; Byers, Clifton 1924-27.

C Carby, Jack 1951-53, C/F; Carpenter, C.C. 1908-10; Carr, Clifford H. 1905-07; Cassell, B. 1904-05; Chipman, Robert A. 1971-73, G; Clark, Ward L. 1947-48, C; Clarke, John Allen 1916-19; Cleveland, H.W. 1936-38; Cody, Jonas 1982-84, G; Coleman, Norris 1985-87, F; Collier, Aaron 1991-93, F; Comley, Larry R. 1959-61, F/G; Cooley, Charles 1943-44; Cowell, E.R. "Shorty" 1918-21; Cowell, W.C. 1919-22; Craft, Les 1979-83, F/C; Craft, Roger L. 1953-55, C; Crist, Guinn 1943-44; Cronkite, H.O. 1929-31; Cunningham, Deryl 1991-94, F/C; Cushman, J.H. 1915-17.

D Dalton, Lloyd Henry 1930-33; Danner, Dean 1976-80, F; Dassie, Larry 1975-76, F; Davidson, George A. 1960-62, G; Davis, Demond 1993-95, G; Davis, Tyrone 1994-96, F/C; DeAlmeida, Fabio 1987-88, F; Dean, John R. 1946-49, G; Degner, Neal 1982-83, F/C; Derouillere, Jean 1989-91, G; Dewitz, Roy A. 1955-58, G/F; Dickerson, Greg A. 1967-68, G; Dies, Manny 1995-96, F; Dicus, G.B. 1926-27; Diggins, Carlos 1987-89, G/F; Dirks, B. Marlo 1941-43, 1946-47; Dobbins, Mark 1985-89, G; Dobson, Maurille 1921-22; Doolen, A.H. 1922-25; Douglas, Steve A. 1957-60, F/G; Dovlan, Art 1924-25; Doyen, Lee 1943-44; Dreier, Clarence 1938-39; Dresser, William 1948-49, C; Droge, Dan 1974-77, F.

E Eaker, Gerald 1995-96, C; Eddie, Percy 1985-87, F; Edwards, A.R. "Monk" 1925-28; Edwards, E.J. 1908-11; Ekblad, Robert 1943-44; Elder, Eddie 1982-85, G; Evans, Mike 1974-78, G; Ewy, Richard D. 1959-62, G.

F Fairbank, Paul E. 1929-32; Ferris, Frank E. 1905-07; Findley, Donald 1943-44; Fischer, Larry L. 1955-58, F; Flynn, Ronald J. 1954-55, G/F; Foltz, G.A. 1917-19; Fopping, C. 1905-07; Foval, F. 1920-23; Foveaux, Myron 1943-44; Fowler, I. Loren 1910; Frank, Wally 1957-60, F; Frazier, Keith 1975-77, G; Freeland, James R. 1933-35; Freeman, A.H. 1927-30; Frick, Galen C. 1965-67, F; Fritz, Steve 1988-89, 1990-91, G; Fullington, D.M. 1916-17; Fulton, Floyd W. 1937-38.

G Galvao, Eduardo 1980-83, G; Gann, E.L. 1927-29; Gavin, Brian 1992-96, G; George, Robert E. 1965-67, G; Gerlach, Carl R. 1972-76, C/F; Gibson, John P. "Hoot" 1949-52, F; Gilpin, Paul 1934-36; Gish, Norvelle 1943-44; Glover, Buster 1987-88, G; Gottfrid, Joe N. 1961-64, C; Graham, Kenneth 1939-41; Graham, Ralph M. 1931-34; Graham, Robert K. 1958-59, F/G; Green, Benny 1985-86, G; Green, Ronald J. 1970-71, G; Grothusen, L.W. 1922-23; Groves, Frank 1934-37; Guerrant, D.S. 1939-40; Gunning, Harry 1915-16; Guthridge, William W. 1958-60, G; Guy, Tom 1940-41.

H Hahn, Issac 1910-12; Hahn, Ray 1921-23; Hall, David 1969-72, C/F; Hamilton, Stanley 1993-95, F; Harman, Richard J. 1946-50, F; Harris, Dean 1973-74, F; Hatcher, Elliot 1994-96, G; Hauck, John Harold 1949-50, F; Haynes, L.G. 1905-09; Head, Ed 1948-51, F; Heinz, Michael K. 1958-60, F; Heitmeyer, J. Phil 1959-62, F; Henson, Brian 1991-93, G; Henson, Steve 1986-90, G; Hickert, Dan 1977-78, C; Hill, George 1992-96, C; Hinds, G.W. 1917-20; Hinds, J.B. 1917-18; Hitch, Lewis R. 1949-51, C; Hoffman, James N. 1963-66, F; Holman, Bruce 1941-42, 1946-47; Holmes, J.C. 1911-12; Holstrom, Norris 1939-41; Holwerda, Jim R. 1956-59, G; Honeycutt, Steven F. 1966-69, G; Horacek, Jack 1939-42; Howard, Burt 1945-46; Howard, Wylie 1989-92, C; Howe, Daniel 1940-42; Howey, Harold 1946-48, F; Howse, Derrick 1984-85, F; Hughes, Wheeler M. 1968-70, G; Hull, William L. 1954-55, F; Humphrey, LaKeith 1988-89, G; Hutchinson, Don 1933-34; Hutto, L.E. 1912-13.

I Iverson, James 1949-52, G.

J Jackson, Tyrone 1982-85, F; Jackson, Vincent 1991-93, F; Jackson, W. Roscoe 1965-66, F; Jankovich, Tim 1979-82, G; Jedwabny, Robert L. 1955-56, F; Jennings, G.S. 1918-21; Jilka, Bernard 1943-44; Johnson, Jerald F. 1958-59, G; Johnson, Louis G. 1961-63; Johnson, O.L. 1914-15; Johnson, Robert A. 1948-49, G; Jones, Askia 1989-90, 1991-94, G; Jones, E.C. 1912-15; Jones, Walter 1927-28; Jung, Jerry 1952-55, C.

K Kecker, K.H. 1916-17, 1918-19; Kiddoo, Clyde H. 1955-57, G; Kincheloe, Jack 1944-45; Klimek, Ed 1935-38; Knostman, Richard W. 1950-53, C; Knostman, William 1916-17, 1919-21; Koch, Fritz 1923-26; Kohl, Fred 1941-43; Kohl, William F. 1953-54, G; Kramer, George R. 1936-39; Kramer, Karl 1945-46; Krone, Lloyd A. 1946-50, G/F; Kruger, Lonnie D. 1971-74, G; Kusnyer, Ernest J. 1970-73, G/F; Kuykendall, Charles G. 1920-21.

L Ladson, Tyrone 1976-77, G; Laketa, Parker 1982-84, F; Lallott, J. 1908-09; Langton, Allan L. 1946-50, G; Langton, Scott 1975-78, G; Langvardt, Chris 1939-41; Larson, E. 1908-11; Larson, H. 1906-07; Lawrence, David 1968-70, F; Leonard, Lawrence 1913-16; Lewis, Kevin 1993-96, C; Lill, Dean 1940-41, 1942-43; Litton, Kent D. 1967-70, F; Long, Glen C. 1957-60, F; Lucas, Ron 1992-94, F; Lull, Dennis S. 1970-72, G.

M Mahoney, Kenneth J. 1947-49, G; Marriott, Gary A. 1961-63, F; Marshall, Fred 1982-83, G; Marshall, Glenn 1978-80, G; Martin, Roy 1906-07; Massop, Tony 1988-90, F/C; Matuszak, Don V. 1956-59, G; Matuszak, Edwin J. 1960-63, G; May, Ayome 1995-96, G; Maydew, Troy 1988-89, G; McCallum, D.C. 1910-13; McClaughry, Larry 1944-45; McConnell, James R. 1963-64, G; McCoy, Fred 1987-89, F/C; McEntyre, Kenny 1992-93, G; McIlrath, C.F. 1913-16; McKee, Andrew J. 1921-22; McKenzie, Patrick B. 1959-62, F; McMillan, R.I. 1914-17; McNall, P. 1908-09, 1910-11; McVey, L. Eugene 1971-74, C; Meives, Joseph R. 1968-69, F; Mendenhall, George 1940-43; Mertel, Elmer 1925-28; Merten, Robert L. 1956-57, F; Messner, Kenneth 1941-42; Meyer, Ron 1984-88, C/F; Miller, Ernest 1938-40; Miller, Jack 1935-37; Mills, Arnold 1934-35; Mills, Marvin 1952-53, G; Mitchell, Ben 1982-85, F; Mitchell, Steve 1970-73, C; Molinari, James R. 1973-75, G; Morgan, Lee T. 1933-34; Mourning, Judd 1993-94, G; Moss, Max R. 1961-64, G; Muff, Kevin 1984-86, F; Murphy, Brent 1977-79, F; Murrell, Willie V. 1962-64, F.

N Nealy, Ed 1978-82, F; Nelson, David E. 1960-61, 1962-64, F; Nelson, Mark 1986-88, G; Nickerson, Gaylon 1991-92, G; Nigro, Alex 1928-31; Noland, Belvis 1993-95, F; Noland, Robert F. 1973-76, F; Nystrom, Amer B. 1905-07.

O Oberg, Kenneth D. 1945-46; Olson, John W. 1964-65, 1966-67, C; Olson, Norris 1943-44; Osborne, R.R. 1925-26.

P Paradis, Ronald E. 1963-66, G; Parks, F.T. 1909-10; Parr, John "Jack" 1955-58, C/F; Patrick, Gerald H. 1946-47, C/F; Payton, Jay 1944-46, G; Peck, Richard B. 1949-52, F; Peithman, Allen E. 1960-63, G; Pethman, Loren E. 1967-70, G; Pino, Nick 1965-68, C; Plagge, Ernest D. 1955-57, F; Poma, Louis L. 1962-65, F; Poore, Lee Kent 1953-55, G; Poppenhouse, Gerhard 1936-38; Powell, Larry Joe 1954-56, C/F; Price, Cedric L. 1958-61, C; Priscock, Jesse W. 1951-54, C/F; Prudhoe, Greg 1979-82, C.

R Railsback, Lee T. 1934-36; Ramsey, Earl 1914-16; Redding, Curtis 1976-78, F; Reed, Randy 1980-82, F; Reid, Ervin 1937-40; Reid, Steve 1980-81, G; Rettiger, John 1988-92, C/F; Reynolds, F.I. 1914-17; Rhodes, Shawn 1995-96, F; Richards, Donald E. 1955-58, G; Richards, William H. 1945-46; Richardson, C.D. 1928-30; Richmond, Mitch 1986-

88, G/F; Ridgway, Joe 1942-43, 1944-45; Robertson, Joe 1938-40; Robinson, Bernard 1972-73, G; Robinson, Sammy J. 1963-66, G/F; Roder, Jim 1982-84, G; Rogers, Courtney G. 1969-70, F; Root, Frank 1912-14; Rousey, Robert L. 1950-53, G; Roy, Jerry 1960-61, G; Rumold, Perry 1922-23; Russell, Ray 1928-30.

S Salter, Eric 1979-80, F; Sams, Patrick 1989-91, G; Sanders, Martin 1910-13; Schierlamann, Charles 1935-37; Schmidt, Todd 1993-94, G; Schneider, Frederick R. 1954-56, F/G; Schultz, William 1944-46; Schuyler, Dan C. 1950-51, G; Schwirtz, Robert 1943-44; Scott, William 1986-88, G; Sechler, Phillip 1942-43; Seelye, Melvin 1938-40; Seyfert, Earl H. 1965-68, F; Shadd, Marlon 1990-91, G; Shannon, Howard 1947-48, F/G; Sharp, Guy "Jack" 1945-46; Shull, Dave 1912-14; Shupe, George E. 1967-68, F/G; Silverwood, Kermit 1928-30; Simmons, Lance 1985-87, 1988-90, F; Simons, Jeffrey C. 1962-65, F; Skradski, Andrew 1930-33; Skradski, Ed J. 1926-29; Smith, Billy Ray 1988-90, F; Smith, Eddie C. 1968-71, F; Smith, Lynn 1985-87, G; Smith, James A. 1952-55, G; Smith, Robert W. 1953-54, G; Smith, Roy O. 1964-67, C; Snider, Douglas L. 1972-75, F; Snider, Terry S. 1968-71, G; Snyder, John R. 1953-55, G; Soldner, Steve 1976-79, F; Souders, M.W. 1910-13; Specht, Henry 1948-50, G; Spencer, Dale 1942-43; Spencer, Richard 1944-45; Stanfield, Todd 1987-89, G; Stauffer, Gene A. 1951-54, G; St. John, John M. 1941-42; Stone, Francis R. 1953-56, F; Stone, Jack 1948-51, F; Stoner, Oren P. 1932-35; Strickland, Hamilton 1991-95, C; Stuesser, Ralph 1944-45; Suttner, Roger W. 1961-64, C; Swartzendruber, Aaron 1994-96, G.

T Talbott, J. 1908-09; Tebow, E.T. "Eric" 1923-26; Tellejohn, Arthur 1934-35; Third, Michael 1967-68, F; Thomas, Jack Lee 1969-72, G; Thomas, Keith M. 1946-47; Thornbrough, G. Wayne 1934-36; Thorton, Joe 1947-49, G; Thruston, Jerry 1972-73, F; Thuston, William 1947-48, F; Turner, Lewis 1945-46.

U Underwood, Brad 1984-86, G; Upson, Donald 1949-52, F.

V Vale, Joe 1911-12; Vance, Warren 1943-44; Vantrine, R.A. 1915-18; Vawter, Raymond 1949-50, C; Venable, Jerry N. 1968-70, F; Vicens, Juan Pachin 1954-56, G; Vohs, Ralph 1929-31.

W Walker, Ty 1985-86, G; Wallace, Harry E. 1955-57, G; Wann, Gill 1923-24; Warta, Ben 1993-94, G; Watkins, Lafayette 1981-84, F/G; Watson, Eric 1983-85, G; Weatherby, James 1944-45; Weatherby, David J. 1945-48, F; Webb, Jeffrey W. 1967-70, G; Webber, H.G. 1921-24; Weddle, H.M. 1924-27; Weigel, Larry N. 1964-67, G; Weller, Harold R. 1928-29, 1933-34; Wells, Eddie D. 1916-17; Wesche, Homer 1936-39; Whedon, E.F. 1917-18; Whipple, G. 1910-11; White, Linbergh, 1970-72, G; Wiggins, George 1929-32; Williams, Alex 1983-85, F; Williams, Chuckie 1973-76, G; Williams, Eugene 1967-69, F; Williams, Fred 1919-22; Williams, Gary W. 1963-64, F; Williams, Johnnie 1995-96, C; Williams, Kenny 1981-82, G; Williams, Larry D. 1971-74, F; Willis, Ray 1966-68, G; Wills, Jari 1978-80, F/C; Wilson, John L. 1953-54, F; Winston, Darryl S. 1973-77, F/C; Winter, M.S. 1918-19; Wires, Jeff 1989-91, G; Woody, Forrest 1923-24; Woolf, Frank 1939-40; Wooster, David 1916-17; Wright, Joe 1984-86, G; Wright, Walter 1987-88, F; Wroblewski, Mike 1959-62, C.

Y Yelley, Clifford R. 1942-43; Young, Mark 1994-96, G; Young, Spin 1911-12; Youngman, Richard 1927-28.

Z Zeigler, Marcus 1990-92, G; Zender, Robert 1969-72, F/C.

ATHLETIC HONORS

KSU SPORTS HALL OF FAME

(through 1995 induction)
Mike Ahearn (coach, administrator)
Elden Auker (baseball, football, basketball)
Thane Baker (track)
Ernie Barrett (basketball player/coach, administrator)
Bob Boozer (basketball)
Fred Bramlage (donor)
Charles Bachman (football coach)
Rolando Blackman (basketball)
Jim Colbert (golf)
Henry Cronkite (football)
Lynn Dickey (football)
DeLoss Dodds (track athlete/coach, administrator)
Jack Gardner (basketball coach)
Ralph Graham (football)
Steve Grogan (football)
Elmer Hackney (football, track, wrestling)
Jack Hartman (basketball coach)
Ward Haylett (track and field coach)
Porky Morgan (trainer)
Dev Nelson (sportscaster, SID)
Ken Swenson (track)
Veryl Switzer (football, administrator)
Jack and Donna Vanier (donors)
Ray Watson (track)
Tex Winter (basketball coach)

FOOTBALL FIRST TEAM ALL-AMERICANS

1922, Ray Hahn, G
1931, Henry Cronkite, E
1934, George Maddox, T
1953, Veryl Switzer, HB
1970, Clarence Scott, CB
1976, Gary Spani, LB
1977, Gary Spani, LB
1992, Sean Snyder, P
1993, Jaime Mendez, FS; Thomas Randolph, CB
1994, Chad May, QB
1995, Chris Canty , CB; Tim Colston, DT

BASKETBALL FIRST-TEAM ALL-AMERICANS

1917, F.I. Reynolds, guard
1937, Frank Groves, center
1948, Howard Shannon, guard
1950, Rick Harman, guard
1951, Ernie Barrett, guard
1952, Dick Knostman, center
1953, Dick Knotsman, center
1957, Jack Parr, center
1958, Bob Boozer, forward; Roy DeWitz, guard; Jack Parr, center
1959, Bob Boozer, forward
1962, Mike Wroblewski, center
1976, Chuckie Williams, guard
1980, Rolando Blackman, guard
1981, Rolando Blackman, guard
1988, Mitch Richmond, forward

FOOTBALL FIRST-TEAM ALL-CONFERENCE

1912, Jacob Holmes, T
1913, Fred Loomis, T; Art Burkholder, G
1915, Lee Randels, E
1916, Lee Randels, E; Eddie Wells, B
1917, Carl Roda, G
1918, Joe Bogue, E; Johnnie Clarke, B; Ike Gatz, G; Cliff Gallagher, B; Dewey Huston, G; Ding Burton, B
1919, Dewey Huston, G; Carl Roda, G
1920, Dewey Huston, G
1922, Ray Hahn, G; Ralph Nichols. T
1923, Art Stark, B
1924, Lyle Munn, E
1925, H.L. McGee, G
1926, Jerry Krysl, T
1927, Ted Fleck, E; George Lyon, C
1929, Orin Tackwell, T; K.C. Bauman, G
1930, Henry Cronkite, E; Alex Nigro, B

1931, Henry Cronkite, E; Elden Auker, B; Ralph Graham, B
1932, Dougal Russell, B; Ralph Graham, B
1933, Dougal Russell, B; Ralph Graham, B; Homer Hanson, G
1934, Ralph Churchill, E; George Maddox, T; Leo Ayres, B; Oren Stoner, B; Maurice Elder, B; Gene Sundgren, G
1935, Paul Flenthrope, T; Rolla Holland, G; Leo Ayres, B
1936, Rolla Holland, G; Maurice Elder, B
1937, Anthony Krueger, T; Howard Cleveland, B; Elmer Hackney, B
1938, Shirley Davis, T; Elmer Hackney, B
1939, Don Crumbaker, E; Bernard Weiner, T; Bill Beezley, G
1940, Bernard Weiner, T
1941, Frank Barnhart, E; Lyle Wilkins, B
1945, Russell Hardin, G
1950, Harold Robinson, C
1951, Tom O'Boyle, G; Veryl Switzer, B
1952, Veryl Switzer, B
1953, Veryl Switzer, B; Ed Pence, E; Tom O'Boyle, G
1954, Ron Nery, T; Ron Marciniak, G; Corky Taylor, B
1955, Ron Nery, T; Doug Roether, B
1956, Ellis Rainsberger, G
1957, Don Zadnik, E; Jack Keelan, T; Ellis Rainsberger, C
1958, Dave Noblitt, G
1959, John Stolte, T
1964, Bill Matan, DE; Bob Mitts, MG
1965, Bill Matan, DE
1966, Danny Lankas, LB
1967, Dan Lankas, LB; Dave Jones, E
1968, Dave Jones, E
1969, Lynn Dickey, QB; Mack Herron, HB; Manuel Barrera, DE; John Stucky, MG
1970, Lynn Dickey, QB; Mike Kuhn, DE; Ron Yankowski, DT; Oscar Gibson, LB; Clarence Scott, DHB
1971, Mo Latimore, OG
1973, Bill Brittain, OG; Isaac Jackson, HB
1975, Gary Spani, LB
1976, Gary Spani, LB
1977, Gary Spani, LB
1978, Charlie Green, SE
1979, James Walker, DE
1980, James Walker, DE
1981, Reggie Singletary, DT
1982, Mike Wallace, SE; Greg Best, CB; Reggie Singletary, DT
1983, Reggie Singletary, DT
1984, Barton Hundley, DB
1985, Barton Hundley, DB
1989, Michael Smith, WR
1991, Michael Smith, WR; Brooks Barta, LB; Jaime Mendez, FS
1992, Sean Snyder, P; Jaime Mendez, FS
1993, Jaime Mendez, FS; Thomas Randolph, CB; Quentin Neujahr, C; Andre Coleman, WR; Chad May, QB
1994, Tim Colston, DT; Tyson Schwieger, WR; Chad May, QB; Joe Gordon, CB; Chuck Marlowe, FS; Nyle Wiren, DE; Barrett Brooks, OT.
1995, Chris Canty, CB; Tim Colston, DT; Percell Gaskins, LB; Joe Gordon, CB; Kevin Lockett, WR; Chuck Marlowe, SS

BASKETBALL FIRST-TEAM ALL-CONFERENCE

1915, E.C. Jones, guard
1919, John Clark, center; George Jennings, forward
1920, Holman Bunger, forward; E.Cowell, guard
1921, Holman Bunger, forward; E.Cowell, guard
1926, C.A. Byers
1927, C.A. Byers
1932, Eldon Auker, guard
1935, Frank Groves, center
1936, Frank Groves, center
1937, Frank Groves, center
1938, Homer Wesche, guard
1939, Homer Wesche, guard
1946, Jay Payton, guard
1948, Clarence Brannum, center; Howard Shannon, guard
1949, Rick Harmna, forward
1950, Clarence Brannum, center
1951, Ernie Barrett, guard; Lew Hitch, forward; Jack Stone, forward
1952, Dick Knotsman, center
1953, Dick Knotsman, center
1956, Jack Parr, center
1957, Bob Boozer, forwardl Jack Parr, center
1958, Bob Boozer, forward; Roy DeWitz, guard
1959, Bob Boozer, forward, Don Matuszak, guard
1960, Wally Frank, forward
1961, Larry Comley, forward
1962, Pat McKenzie, forward; Mike Wroblewski, center
1963, Willie Murrell, forward
1964, Willie Murrell, forward
1968, Steve Honeycutt, guard
1969, Steve Honeycutt, guard
1970, Jerry Venable, forward; Bob Zender, forward
1972, David Hall, center
1973, Lon Kruger, guard
1974, Lon Kruger, guard
1975, Chuckie Williams, guard
1976, Mike Evans, guard; Chuckie Williams, guard
1977, Mike Evans, guard, Curtis Redding, forward
1978, Mike Evans, guard
1979, Rolando Blackman, guard
1980, Rolando Blackman, guard
1981, Rolando Blackman, guard
1982, Ed Nealy, forward
1986, Norris Coleman, forward
1987, Norris Coleman, forward
1988, Mitch Richmond, forward
1989, Steve Henson, guard
1996, Elliot Hatcher, guard

FOOTBALL BIG EIGHT COACH OF THE YEAR

1970, Vince Gibson
1982, Jim Dickey
1990, Bill Snyder
1991, Bill Snyder
1993, Bill Snyder

BASKETBALL BIG EIGHT COACH OF THE YEAR

1975, Jack Hartman
1977, Jack Hartman
1993, Dana Altman

FOOTBALL NATIONAL COACH OF THE YEAR

1991, Bill Snyder (ESPN)
1994, Bill Snyder (CNN)

BASKETBALL NATIONAL COACH OF THE YEAR

1958, Tex Winter (UPI)
1980, Jack Hartman (NABC)

TRIVIA ANSWERS

1. Bo McMillin guided K-State to a record of 29-21-1 in six years, and then moved on to Indiana and finally the NFL's Detroit Lions in 1948.

2. In 1947, K-State's ends and backs wore white helmets to distinguish them from the linemen who wore purple helmets. The practice was stopped in 1948 by the NCAA.

3. Junior running back Cornelius Davis punched it in from 1-yard out with 3:56 left in the third quarter against Colorado in the 1966 season. Colorado had the final touchdown at Memorial Stadium in the fourth quarter by running back Dan Kelly in a 40-6 Buffalo victory.

4. Gerald Hackney had the longest run in the nation in 1948 with his 96-yard dash, and the mark remains the longest run in K-State history.

5. Jersey No. 11 worn by Lynn Dickey 1968-70 and Steve Grogan 1972-74.

6. Freshman tight end Kent Dean picked up the on-side kick from Colorado and sprinted 47 yards for a Wildcat score to make the final tally 38-6.

7. Out of Brad Lambert's four interceptions during the 1984 season, he returned three of the interceptions for touchdowns, tying the Big Eight mark for a season and a career.

8. 1988. It was the the "Air" Parrish era when the Wildcats threw 443 passes (Carl Straw attempted 358) and completed 51 percent of them during an 0-11 season.

9. Lynn "Pappy" Waldorf was the first inductee in 1966. He coached the Wildcats only one year, but it was the 1934 Big Seven Championship season. Charlie Bachman is the most recent inductee in 1978, coaching K-State eight seasons with a record of 33-23-9. No Wildcat player has ever been inducted into the National Football Hall of Fame.

10. Flanker Eugene Goodlow received the honor in 1978 with 20 catches for 547 yards and 4 touchdowns. He averaged 27.4 yards per catch in that sensational sophomore season.

11. Junior quarterback Dennis Morrison had a big day at Oklahoma State on Nov. 6, 1971, where he threw for 303 yards on 23-43 passing with three touchdowns leading K-State to a 35-23 victory.

12. In the 1911 football season Captain Jacob Holmes played left tackle, and displayed his powerful tackle swings and terrific line plunges to earn first-team all-league in the Missouri Valley Conference.

13. Right tackle Frank Rodman made the Phillips 66 Academic All-Big Eight Football Team his junior and senior years majoring in vet medicine with a "B" average. As a player he was known for playing a fired-up brand of football and being a real scrapper.

14. Cornerback Chris Canty tied for the national lead in interceptions with a school record eight in 1995. Also, place kicker Ben Grosse led the nation with five field goals in 1958. He did play some running back, but his specialty was in field goal kicking. Including a game-winning 13-yarder against Missouri in the 1957 season?

15. After the Kansas victory in 1982, Kilisimasi (Masi) Toluao ignited a celebration at midfield with his traditional Samoan war dance that ended with the fans tearing down both goal posts.

16. Chris Canty returned an interception 96 yards against Oklahoma in 1994.

17. Andre Coleman gained 3,443 yards from 1990-93.

18. Ralph Graham, who played from 1931-33.

19. Linebacker Brooks Barta from 1989-1992.

20. Veryl Switzer was picked fourth in the 1954 draft.

21. Damian Johnson

22. 1988

23. Don Birdsey punted from 1977-1980, and Scott Fulhage took over from 1981 to 1984.

24. Four. J.J. Smith (1994), Eric Gallon (1991), Isaac Jackson (1973), and Cornelius Davis (1966).

25. Andre Coleman, 1990-1993.

26. Yes, Darrell Ray Dickey led K-State in passing from 1979 to 1982.

27. Chad May, 1993-94.

28. Missouri and California.

29. Erick Harper.

30. A campus contest was won by H.W. Jones in 1888.

31. Zero. The Wildcats came closest in the 1951 men's basketball title game against Kentucky. Kansas State is the only school from the former Big Eight Conference not to have won a team title. Here is a list of the other schools and their total titles: Oklahoma State-42, Oklahoma-19, Nebraska-15, Colorado-14, Iowa State-13, Kansas-9, and Missouri-2.

32. Women's rowing, formerly known as crew.

33. The 1992 women's cross country team tied with Colorado at the Big Eight meet in Boulder, Colo., to be the last Wildcat team to win a team title.

34. The 1976-77 men's basketball team were the regular (11-3) and postseason champions in the conference. The Wildcats ended up being ranked No. 11 by UPI, and lost to Marquette 67-66 in the second round of the NCAA Tournament.

35. The women's basketball team won the regular season championship four times in the 1980s ('82, '83, '84, '87).

36. Woods' father, Earl, played baseball at K-State from 1951-03. The elder Woods played first base, outfield and pitched.

37. The Wildcats have the most in the Big Eight Conference with 10 players receiving this honor. Here is a list of winners for Newcomer-of-the-Year in the Big Eight: Bob Zender-1970, Steve Mitchell-1971, Lon Kruger-1972, Mike Evans-1975, Curtis Redding-1977, Ed Nealy-1979, Randy Reed-1981, Norris Coleman-1986, Jean Derouillere-1990, and Anthony Beane-1993.

38. Lew Hitch, K-State's No. 35, made a follow-shot off of teammate Ed Head's miss against Utah State on Dec. 9, 1950.

39. 6 times (Kentucky-1951 Championship Game, Cincinnati-1961, UCLA-1964, Marquette-1977, Louisville-1980, and Kansas-1988)

40. Kansas was ranked No. 1 in the nation and Kansas State was ranked No. 2 in the nation by the UPI. Kansas had a five-point lead at halftime 37-32, and rolled to a 79-65 victory between the top two teams in the land at the time. Forward Wally Frank

led the Wildcats with 18 points in the contest and guard Ray DeWitz scored 16 in a losing cause. Kansas State ended up being ranked fourth by the UPI and Kansas was eighth.

41. Iowa State, 75-69.

42. 14, and former coach Tex Winter led K-State to eight league titles in his 15 years as a Wildcat coach. Two of the championships were won in the Big Seven and the other six in the Big Eight.

43. Guard Tyrone Adams was taken by Chicago in the third round, forward Randy Reed was drafted by the Cleveland Cavaliers in the seventh round, and in the eighth round Ed Nealy was drafted to the Kansas City Kings.

44. Bob Boozer in 1960.

45. Dana Altman in 1993.

46. K-State ended the 1959 season ranked No. 1.

47. Norris Coleman with a 21.8 average in the 1985-86 season, although it was later determined Coleman should not have been considered a freshman.

38. Mike Wroblewski poured in 46 against Kansas in 1971.

49. 1978. K-State won the game 57-54 in what many longtime observers of Ahearn games call the loudest in history.

50. Tony Massop grabbed 17 boards on March 3, 1990, against Nebraska.

51. Greg Anderson of the San Antonio Spurs during an NBA exhibition game with the Dallas Mavericks in November of 1988.

52. Graham Hunt won in 1951 with a three-day total of 226 to take first-place honors.

53. Phil Wilson only coached the Wildcats for five years (1973-77), but his record was very impressive. He had only one losing season and his career winning percentage is .568 (138-105). His 1976 team has the most wins in a season by a K-State team with 35 victories.

54. Two, the 1930 team went 9-3 in conference play and tied with the Oklahoma Sooners. In 1933 the Wildcats only had five conference games, but they ended up 3-2, tied again with Oklahoma for the conference crown. Former coach C.W. Corsaut led both of those conference championship seasons.

55. Designated hitter Jon Yeagley in the inaugural year of the Big Eight Tournament in 1976 hit .500 out of 12 plate appearances in three games of competition. Yeagley was only All-Big Eight honorable mention that year.

56. Wildcat pitcher Tom Smith on the week of April 29th pitched a solid nine-inning game for a 5-4 victory over Missouri. Teams played seven-inning games in 1984, but Smith went the distance in the extra-inning affair giving up four earned runs on seven hits and collecting four strikeouts. Then two days later he came in to close out a Missouri rally in the seventh for a 12-6 Wildcat win.

57. Outfielder Sean Collins was the first Wildcat to receive the honor of first-team All-American, while batting .361 with seven home runs and having stolen 33 bases on 42 attempts. The other All-American was Craig Wilson in 1992 when he hit .416 for fourth place on the all-time single season charts with 87 hits to put him behind his own mark of hits in a season with 88 in 1991.

58. Lon Ostrum tossed a no-hitter against Oklahoma State, but the score ended up being 2-1. The Wildcats committed three errors, and Ostrum pitched to 23 batters with three strikeouts and no walks. Ostrum had nine wins in the 1976 season to put him tied with three others for the lead in victories in a single season.

59. It only took 1 hour and 35 minutes for the Wildcats to dismantle Ottawa 3-0 in 1969, but all the credit should go to pitcher Mark Arnold who threw seven innings for the only perfect game in Wildcat history. This was Arnold's first win of the season, but his record would end up at 3-4 on the year with a ERA of 3.99, and K-State finished the season 17-15.

60. Tom Rodda did it for the men in 1958 earning All-American honors and placing fourth in the NCAA meet. In 1986 Chris Vanatta placed sixth in the NCAA cross country meet in Tuscon, Ariz., and she also earned All-American accolades that season.